The Real Business of Web Design

John Waters

ALLWORTH PRESS
NEW YORK

07 06 05 04 03   5 4 3 2 1

Published by Allworth Press
An imprint of Allworth Communications, Inc.
10 East 23rd Street, New York, NY 10010

Interior and cover design by Cheryl Oppenheim Waters

Page composition/typography by Integra

ISBN: 1-58115-316-3

Library of Congress Cataloging-in-Publication Data

Waters, John, 1942-
The real business of web design / John Waters.
p. cm.
1. Web sites--Design. 2. Electronic commerce. I. Title.
TK5105.888.W365 2003
005.7'2--dc22
2003022107

Printed in Canada

Contents

Acknowledgments

Central to this book is the premise that, as people share ideas—through a myriad of connections—they create new ideas and artifacts. Nowhere is this premise more evident than in the variety of ideas, inspirations, and criticisms that led to the creation of the book itself. Primary among the contributors who must be acknowledged is my partner in business and life for the last ten years. My wife Cheryl, a gifted designer and interaction architect, has repeatedly tested, revised, and implemented on behalf of our clients many of the ideas put forth in this book. I am eternally grateful for the inspiration, energy, and clarity she brings to our constant collaboration.

Foremost among the other contributors I wish to thank are the clients who not only permitted me, Cheryl and our associates to practice Web design on their behalf, but dared to go along with our recommendations. Among them are Mark Caliquire, Frank Carrigan, Lisa Charmichal, Art Coles, Patty Collins, Key Compton, Jon Cooper, Mitchell Engelmeyer, Mark Feldman, Alan Gaynor, Ann Greer, Ilene Gutman, Paul Hoffman, Cathy Hofknecht, Dan Hucko, Judi Jedlicka, Andrew Lona, Mark Levin, Charles Moretz, Paolo Pianezza, Liz Quinlisk, Ed Rosenfeld, Mark Suroff, Nina Terrell, and Jeffrey and Ellen Van Zandt.

During the first decade of Web design, I have had the good fortune to work with many talented designers, programmers and producers. It is impossible to thank all of the people from whom I have learned, but I am particularly grateful for the experience, insight, and knowledge gained from working with Jennifer Baldwin, Eric Bernhardt, Jason Crowl, Carol Eng, Mike Giangrasso, Crystal Harris, Amando Jimarez, Henry Kuo, Phillip Lockwood Holmes, Carolyn McCarron, Yosh Oshima, John Paolini, Dominic Poon, Amit Pradhan, Rick Ramhap, Tyler Rayner, Kay Pee Soh, Colleen Syron, and Norman Vino.

Innumerable writers have influenced my thinking about communications, design, business, and the Web. But special thanks go to John Seely Brown, Alan Cooper, Richard Lederer, Geoffrey Moore, Steven Pinker, and Neil Postman.

This book would not have become a reality without the sage advice and remarkable patience of its publisher Tad Crawford. Thank you for encouraging me to write this and for putting up with my delays and missed deadlines as I struggled to do so. And finally, a special thank-you to Helen, Sasha, Nell, and Emma. You have taught me much about the rich and complex nature of human communication and I am indebted to each of you for your patience and creative inspiration.

John Waters

Introduction

This book is about communication, design, and business in the first decade of the twenty-first century. It is about fulfilling the astonishing *Promise* of the Web, simplifying the complex *Practice* of Web design, and improving the relationship of the *Players*—designers, engineers, and business executives—creating the Web sites we love and hate. It is about the vital changes continuing to occur in *Markets and Marketing* in every industry, and it is about the potential for *Increasing Returns*—economic, social, creative, and humanitarian—from Web initiatives driven by design.

The book is written for designers in the broadest sense of the word. Those that in any profession are charged with making sense out of data, and shaping information or matter to a purpose. This includes graphic designers, information architects, interaction and experience designers, and industrial designers. It also includes designers of software, information technology systems, marketing programs, management processes, businesses, and governments. This book then is written for everyone involved with the Web, and that means everyone.

Despite the greed, uncertainty, and despair often associated with the Web because of its perceived misuse, awkwardness, and ugliness, the impact of the Web is inescapable. It is a fact of our lives. It is almost everywhere and everyone knows it, even if they are not spending time online. Far from being over, the social, business, and political revolution promised by a global digital network has barely begun. Its influence on our institutions, economies, language, and daily activities is just beginning.

With all of its problems—and there are many—the Web is the single most profound communications design effort of the twentieth century. This book is about realizing the promise of that effort—turning the creative, humanitarian, and economic potential unleashed by the Web into a reality.

In 1986, I gave a talk in Boston on computers and design for the Design Management Institute, in which I compared designers to chicken farmers. My brother-in-law, who was a chicken farmer in North Carolina, provided me with what I thought was the perfect analogy. He had, at that time, two fully automated chicken houses, into which every eight weeks 52,000 baby chicks were deposited, to be fed and fattened for the market. A computer controlled all of the feeding, watering, ventilation, and alarm systems. My brother-in-law delivered 312,000 plump birds a year, and his sixteen-year-old son ran the entire operation.

My presentation was titled, "Expanding the Possibilities of Design with a Computer," and my point was that designers, using computers, could improve the quality of their output in much the same way as my brother-in-law. By using computers, designers could expand their creative potential and their business opportunities. Now, seventeen years later, sure enough, nearly all designers are using computers—nearly all people are using computers, even computers are using computers—and the output is prolific. There are more mailers, manuals, magazines, books, brochures, annual reports, packages, posters, e-mails, Web sites, portal sites, databases, languages, and metalanguages, than at any time in our history.

Two years ago, when my brother-in-law sold his six chicken houses, he was producing over one million chickens a year. His biggest problem: Every eight weeks it took two tractors all day to clean out the chicken shit.

It's time for us to bring in the tractors, to go through this cleansing process. It's time to take a look at all of the stuff we produce and ask of each new thing: Is it necessary? What value does it provide? Can it be produced in a more useful, efficient, accessible, or meaningful way? *The Real Business of Web Design* is about finding the answers to these questions and many more. It is about cleaning out our waste and planning our new Web initiatives to be increasingly valuable and sustainable contributions.

We are living in the global village but continue to act and speak as if we are isolated in Greenwich, Connecticut; Akron, Ohio; or Sausalito, California. We are shopping at the global mall; attending the global university; taking books out of—and putting new ones into—the global library; using the global post office; reserving our cars, buying our airline tickets, and making our travel plans on the global network; bartering our services and goods at the global bazaar; developing and producing services and goods with global partners through the network; participating in a global economy; attending the global theater; and voicing our opinions in the global political arena. Although today, many business Web sites are downloading faster, looking a little nicer, making slightly more sense than just a year or two ago, the look on most is still a veneer, too many are inaccessible to everyone, and far too many don't work at all.

The Real Business of Web Design is about how to make Web sites work, make them friendly, useful, valuable, and accessible to people. It is about understanding the new language of business, the real meaning of brand, and the new approach to marketing necessary for success in a networked world. The book is not about the Web as a disruptive technology. It is about designing for a sustaining technology and the emerging values that come with it. The Web is not a revolution, although it appeared to be five years ago. It is just another step, albeit a big one, in human evolution. There have been reports for years about the end of humankind—research that shows how we are overpopulating the earth; how we will not be able to produce enough food to feed the people; how we are destroying the rain forest, the lakes and oceans, the air quality, and the ozone layer. There is truth in many of the statistics presented, yet we continually manage to come up with new ideas, new things that allow us to improve, preserve, and even enhance our existence. The Web is one of those things. And designers of the Web have an opportunity and an obligation to make this thing work.

The Web is about expanding human potential. And that expansion begins with the exchange of ideas. It is about human communications, and increasingly, it includes machine communications. So Web design is about creating the individual components, the infrastructure and the language for multi-level, multi-directional human and machine communication.

This book, however, is not about technology. Although it discusses several larger trends in technology, the "tech-talk" has been kept to a minimum. It makes very few references to specific computer-based tools, platforms or browsers, programming languages, or protocols. There are two reasons for this: One, this would be at least ten books if it tried to cover even the most popular tools, languages and tricks; and two, many of those would be outdated or at least modified by the time you read this. Readers who may be looking for "how-tos" regarding these issues will find better sources on the Web. Included are some of my favorites in the resources section on page 230.

Although some favorite design tools, and many useful "real-world" examples of development practices and methodologies are included, this is not a how-to book in the sense of offering details on how to code a Web site, or how to make money on the Web, or how to increase traffic to your site. Instead, the book attempts to say something about an approach to Web design and Web use that may help make the process of site development easier, and the results far more meaningful and valuable for individuals, organizations, and companies.

I was fortunate to be working with IBM in 1994 when the Web first began to be perceived as a business asset. Over the next five years, my associates and I designed and built a number of sites for IBM. We went on to design and build sites for the National Museum of Women in the Arts, the *Wall Street Journal*, the United Nations and a host of other companies and organizations. We also developed many integrated, Web-based marketing programs. In the process we spent a huge amount of time on the network, exploring, testing, using its resources, and we learned something about the Web. It functions like a living organism—a living system that self-organizes into greater and greater levels of complexity. As with all living systems, it is the relationships—the connections and the patterns formed by connections—of multiple components that provide expanding creative potential, business opportunities, and humanitarian benefits. The potential for fraud, corruption, loss of privacy, and authoritarian control are also extremely high. What we do with this potential, how we choose to use the Web in our business and personal lives, is up to us—each of us.

•

As the networked world draws us all closer together, even with the frightening world events of recent years, the possibilities for meaningful contribution by designers and the opportunities for business are greater than ever. In fact, because of the frightening recent events of global terror, corporate scandal, and failing infrastructures, our obligation is more urgent than ever. The important thing now is for each of us to respond to this obligation and help realize this golden opportunity.

The Promise

It began long before the Web originated in 1991. It was ruminating in the minds of lab assistants, librarians, and researchers in universities around the world. The notion of change, of a new world order, of utopian possibilities mixed with the risks of catastrophic disasters, both possible results of information growth and the increasing rapidity of its exchange. In this first section, we will review critical issues related to the origin and promise of the networked world brought about by the Web, and touch on the business and culture changing events of its first decade.

Social thinker Alvin Toffler rocked our world with Future Shock *in 1970 when he announced the "premature arrival of the future." He nudged us forward again in 1980 with* Third Wave, *a synthesis of sociological, economic, technological, and psychological "colliding waves of change." And in 1990 with* PowerShift, *he foretold the rise of a new "system for wealth creation," which would cause dramatic change in the distribution of power. "This new system for making wealth," Toffler declared, "is totally dependent on the instant communication and dissemination of data, ideas, symbols, and symbolism."*

The following year Tim Berners-Lee, a little-known physicist, quietly released on the Internet three tools he had developed which would allow the instant communication of data Toffler spoke of. Berners-Lee had the chutzpah to name his tools, or rather the space provided by the tools: the World Wide Web. The "super-symbolic" decade that followed, as we shall see, was filled with radical change—new magazines, new books, new technologies, new rules for business, and new theories of growth. Toffler's "waves of change" became a windstorm of economic euphoria that drove people to the edge of sanity and beyond. Web designers came out of the woodwork, business boomed, and Web consultancies became global corporations. Then the bubble popped. Fortunes were lost. Careers were destroyed. The fires went out, but the world had changed.

Now here we are. Living with what was once science fiction. A world filled with promise and fear. Berners-Lee's vision had an impact on virtually every business and institution in America, and many around the globe. It shifted the focus of communications by businesses, educators, and politicians. It altered the time and space in which we live and work, and fractured the very foundations of cultures and societies. But the promise of the Web, as we will discover, is far from fulfilled; its exponential growth, impact, and influence have just begun.

1

Linking and Thinking

Cold air hit me hard in the face as I ran out the front door on my way to pick up my daughter from her after-school program. It was February in New York and the wind was blowing. I was instantly reminded of being hit by a blast of hot air, a number of years ago, as the door was opened on our airplane, which had just landed in the desert of Doha, Qatar. It was 112 degrees and the wind was blowing. I am always amazed at the way my brain makes these unlikely, seemingly useless connections. Connections that instantly transport me through space and time.

The brain is like that. Composed of millions and millions of individual neurons which are not really connected, but have input and output devices and a simple "firing" mechanism which allow any single neuron to connect with another, or with a series of other neurons. This is how we think. It is how we create, organize, grow, interact, and participate in our world—by making connections.

The World Wide Web is also like that. Composed of millions and millions of independent documents that are not connected, but with a simple mechanism can be linked in a variety of ways, allowing viewers to expand their ability to create, organize, grow, interact, and participate in the world.

A Philosophical Change
A desire to represent this connective aspect of information was a driving force in 1989 for Tim Berners-Lee, a physicist in his mid-thirties working

at CERN[1] when he conceived the World Wide Web. "Inventing the Web involved my growing realization that there was power in arranging ideas in an unconstrained, Web-like way . . . A computer typically keeps information in rigid hierarchies and matrices, whereas the human mind has the special ability to link random bits of data."[2] The idea Berners-Lee pursued was to program computers to create a space in which they could link otherwise unconnected information. And the users of these linked documents from connected computers could become much more knowledgeable and more creative.

This approach to computers is a philosophical change from the way we generally think about computing. The principles underlying the Web are a fundamental change from the way people previously viewed and used information. A shift in the way we think about and connect with one another. A change in the way marketers think about marketing, and how businesses, institutions, and governments think about communications.

The foundation of the Web stretches all the way back to 1945 when Vannevar Bush, an engineer from MIT, head of the Wartime Office of Scientific Research and Development under Franklin D. Roosevelt, wrote an article in the *Atlantic Monthly*, which focused on global information sharing. He envisioned a personal, searchable machine for storing and cross-referencing microfilm documents with information "trails" which linked to related text and illustrations. His Memex machine was never built, but the concept of organizing information similar to the way the brain worked was not forgotten.

In 1965 Ted Nelson, a visionary who developed a "non-sequential writing system"[3] while at Harvard, presented a paper at the Association for Computer Machinery conference in which he talked of "literary machines" that allowed people to publish documents in what he called "hypertext." He described Xanadu, a project which would contain all of the world's information published in hypertext, allowing the reader of one document to link out to other related documents following the reader's train of thought. Nelson, like Bush, was too far ahead of his time. Xanadu was never realized.

Throughout the sixties and seventies, numerous other people pondered the complexities of our ability to share growing amounts of information. Several ideas in publishing and computing eventually jelled to provide the underlying structure for the concept of the Web. Historically, writers, editors, or graphic designers in publishing, would "markup" a manuscript for typesetting. This essentially told the typographer what size typefont, length of line, and how much spacing to use when setting the type. There were also marks that described page elements or the format to be used. As we progressed to word processing with electronic text, people at IBM developed this into an electronic tag known as Generalized Markup Language (GML), which gave meaning to page elements. By separating the presentation of a document from its content, GML provided a way for many people to edit, share, and reuse the text. More importantly, it was developed so multiple electronic devices could share it. The concept quickly spread within the publishing and computing industries and sometime in the mid-eighties became the Standard Generalized Markup Language (SGML).

The notions of separating content from its structure and of using names for markup elements to identify text objects descriptively—a formal grammar to describe structural relationships between objects—was the basis for the future development of the Web. Understanding the interplay of content with its context at a structural level is fundamental to grasping the "mechanics" of the Web. And as we shall see later, it is also essential to understanding the global creative possibilities of the Web.

Most of us do not think of such things when we sit at our computers. We see computers as highly organized, rigid, dumb machines that may help us accomplish certain tasks if we are patient enough to learn the procedures. Although they began as mechanical counting devices, a means of calculating or "computing" mathematically, following the information explosion of the seventies and the desktop revolution of the eighties, which was stimulated by the use of SGML, we have viewed computers primarily as information storage devices.

In the past, most of us thought all of the information on our computers were proprietary. Even if connected to a local area network (LAN) within the office, or wide area network (WAN) within the organization, "information silos" was—and to a large extent still is—the prevailing structural view. We "drill down" through a data hierarchy to find the document we want. Though an individual or a company may own some of this data, much of it is thought of as proprietary simply because of this storage structure.

Like the hierarchical management of corporations, the structure itself has a powerful and sometimes debilitating influence on the ability of a company to perform. Connections, when they can only be made in a linear fashion—up and down the command ladder—may be rational and strengthen control, but do nothing for spontaneity or creativity. Changing the structure of information expands the creative potential. As any designer knows, most new ideas arrive serendipitously. And anyone who has spent a little time on the Web—having gotten beyond the preconception that computers cannot contribute to imagination— knows it is a tremendous creative resource.

Unleashing Creative Potential
With the introduction of three simple tools, Berners-Lee changed the way we think about information. He did not ask us to give up owner- ship. His view was that the Web was like a market economy where anybody could exchange information with anybody, from anywhere, and in nearly any form. All that was needed for the exchange were some basic standards everyone could agree on.

The three tools he provided, which have now become universal standards are:
1. Universal Resource Locator (URL). This is simply a method for locat- ing documents by an address, similar to the way the postal service delivers your mail to a street number, city, state, and zip code.
2. Hypertext Transfer Protocol (HTTP), is a standard for how computers speak to one another.
3. Hypertext Markup Language (HTML); a simple coding metho- dology—simplified SGML—that allows people to specify what a line of text may do in a document (i.e., appear as simple text, a large headline, or as a link to other text or another document).

In August of 1991, Berners-Lee placed his tools on the Internet mak- ing them available to all who were interested. This was the beginning of "information space." The world has talked about, played with, worked with, complained about, and exclaimed the virtues of this space for over twelve years now, but the concept and its implications are still hard for many to grasp. The Web is not a "place." It is not a "thing." There is no central computer, single network, or single organization controlling it.

Although the World Wide Web Consortium (W3C, *www.w3c.com*)—a nonprofit organization founded by Berners-Lee in 1994—does provide "guidelines" for Web development, the Web is essentially an enormous, unbounded, chaotic world of information. By connecting documents from all over the world, information has not only grown; it has changed. The Web is not just providing more information; it is not only a giant library, or a new publishing medium, or a marketing method. It is what Michael Dertouzos, director of the MIT Laboratory for Computer Science, calls "a gigantic Information Marketplace, where individuals and organizations buy, sell, and freely exchange information and information services among one another."[4]

Chaos theorists would call this change in information structure a "phase transition." Something like what happens to water when it changes into ice or steam. It has not only gotten hotter or colder, it has changed fundamentally—at a molecular connectivity level. Another "phase transition" in communications was the invention of the telephone. Although not intended as such, the telephone was one of the first great idea of connectivity. Alexander Graham Bell originally thought of it as a broadcast medium, but to his surprise, the telephone provided real-time, two-way communication, a revolution in information exchange that we often overlook because we use it so frequently.

With the exception of the telephone and its forefather, the telegraph, just about all public communication channels prior to the Web were one-way streets. Radio and television broadcast information over airwaves. Newspapers and magazines broadcast via print. Most business and organizational communications, whether by public channels or private (newsletters, memos, videos, or closed-circuit TV), are essentially one-way transmissions.

The mind-set of advertisers who supported this kind of information distribution was "tell and sell."[5] Look at any print or broadcast advertising over the last 100 years and you will see one-way talk about the features, advantages, and benefits of products, services and organizations: *Here is what we have, what we know, what we believe, and what we think you should also know, believe and buy.* Ultimately the goal was to direct the receiver of this information to visit the "store" and make a purchase.

Much of what exists on the Web today, even after twelve years, is still following the old model, when what the Web is about is a different, totally new approach. The Berners-Lee vision was of an information space "to which everyone has immediate and intuitive access, and not just to browse, but to create . . . a universal medium for sharing information . . . "[6] Sharing is the key word here. After centuries of clinging to what we have and what we know, feeling pride in the ownership of things and knowledge, protecting our knowledge in silos, it is difficult to grasp the extent of change a phase transition requires. It is nearly impossible to reverse our thinking, to open our doors and let others in.

To realize the promise of the Web we need to review everything we are currently doing in business and in our personal lives. We need to let go of many of our favorite habits, old models, best practices, and much of our current language to "make room" for new things, new knowledge, new languages, and new possibilities. As we will see in the following chapters, the real business of Web design is about broadening knowledge, enlarging our capacity for imagination, expanding business markets, creating new opportunities, saving time, reducing costs, and improving the quality of life by connecting people to people. Although most businesses on the Web have not gotten it right yet, the human desire to connect is clearly there.

$\bullet$

2

New Rules for Growth

The idea of a super-symbolic society that Toffler introduced in 1990, and Berners-Lee made possible in 1991, began slowly but became a roaring reality by the end of the century. It was hyped, pumped, fanned, and fed at every turn. This chapter reviews the highlights of this whirlwind decade, the insanity that drove economic markets, the books and magazines that drove the insanity, and some of the critical ideas that survived and continue to influence Web design.

From Little Acorns
Checking the logs in 1992 showing traffic on the first Web server, info.cern.ch, Tim Berners-Lee saw a doubling of traffic every three to four months. Starting with about one hundred hits a day in 1991, it jumped to one thousand by the summer of 1992 and ten thousand in the summer of 1993. At the same time additional servers were coming online, as well as a variety of browsers, mostly developed by students, each seeing the creative potential and adding their own features or tweaking a feature they had seen on another browser.

By 1993 there were 90,000 Web viewers and two years later there were three million. Yes, people wanted to connect, but the real explosion followed the introduction of Netscape, an intuitive point-and-click graphical browser that in less than two years helped take the Web audience to 30 million. I would like to say here that the rest is history, but what the founders of Netscape did had such a profound

•

effect on commerce, business culture, and society that it deserves some attention. Many of the fundamental rules of business were turned on end, and the basics of a network economy, which continues to grow, were established.

It began when two young programmers, Marc Andreessen and Eric Bina, working for the National Center for Super Computing Applications (NCSA) at the University of Illinois at Urbana-Champaign, wrote the code for the first graphical browser, named Mosaic. It was launched on the Web in February 1993 and rapidly gained users from other browsers because its graphical interface was easy to learn and use. Knowing that Mosaic was oriented more as a commercial product than a research tool, NCSA seized the opportunity to portray Mosaic as the center of the Web. Meanwhile, Berners-Lee did not gain full freedom from CERN to distribute the Web protocol and code to anyone without royalty or constraint until April 30, 1993. Everyone involved saw that the Web was spreading like wildfire and power struggles ensued between different factions that wanted control or profits.

When Andreessen met businessman Jim Clark they formed the Mosaic Corporation in early 1994, hired the core Mosaic development team away from NCSA, moved to California, and to avoid all legal problems renamed the company Netscape. In just six months they released a beta version of their browser software code-named Mozilla, the Mosaic killer. Mosaic, of course, was first to the market and by the fall of 1994, while the Netscape team of developers worked around the clock to complete their new code, Mosaic had become a basic tool for three million users of the Web, accounting for roughly 60 percent of all Web traffic.

Knowing that NCSA had licensed the Mosaic code to others and that Microsoft was also developing a browser, Andreessen and Clark figured that the browsers would rapidly become commodities and their best chance at commercial survival was to conquer market share quickly. To do so, on December 15, 1994, they released Navigator 1.0 for free over the Internet. Within four months, without advertising, sales, or distribution through retail stores, six million copies of Netscape Navigator 1.0 were in use. By the spring of 1995 Navigator was used by more than 75 percent of all Web traffic, and Mosaic was left in the dust with only 5 percent of the market.

On August 9, 1995 the Netscape Corporation went public, creating an IPO frenzy that is now legend. Netscape stock opened at $28 and closed the day at $58.25. The company, which many people had never heard of, with just $16 million in revenues, and barely a year old, was worth about $2 billion dollars. Cofounder Marc Andreessen, at twenty-four years old, held shares worth nearly $60 million and his partner, veteran Jim Clark had shares worth half a billion dollars. This was the beginning of our national dot.com IPO addiction. It was also the beginning of radical change in the way businesses would develop, launch, market, and charge for new products in the future.

Winning on the Web

In November of that year, in the premiere issue of *Fast Company*—the magazine founded on the premise that "a global revolution was changing business, and business was changing the world"[1]—the Netscape story was finely captured in a feature article by Tom Steinert-Threlkeld titled; "Can You Work in Netscape Time?"[2] According to Steinert-Threlkeld, Netscape time was certainly about speed, but it was also about the mind-set of "hungry young programmers" doing what they love to do. It was about a "company in overdrive" knowing what it wanted to do and doing it; a company "whose headcount, in 15 months, has gone from two to 330." The principles of Netscape time outlined by Steinert-Threlkeld included:

Fast Enough Never Is

In the fall of 1994, Mosaic was gaining users at a rate of 600,000 per month while the Netscape developers were continuing to program. Working insane hours was imperative. "If we had been six months later," Jim Clark would later say, "we would have been lost in noise."

The Paranoid Predator

Even with the huge success of Netscape's IPO, Clark said his role was to create paranoia, "to undermine the glowing publicity, subvert the evidence of success, and instill fear and urgency at all levels."

All Work, All The Time

The Netscape team of developers worked 110, 120, even 130 hours a week, sleeping and eating at their computers in order to complete the first launch in six months. Even after the initial success the company culture required twelve to fifteen hours a day from nearly everyone.

All of this sounds too familiar to anyone involved with Web development over the last ten years. The 24/7 x 365 business world had become a reality overnight. The Web design world exploded with companies following the Netscape model, working in Netscape time.

Speed, commitment, focus, and urgency were all important to Netscape's success, but what Netscape really did was use the Web to win business on the Web. By avoiding the manufacturing of discs, distributing over land to retail outlets, advertising to find customers—the standard "tell and sell" of the past—they reduced time to market and cost to market. Even more importantly, they built immediate relationships with their customers by allowing them to "link and think," to download software, use it, and provide feedback on the product through the Web. The Netscape site became a forum for ideas, ideas from outside the company about improving the company's product. Netscape 1.0 was released in December, less than three months later version 1.1 with many new features was released, and a beta version of 1.2 designed to run on additional platforms was released in another three months. As Steinert-Threlkeld says, "Netscape engineers don't develop software; they co-develop it with their customers. The product is the process is the product."

It is now common practice for software developers to release beta versions for free over the Internet, for manufacturing and service companies to give away basic products and services in order to drive traffic to their sites, and thereby increase sales of other products and services. This is often referred to as freeware. A more accurate label comes from Jim Clark who says, "This is not freeware, this is marketware." The tools that Berners-Lee had provided were getting slightly more complex. More importantly, they were being used by millions of people to create a marketplace for ideas.

Less than a year after Netscape's IPO—on April 12, 1996—Yahoo!, the search engine site that Stanford students Jerry Yang and David Filo created to keep track of their bookmarks, made headlines when its initial offering jumped from $13 to $24.50 at the opening bell, and closed at $33. At the end of the day their market cap was over $1 billion. Everyone was so crazed by the money that we nearly missed what made Yahoo! important. By comparison with Google today it would be considered crude, but Yahoo! was the first search engine that helped us find our way through the growing maze of available information.

Over thirty million computer users had access to the Web in 1996. There were 12.8 million Web hosts and half a million Web sites. This was only five years after Tim Berners-Lee made his first tools available.

The Winds of Change

By 1997 the business revolution was in full swing, "paradigm shift" had become a common phrase, and new rules for the new world were popping up everywhere. Publishers still using the old media, while attempting to understand and use the Web, were feeding the forces of change with an endless stream of new books and magazines in hard copy form, with digital versions available online. Magazines such as *Wired*, *Fast Company*, *Industry Standard*, *Red Herring*, and *Business 2.0* and books such as *Webonomics*, *Net.Gain*, *Killer App*, and *Customers.com* are a few examples. Following are brief notes on just a few of the books that gave us the "rules for success" in 1997 and 1998. Some of them still apply and will be explored further in subsequent chapters.

Webonomics by Evan Schwartz, a reporter for *Business Week* and contributing writer for *Wired* magazine, gave us "nine essential principles for growing your business on the World Wide Web."[3] Three of the most important principles are still relevant and worth repeating:

1. *"The quantity of people visiting your site is less important than the quality of their experience."* To any designer worth a grain of salt, this is unbelievably obvious, yet the visitor experience today remains awful at most sites. So awful, in fact, that a whole new category of design—Experience Design—has developed. In 2000 the American Institute of Graphic Arts (AIGA) held its first special interest group on experience design. SIGCHI, the leading international group of professionals, academics, and students concerned with Human-Computer Interaction (HCI) launched the Experience Design Forum in 2002. And the first DUX (Designing for User

Experiences) conference, orchestrated by AIGA, SIGCHI, and others was held in June 2003.

The issues surrounding the interface between humans and computers have been around for years. With the Web, the importance of this interface accelerated. The primary difficulty has to do with who controls the user experience. Marketers, editors, and designers continue to struggle with the idea of relinquishing control to visitors, allowing them to participate in the conversation. Often the most critical part of creating a positive experience on the Web is allowing visitors to get the information or entertainment in the form, fashion, and time each visitor wants.

2. *"Marketers shouldn't be on the Web for exposure, but for results."* Schwartz called attention to Prudential Securities as one of the early financial sites to allow customers to set up their accounts online, check their status, transfer funds, and communicate with representatives of the company. The site was unbelievably ugly and clunky, but the thinking was certainly what the promise of the Web is about. Today this is common practice (though frequently not well done) with nearly all major financial service companies, many retail stores, manufacturing companies, and some professional service firms. However, a surprising number of major corporations, middle market and smaller companies still have "brochureware" sites, brandishing their image but not providing for transactions, not allowing for two-way communications. This is like putting beautiful signs on the front of your building or enticing window displays but never opening the door.

3. *"Consumers must be compensated for disclosing data about themselves."* Although many people give up more information about themselves offline than they do on the Web—by using credit cards and supermarket or retail outlet discount cards—most at least think they are getting a bargain in the process. This was Schwartz's real point: People (not consumers) on the Web must be treated with respect. Any transaction has two sides and they both should benefit.

Net.Gain by John Hagel and Arthur Armstrong, former McKinsey & Company consultants, was a "must read" for corporate marketing executives in '97 and '98. Hagel and Armstrong saw the connectivity happening at The Well, an early online community of thinkers at the crossroads of technology and culture, as a "kernel of a fundamentally new business model."[4]

Their concept was to use the purely social phenomenon that was happening on the Web—virtual communities being formed by people gathering to discuss what they were passionate about—as a guide for corporations to create and manage a "virtual community as a commercial enterprise." The concept is not without merit, and many of the recommendations of Hagel and Armstrong are valid. The reality was another story. Many "corporate-sponsored communities" failed because visitors correctly perceived them as just another profit-making scheme. Balancing the profit motive of the commercial enterprise with the passions of a community requires one essential ingredient—trust.

Customers.com by Patricia B. Seybold, founder of the Patricia Seybold Group, a business technology-consulting firm in Boston, certainly appeared to have the focus right. The subtitle is, "Make it easy for your customers to do business with you."[5] A critical point that is even truer today than when it was written. Unfortunately, the language of most of Seybold's case studies focuses on the customer through the eyes of the company and their technology investments rather than the eyes of the customer. Companies should never talk about "owning the customer's total experience." Customers are not slaves. Although the book is filled with this language bias, it was widely acclaimed for its knowledge of how to build profitable business on the Web.

Magazines also fanned the fires of change with breathless urgency. The February/March 1997 issue of *Fast Company* provided "The Startup Manifesto" on its cover: "Quit your Job, Work Your Butt Off, Screw Up." Then in April/May it was the "CHANGE" issue with articles like: "Anything, Anywhere, Anytime" by Net visionary Michael Saylor, and "Brainstorming the Future," a review of Xerox's famed Palo Alto Research Center.

Unquestionably the most unique voice and one of the most provocative was Kevin Kelly, editor of *Wired* (1993), the first technocentric publication that rapidly became the guiding light for early Internet users and, as some readers thought, pushed the concept of the future to the level of science fiction.

In 1998, building on his *Wired* article from 1997, Kelly produced his book, *New Rules for the New Economy: 10 Radical Strategies for a*

Connected World. "This book is a shock to the system," the *Wall Street Journal* said, "Practically everything you ever learned from that back-breaking economics text is going out the window . . . ."[6]

What Kelly said, in a nutshell, is that the new economy "has three distinguishing characteristics: It is global. It favors intangible things—ideas, information, and relationships. And it is intensely interlinked."[7] As we will discover, what many have called the "information economy" is in the digital world, a communications economy. Communication is not just part of the economy, but as Kelly says, "Communication *is* the economy." The rules he went on to provide, the language they were presented in, and the thinking behind them were nothing short of breathtaking. "Embrace the Swarm, Follow the Free, Feed the Web First, No Harmony, All Flux." They were lyrical, emphatic, empowering. They stirred the independent spirit and begged for participation in this now, clearly obvious, boom economy.

Webmania

By late 1998, everyone was clamoring to be on the Web or be a Web consultant. Why? Because it was easy, just learn the basics of HTML—the rules were available from the books and magazines mentioned, as well as many, many more. It was hot! Major corporations, nonprofit organizations, long-standing institutions and start-up Web-based businesses could not get there fast enough. And it was financially rewarding—venture capital was flowing like a ruptured fire hydrant. There were over a million Web sites, 300 million pages with 1.5 million more being added daily. Internet traffic was doubling every one hundred days.

The pace became so intense it drove people to the edge of sanity. One afternoon in the spring of 1999 my receptionist paged me, "You have to help me," she said. "There's a guy on the phone screaming and swearing so much I can't understand him. He is so busy calling me names I can't figure out who he wants to talk with." I picked up the phone and immediately recognized the voice of a young "entrepreneur" who had retained us just two months earlier.

At the time of his first call he had just named his business and was still working at desk space in his Venture Capitalist's (VC's) office. His plan had been approved for an initial round of $3.5 million in venture capital and he needed all the business start-up basics: branding, business communications papers, a marketing folder to take to a trade show, a trade exhibit, and a small Web site that would both demo the business model and rapidly grow to become the transaction center of his business. He had purchased his URL and hired an assistant who was interviewing future employees while he searched for office space. In order to meet the deadline given by the VC he needed all of his materials in eight weeks. With some reservations, but with money upfront, we took the assignment.

It was now the seventh week. He had signed a lease on space, installed phone lines, purchased furniture, and hired over thirty people. We had developed the logo and key positioning documents. The business papers and the marketing brochure were to be delivered in two days from the printer. We were in the final testing stage of his initial site. "Just stop it!" he yelled. "You've got to stop everything immediately!" he was screaming. After several minutes of listening to his rants, I finally got to the heart of the problem. Although he owned his URL, he had failed to have his lawyer clear ownership of his business name. He did not own it, and even worse, he could not buy it from the people who did. Webmania was in full bloom.

The freneticism was not limited to "young entrepreneurs." Mom and Pop investors, day traders, experienced corporate executives, Wall Street analysts; all were caught up in the swirling "boom economy."

In June of the following year, I received a call from the director of marketing at a *Fortune* 500 company with whom I had worked for a number of years. "You're not going to believe this," she said, "I quit my job." I didn't believe it. She had been with this company for fifteen years, was highly respected and highly paid. "I've joined a dot.com," she went on. "They offered to match my salary plus I have tremendous stock options. You are going to have to help me. I just started this week as the Brand Steward, and these people really need help. They don't even know what brand means. I'm scared to death, but you know at my age, I figured I can do this and if it doesn't work out, I'm still young enough to get back in."

Nine months later she lost her job. A few months later the company was gone. She was out of work for the next sixteen months. Even as the press continued to herald the new economy, it had begun to falter.

3

After the Bubble Burst

The logic that drove ordinary people to sell their businesses, mortgage their homes and invest their life savings in slips of paper representing future flowers in Holland between 1634 and 1637 came to be known as "the greater fool theory." By any conventional measure, it is absurd to pay thousands of dollars for a tulip bulb. However, as long as there is one greater fool somewhere prepared to pay more, doing so is logical.

On February 2, 1637, Tulipmania, a speculative frenzy that sucked people from all walks of life into its whirl, came to a halt. On that day, the florists gathered in a tavern college of Haarlem, Netherlands, the capital of bulb trade, and began their auction as usual. "A florist sought to begin the bidding at 1,250 guilders for a quantity of tulips . . . finding no takers, he tried again at 1,100, then 1,000 . . . and all at once every man in the room—men who days before had themselves paid comparable sums for comparable tulips—understood that the weather had changed."[1] Word spread rapidly across the country that there were no buyers and within days tulip bulbs could not be sold at any price. "In all of Holland a greater fool was no longer to be found." Within months hundreds of people had lost fortunes.

The Results of Wind Trade
Tulipmania had nothing to do with the beauty or practicality of tulips. This was a frenzy of purely financial speculation. So, too, was the dot.com frenzy that helped to drive the Nasdaq Composite Index—the

technology-stock bellwether in the United States—to its all-time high of 5,047 on March 10, 2000. It took only four months to soar from 3,000 past 4,000 to this new record. On March 11, the weather changed. The Nasdaq fell 25 percent in the next 30 days. It closed the year down 65 percent, and has been struggling to see 2,000 ever since. The greater fools lost a fortune.

In the eighteen months prior to the crash, a number of high-profile Web consulting firms had gone public, including iXL, Organic, Rare Medium, Razorfish, Scient, Sapient, US Interactive, and others. With their dot.com focus and alleged Internet expertise, they had made the hot list of highly respected investment firms. When the market fell, the funding to dot.coms disappeared, and the consultants were caught short. "We were geniuses six weeks ago," Christopher Lochhead, chief marketing officer at Scient said in a CNET article on September 27, 2000. "And we're idiots now."[2]

Quickly they shifted their marketing focus to large corporate clients. It was too late. Major corporations, having spent fortunes in the previous few years on portal sites, multiple B2C and B2B sites, and Intranets—many of which produced little to no returns—had already slashed their IT budgets. The change had come much faster than anyone expected.

Many of the Web consultancies had started only a few years earlier. With little more than two engineers, a few computers in a small office, and VC funding, they rapidly acquired other development firms, graphic design firms, and industrial design firms; growing to global operations with offices around the world, thousands of employees and hundreds of millions of dollars in revenues. The premise was, "It's a new day that requires a new strategy; a digital strategy. You guys (the suits) don't understand the Web and we (the developers) do. Therefore we will advise you on your business strategy. (A major leap of faith!) And, by-the-way, it will cost you a huge amount of money." Millions of dollars were being charged to corporate clients for Web initiatives, and hundreds of thousands to dot.com start-ups.

The IPOs from the consultant companies followed the skyrocket fashion of Netscape and Yahoo! turning young developers into millionaires overnight. The media gobbled up the press releases of these firms and spit back stories of fabulous parties, new cars, and the glamorous lifestyle of young high-tech entrepreneurs. The fact that

•

their costs were exorbitant, their work questionable*, and their profits nil, did not seem to matter. For client companies accustomed to detailed planning and project management, the culture and practices of the consulting firms were a shock, but the old standard of "ready, aim, fire" had long since given way to the new rule, "fire, aim, ready."

It was all so new and happening so fast that corporate managers had little to base their hiring decisions on. It seems investment advisors also had nothing more on which to base their company valuations than what was known in Holland 300 years earlier as *wind trade*. Buying and selling Web promises was like buying and selling a product as invisible as un-sprouted flowers. The prices were made up out of thin air.

In the public's mind, the new economy—the networked economy, the Web—had come to be associated with the Nasdaq, dot.coms, and Web consultancies. When the market fell, many thought the promise of the Web was history. The technology landscape was certainly strewn with dot.com remains, including Boo.com, Furniture.com, Garden.com, Mortgage.com, Pets.com, and the carcasses of Web consultancies.

By the end of 2002 most of the consulting firms mentioned above were gone. Sapient continues to hang on but has substantially reduced its size, and Razorfish, in January 2003, agreed to have its remains acquired by SBI, a large professional services firm.

Most of the so-called New Economy magazines, *The Industry Standard, Forbes ASAP, eCompany Now*, and *Upside* were also gone. As of February 2003, *Red Herring* was desperately looking for a buyer but had no takers, and the founding editors of *Fast Company* had resigned.

Comic Tragedy

Just as the New Economy went into a nosedive, FuckedCompany.com, run by Philip (Pud) Kaplan in New York, stepped in to provide needed relief. The name itself was a parody on *Fast Company*'s stated purpose: "To chronicle how changing companies create and compete, to

---

* In the middle of 1999, International Data Corporation (IDC) issued a report that found that 35 percent of Internet-project decision makers had fired their consultants before the project was complete; most because of dissatisfaction with project management.

highlight new business practices, and to showcase the teams and individuals who are inventing the future and reinventing business."[3]

Beginning in June 2000, Kaplan encouraged employees and former employees of "troubled" companies to post their stories; rants and rumors about management, practices, and other employees. Many were fantasies, but more were real scoops about upcoming layoffs, payrolls not being met, and pending office shutdowns. The site became an obsession with many in the technology sector, as second, third, or fourth rounds of layoffs were rumored before the formal announcements.

News from the trenches of dot.coms dominated the stories on FuckedCompany.com in the early days, but was soon followed by stories from the consultancies, professional service firms, investment firms, media, and major corporations. These were not "missives" from the front office. They were thoughts, comments, stories, and worries from real people who worked within these companies. Often they attached memos from management along with their comments. These were what made the site such fun to read. The differences in language were amazing, from the stilted corporate speak of management to the more direct "screw you" that came from employees interpreting the memos.

The good news is that FuckedCompany.com, like so many more community bulletin boards, discussion groups, and chat forums, confirmed that the people-connectivity promise of the Web was still alive. As Christopher Locke, author of the *The Cluetrain Manifesto: The End of Business as Usual* said, "People didn't love the Net because it let them shop in their underwear. They loved the Net because it let them talk to other people, gave them a voice, and let them do their own thing in a public space that had never existed before."[4]

What Did We Learn?

The litany of mistakes made by dot.coms, the consultancies, investment advisors, and the media can be summed up with two words: hubris and inexperience. Surely the advisors should have known better, you say. So should the media, and the others. Maybe so, but it doesn't matter now. What matters is what remains. What did we learn? How can we use what we learned to everyone's advantage going forward?

Five things we learned:

1. *People drive the Web, not business.* The Web has given people—not consumers, or customers, or target markets, but people—the opportunity to connect to other people; to talk, complain, create, act, do, and be who they want to be. Most businesses missed the point. They saw the Web as just another "market opportunity," a new place to sell more "stuff." As they clamored over one another to post their catalogs and take advantage of this new e-tailing medium, people— as individuals, twosomes, small groups—were turning their own computers into Web servers, building their own sites, and joining discussion groups. Most were laughing at the "shovelware" coming from corporations. People, using the Web, exposed the underbelly of inflated dot.com egos, pompous corporate positioning, and bloated digital strategies.

2. *Technology changes faster than people.* Overestimating the speed at which people would adopt to technology innovations—buying, selling, and trading on the Web—was one of the biggest mistakes made by dot.coms. Investors pushed entrepreneurs, and entrepreneurs pushed designers, to get to market fast and get returns fast. Meanwhile, people went about their lives as they always had, going to their local grocery, butcher, cleaners, and pet shop. Change may be the only constant, and rapid change is a given in the technology sector; but people do not like change. People like the comfort of the familiar, the reassurance of repetition, the stability of certainty, the connections they have with other people. Yes, we change, but we change incrementally, while technology changes exponentially.

3. *The Internet is still in its infancy.* Many dot.coms came to market long before the infrastructure was in place to support them. Boo.com is a prime example. It launched as a global e-commerce fashion store, with stylish imagery, motion, sound, and a back-end that was to support multiple languages, multiple currencies, tax calculations on the fly, and multiple fulfillment partners. It was doomed before it got out of the gate. Not because these things are not technically possible. It was doomed because management did not realize the extreme complexity of the technologies involved, and even more important, the complexities of communication between all of the people required to make it work. The communications infrastructure was not in place to assure

that designers, developers, interpreters, lawyers, and accountants were all talking together, working toward a common goal.

4. *New channels do not replace old.* During the late nineties many businesses acted on the fear—spread by the new media—that online sales would replace offline sales. Middlemen, the agents and distributors that have traditionally mediated between companies and customers, feared "disintermediation." If buyers and sellers can find each other easily over the Web, who needs the middleman? History shows us repeatedly that communications innovations do not replace existing methods of communicating. Television did not replace radio and telephones did not replace the need for face-to-face meetings. They merely broadened the available possibilities for information exchange. The Web with its two-way, multiple channel, many-to-many connections has only enriched our communications palette.

5. *New channels require new thinking.* Too many companies tried to use the new media as if it were the old. Broadcasting their standard messages, putting up "brochureware" to tell us about their products and services, rather than thinking about the creative possibilities of the Web. The more successful businesses leveraged available tools; person-to-person trading; name-your-price bidding systems; manage your own account systems with automated and personalized notices of product/service changes, inventory changes, and wish lists fulfillments; and collaborative product design, collaborative purchasing, and collaborative thinking about what's working, what's not, and what else might be done.

A Legacy of Expansion

An interesting post appeared in *The Well* on September 20, 2002, from designer David Greene. He was commenting on a *Reuters* news report of a just-released survey showing that almost 20 percent of dot.com start-ups backed by venture capital failed before first stage investors could sell their shares. The article was a picture of gloom, discussing the bad business models and the investors' loss of billions of dollars from 1999 through 2000. Greene's take on the survey was just the opposite, "My reaction is excitement and optimism that over that two year period, it appears that somewhere in the neighborhood of 80 percent of the start-ups WERE successful."[5]

Probably not. Many did succeed and have continued to grow, but many others failed after first-stage or second-stage investors had escaped. Either way, it can all be chalked up to the unique uncertainties, inevitable risk, growing pains, and cost of experimentation to create something totally new. And this new thing is continuing to grow.

- As of February 2003, according to findings from Nielson/Netratings, 580 million people had access to the Internet with 168.6 million attributed to the U.S. Even with the market crash and the dot.com implosion, nearly 10 million people in the United States over the age of 16 gained access to the Internet between the end of 2001 and 2002.

- Almost three quarters of all Web visitors have incorporated applications including instant messengers, peer-to-peer file sharing, and media player viewing into their daily online experience.

- In December 2002, readership of the *New York Times* Web site overtook the paper's daily circulation numbers by about 100,000. This does not mean the paper will disappear. They will both feed into and off of one another.

- In early 2003 the U.S. Commerce Department's Census Bureau confirmed what other surveys had found; online retail sales were very good. Total e-commerce sales for 2002 were estimated at $45.6 billion, an increase of 26.9 percent from 2001.

The ultimate legacy of the dot.com boom may be the expansion of the Internet itself.

·

4

Business Fundamentals

The basic premise upon which every business is founded is to provide those who invest their time, energy, and money with returns commensurate with their investment. How this is achieved continuously changes. In this chapter, we will review two fundamental transformations that have occurred in business over the last twenty five years: the business, social, and cultural implications of these changes, and a number of related changes linked to the Web.

Change Begets Change

For the past one hundred years, the business of business has been business. It has refined its understanding of itself—its purposes, processes, and benefits. It learned to segment work into tasks, and to manage and direct masses of employees to accomplish the tasks. It improved on Ford's "any color they want as long as it's black." It reversed inventory management from LIFO to FIFO. It learned to segment markets and target messages. It implemented outsourcing to shift cost from fixed to variable. It embraced the principles of Total Quality Management and realigned its methods with its motives. Businesses have upsized, downsized, and right-sized. And in the last half of the final decade of the twentieth century, productivity boomed, the economy skyrocketed, and the business of business became the business of life.

Many of the economic fundamentals that drove the productivity boom that began in 1995 can be directly attributed to information technology. That year, the semiconductor product cycle quickened from three years to two. Intel pumped up their development, semiconductor prices plummeted, processing power rose, and companies took advantage of the cheaper prices by investing more in information technology. Sure, wild-eyed optimism caused many to get carried away, but as Harvard economist Dale Jorgenson says, "Many of the truisms of the boom, it turns out, were true."[1]

"Information technology is certainly a crucial part of the productivity story," says Kevin Stiroh, an economist with the Federal Reserve Bank of New York. "But it's a complex process. Without complementary innovations in organization, changes in the way companies use human capital, and changes in the workforce, the story would look very different."[2]

Two fundamental changes emerged in the last quarter-century that have had profound implications for any business:
• Soft assets are now more important than hard.
• Abundance is now more valuable than scarcity.

These two are intimately connected. They are strongly influenced by the connectivity of the Web. And, they result in a host of other changes with substantial consequence not only within an organization, but for society as a whole.

Soft Assets Are More Important Than Hard
The critical business assets of the "bricks and mortar" industrial economy were relatively easy to identify, label, and assess. Buildings, equipment, inventory, and accounts receivable all have "hard" depreciable value. On the other hand, things referred to as soft assets—brands, industry knowledge, intellectual property, human capital, strategic alliances, and customer/market data—are much harder to assess. These are intangible assets.

The value of intangibles, though hard to measure, is intuitively easy to grasp. Which would you rather own, the ability to manufacture tennis shoes, or the Nike brand? What is more valuable to today's game of basketball: the ball, the nets, the gym, the bleachers, or the players? Which would you rather buy, the latest Encyclopedia Britannica print set, or a computer with access to the Web?

This does not mean that hard assets are no longer important. Nike certainly needs manufacturing facilities to produce its shoes. But, the cost of materials, manufacturing facilities, and distribution that goes into getting a pair of Nike shoes into the store, is a small fraction of the price you pay. The balance is the cost of the brand. The strategy, design, advertising, promotion, training, service, and entertainment assure that the shoes in the store make it to your feet—and you like them. Since anyone with a little effort and capital could produce tennis shoes, the brand asset is more valuable than the hard assets.

Two of the three things Jack Welch, former chairman of General Electric (GE), thought were the most important things to measure in business were soft assets: customer satisfaction, and employee satisfaction. He often talked about the need to win "the hearts and minds" of employees, and believed that managers should be "hardheaded but softhearted." Speaking of creating business change, Welch said, "We're all working harder and faster. But unless we're also having fun, the transformation doesn't work. Our concept: Direct, personal, two-way communication is what seems to make the difference. Exposing people—without the protection of title or position—to ideas from everywhere."[3]

GE, like Nike, Coke, Ford, IBM, Merrill Lynch, and hundreds of other companies may not have it all right yet, but they are investing more and more in their soft assets.

Prioritizing Expense
In the early nineties, while attending a computer graphics conference in Florida, I slipped into a breakout session being held for commercial printers. The room was packed with two hundred to three hundred people facing a panel of five leading technology visionaries. After brief introductory remarks were delivered by each member of the panel on the radical changes occurring in information technology, the room exploded with questions. They were all—without exception—about investment in equipment decisions. "We are a moderately small company doing approximately $70 million in annual sales and are seriously considering a $2.5 million purchase of a new offset press. After hearing the comments today, maybe we should be looking at more digital prepress, or digital printing, or direct to plate printing, or . . ."

The tension in the room was high, and the conversations in the halls later convinced me that these printers were legitimately concerned about their futures. The problem was they all talked about investing in hard assets. Not one mentioned the knowledge they had about their clients' communications needs and how they might invest in that instead of equipment. None of them mentioned the possibility of investing in new technology and new skills to help their clients communicate in new ways. Most of them had databases filled with client information—stories, images, personnel lists, distribution lists, but they did not think of themselves as information managers or coordinators or even communication assistants. They were printers.

Printing presses, like all hard assets, wear out. That's why they depreciate. Knowledge, on the other hand, does not get used up. It grows over time. The more it is used, the more it is shared with others, the richer it becomes.

Increasing Value

One example of a company that has used its knowledge base to thrive even in an economic downturn is Arrow Electronics, Inc., the world's leading distributor of electronic components and computer products to industrial and commercial customers. Arrow is one of those "middlemen" that were supposed to be disintermediated by the Web.

Throughout the seventies and eighties, Arrow invested heavily in strategic acquisitions, infrastructure, and systems. It opened the first Automated Distribution Center, a robotic warehouse for parts packing and shipping, in 1985. In the same year, it became the first North American electronic components distributor to establish a presence outside of the Americas. Today the company has more than 200 sales locations and distribution centers in forty countries. When the Web began to take off in late 1996, Arrow did not get caught up in the hype. The company quietly went about its business, having extensive conversations with its customers about the customers' wants and needs.

Then in the fourth quarter of 1999, the company launched a suite of online supply chain management tools giving their customers Web-based, 24-hour access to Arrow's inventory of 3 million parts, plus the ability to place, modify, monitor, and manage every order online.

Over the following years Arrow has refined and added to its initial tools, becoming an integral part of its customers supply chain. Today, it is no longer a "parts picker," as distributors are often called. It is recognized for their turnkey design, product lifecycle analysis, technology feasibility analysis, inventory profiling, and materials management. These are all knowledge-based, value-added services. Arrow has also invested in its people, providing the tools, training, support, and flexible work schedules to make their lives more productive and enjoyable. The more Arrow has expanded its knowledge networks, the more tightly entrenched it has become with its customers and the stronger the relationship it has with employees.[4]

Abundance Is More Valuable Than Scarcity

In the industrial economy, scarcity of supply established value. Natural resources such as oil, gold, and diamonds were scarce and therefore considered valuable. As new products were introduced—cars, refrigerators, telephones, radios, and televisions—initial development and manufacturing costs limited quantity and made prices high. As manufacturing processes improved, prices came down, and products proliferated. Conventional, industrial-economy thinking believes these now-common products have less value.

For ages, economists have modeled economic growth by adding two factors, labor and capital, to create goods. The problem with this model is "diminishing returns." At some point the value of the goods produced equals the cost of the labor and goods used to produce them, and you have no more growth. In the last couple of decades, economist Paul Romer and other theorists have proposed a model that has come to be known as the New Growth Theory. In this new model, the principle of scarcity is turned upside down.

The new theory essentially divides the world into two productive inputs: "things" and "ideas." Only one person at a time can use things such as a hammer, a telephone, a lawnmower, or a car. On the other hand, ideas can be used by many people simultaneously, i.e., recipes, blueprints, formulas, methodologies, and software. They can be used to rearrange things. They can be copied, shared, and connected, thereby leading to more ideas. "Economic growth," Romer says, "arises from the discovery of new recipes and the transformation of things from low to high value configurations."[5]

The fax machine is the most obvious example. After millions of dollars were spent on development, the first machine produced was worth nothing. It took the second machine to give it value. The third, fourth, fifth, and one hundredth gave it even more value. The more fax machines that are connected, the greater the value of the fax network. As Kevin Kelly said, "When you buy a fax machine, you are not merely buying a $200 box. Your $200 purchases the entire network of all other fax machines in the world and the connections among them—a value far greater than the cost of all the separate machines. In the network economy, the more plentiful things become, the more valuable they become."[6]

Increasing Returns

Robert Metcalfe, the founder of 3com and the designer of the networking technology known as Ethernet, was the first to formulate a mathematical rule to explain the "increasing returns" tendency of networks. What has become know as Metcalfe's Law states: the usefulness of a network equals the square of the number of its users. All networks begin with a few participants. Depending on the value derived from belonging to the network, word spreads and more people join. As more people participate, the usefulness increases, word spreads even more, and even more people join. On a graph, this may appear as a horizontal line gradually rising. As more people join, the line continues to rise more steeply, creating an upward curve that eventually becomes a near-vertical line.

Microsoft is the classic example of Metcalfe's Law and of increasing economic returns. It may cost Microsoft millions of dollars for the first copy of Windows 98, but each copy thereafter is merely the cost of the disk on which it is stored. The more people who use the Microsoft platform, the more attractive it becomes. The more people who participate in the Microsoft business network—product users, developers, distributors, and resellers—the more powerful the network becomes. "The value of Windows increases exponentially as its users increase arithmetically."[7] This has made Bill Gates and the shareholders of Microsoft very wealthy. Another way to state the power of increasing returns is: "The more you sell, the more you sell."[8]

Although the pace may be quickening, most networks that exhibit increasing returns do not happen over night. The fax machine had been around for twenty years before it rounded the Metcalfe Curve sometime in the eighties. Then overnight it became a requirement of every business.

The technology productivity boom of 1995 was the result of some twenty years of "chip power" doubling every eighteen months. Microsoft was in business for eleven years before it went public in 1986, but it was the introduction of Windows NT in 1993 that took it around the curve and sales skyrocketed.

The Internet is the prototypical example of all the facets of increasing returns and the value of abundance. Though few noticed, the Net was around since the seventies gradually building a base of dedicated users. Then in 1991, when Tim Berners-Lee introduced the Web, the number of participants mushroomed and by the end of the decade the network had exploded around the world.

Today, for the relatively small (and continuously reducing) cost of a computer and a phone line, you have access to billions of documents from all over the globe, a growing world of information, an unbelievable range of human opinion, and purchasable products and services, plus the added value of the ability to copy the documents that interest you, to rearrange the information to suit your purposes, to throw your own opinion into the mix, and to sell your own products or services. The more people, businesses, institutions, and governments that join the network—regardless of how or what they contribute—the more valuable the network becomes. The added value resides in the abundance of related opportunities. The creative possibilities are nearly infinite. As Romer says, "We consistently fail to grasp how many ideas remain to be discovered. The difficulty is the same one we have with compounding. Possibilities do not add up. They multiply."[9]

The Web Advantage

The Web is now as necessary to business as the telephone. Yet many businesses continue to use it as nothing more than an expensive business card. And many designers seem content to design and redesign these animated, extravagant, corporate "hellos."

There is nothing wrong with Generation 1, "brochureware" Web sites for companies that have not been on the Web before. This is a good way for any company to get its feet wet. The problem arises when Generation 2, 3, 4, and more are still brochure sites, and many are.

Brochure sites do not take advantage of the unique capabilities of the Web: the ability to connect with people, get feedback, customize information to meet specific needs, provide for easy and immediate transactions, collect, analyze and store data, and collaborate on the development of new products and services.

Brochure sites do not reflect the changes now required to succeed in a knowledge-based network economy. If I can get the same product or service that you are offering from numerous other companies online (and I can), and all of these companies are only a couple of clicks away (which they are), why should I waste my time with you?

Changes in business have occurred in the following five areas as a result of the growth of the Web. These changes will grow in importance as the network economy continues to grow.

1. *Structures.* Since the fall of the Berlin Wall in 1989, we have seen walls crumble within and between business organizations. Physical environments have switched from "the corner office" to the "open plan" to, in many cases, "virtual offices." In a networked economy, the important organizational structure is connectivity—of all to all. Management hierarchy flattens and collaborative teams respond directly to the market. Employees are treated as equals in the business of a company's success. Information systems are no longer proprietary; they are open, not only within the company, but to suppliers, partners, and customers all via the Net. Departmental systems including inventory management, order management, warehouse management, customer data, product data, and accounting, are connected parts of the same system. All of the participants in the network are treated as equals in the success of the network.[10]

2. *Decision making.* Command and control may never go away but the networked environment favors more democratic forms of decision making: consensus, majority rule, small teams that select their own leaders, flexible teams that form to satisfy an immediate need, then reconfigure to meet another need. Five-year plans give way to a "mission" orientation—a sense of direction with a number of possible scenarios. Rapid adoption and incremental improvement move at the same pace. Flexibility is more important than "hard" decisions, and fixed procedures are replaced by playful new attempts. Yes, mistakes will be made. Learn from them and move on.

3. *Corporate culture.* The nine-to-five, by the book, blue suit and tie culture of early twentieth century business began to disappear in the eighties with "dress-down Fridays." The dot.com explosion of the nineties brought the "massage therapist, foosball, fun days and party nights" to the office. Most of these things did not survive. But the concepts of flexible schedules and work-life balance have lived on, and become increasingly important. In the networked economy, employees working together on a daily basis may be thousands of miles apart, in different time zones, yet working on the same project and deadlines. What was most important in the past is even more important today: personal commitment, responsibility, accountability, and trust.

4. *Marketing.* Demographic market segmentations no longer work. In the network economy, individuals, not statistics are what count. People do not think of themselves as "female upscale homemakers," or "male suburban teens." If you treat them as individuals, with respect and honesty, they may permit you to collect profile characteristics, which in turn will allow you to further customize your offer to them. This is a win-win proposition. It begins by thinking like a demanding customer:
   - Don't waste my time
   - Don't make me feel stupid
   - Make it easy for me to find and get what I want
   - Remember who I am and what I like
   - Customize your offering for me

5. *Making money.* Cash is still king. The third item Jack Welch thought was most important to measure was cash flow. If a company does not know where its cash is coming from and how it is being used it probably will not survive. Profits are a requisite of any business, but how cash is used to generate the profits has shifted. Highest quality, fastest service, and lowest price are now expected. So, how do you make a profit? A recent research report, from customer value research firm Miller-Williams, suggests that companies that understand customer value the best enjoy "pricing power" within their industry. These companies, which in the Miller-Williams study included Apple, Dell, Amazon, eBay, Toyota, and Volkswagen among many others, have moved away from traditional methods

of setting prices such as the cost-plus model or benchmarking competitor's prices to what is called "value pricing."[11] The companies that can identify what's truly important to their customers—what they think is of value in the purchase decision—and can meet their expectations, gain pricing power over their competitors. To identify what's important to your customers and increase their satisfaction, open your information systems to the customer, multiply the touch points, and customize to exceed the need at each point.

The Hard Voice of Business Softens

For over a hundred years the *Wall Street Journal* has been the leading voice of business, the scorekeeper for the industrial economy. It recorded the market prices, tracked the ups and downs, and delivered the facts of business. In black and white text, without photography, it painted our pictures of the Herculean efforts of corporate titans as they built America. It followed the global leaders and led a world of followers, cautiously revealing the business practices that led to either pitfalls or prosperity. There were no frills, no sports, no travel, and no leisure. The *Wall Street Journal* was about the work, and works of business.

In 1995, the *Wall Street Journal Online* was launched. It has become the largest paid-subscription news site on the Web. *CareerJournal, CollegeJournal, OpinionJournal, StartupJournal, RealEstateJournal* are just a few of the *Journal*'s additional, value-added, Web-publishing ventures launched in the last few years.[12]

In April 2002, the printed *Journal* made the most radical changes to its front cover in over sixty years. Among other things, it added color. The paper also added new features and sections, such as the *Personal Journal*. It now includes photographs and color illustrations as it covers an array of new topics, which in the past were considered "soft issues," topics such as health care and family concerns, personal finance, travel, and consumer electronics and automobiles. The *Journal* now provides readers with information that affects their daily lives beyond the workday. As its new marketing slogan suggests, the new *Wall Street Journal* is: Business. And the Business of Life.

5

Expanding the Circle

"The ultimate goal of the Web," Berners-Lee said, "is to support and improve our Web-like existence in the world . . . I designed it for a social effect—to help people work together—and not as a technical toy."[1] This does not mean some people. It means all people. If the Web is about expanding human potential then all humans must be included. What has come to be known as the Digital Divide—the gap between those who have access to the network and those who do not—is a real and serious issue. As we will discover in this chapter, it is also a huge opportunity, to which many creative people are responding.

The challenge is to find ways to make the Web more available. The benefit—following the theory of increasing returns, and abundance being more valuable than scarcity—is that the more people who are included, the better it is for everyone, socially and economically.

Even though the price of access to the Web continues to come down, it remains substantially beyond the reach of millions of people. Underprivileged people who do not come close to having the financial resources required, as well as people who may have the resources but because of physical disabilities cannot use 90 percent of what's available. For both of these groups there are new glimmers of hope.

Access for the Disabled

The opportunities provided by the Web for people to connect with people, to learn, to work, and to shop are most important for the people who have difficulties doing these things off the Web. Some people have disabilities that prevent them from easily going to the mall, the office, or to the library. This is a larger group than you may think. According to the Center for Applied Special Technology (CAST), a not-for-profit educational organization, more than 21 million people have disabilities that impact their ability to use the Web.[2]

For the past six years, the goal of CAST has been making Web sites available to these people. CAST is the group that developed Bobby, the market leader in Web site accessibility software. This analysis software and testing tool identifies Web site accessibility problems, and allows designers to test critical accessibility issues while still in the development stage. Bobby checks for compliance with government standards, including the U.S. Government's Section 508 (see below), and the guidelines provided by W3C's Web Accessibility Initiative.

In the fall of 2002, the Watchfire Corporation acquired Bobby from CAST. This could be very good news. Watchfire management has expressed strong commitment to Web site accessibility and they undoubtedly have the development resources and marketing expertise to take Bobby to the next level.[3]

The one potential problem is that Bobby is not an open source code, and Watchfire is a for-profit company. This means Bobby becomes a proprietary tool of Watchfire that they will sell to others. The company has already limited what was a free testing capability available online. This almost guarantees that a large number of the very people the technology is meant to help will no longer be able to afford to use it. If Watchfire management is wise, they will continue to allow use of a free current version of Bobby, and only charge for advanced versions. By using the "currency" of good will and trust, Watchfire can build on the established market base. If they do not, many current users will simply find other sources. And there will be many other sources.

Since the U.S. Congress amended the Rehabilitation Act in 1998 establishing the Section 508 accessibility standards, more organizations and leading companies have begun to address the issue. Section 508 requires that federal agencies' electronic and information technology be accessible to people with disabilities. This means that any organization working with federal agencies on Web initiatives must also make their electronic and information technology accessible. Forrester Research has reported, "government action and an aging population will make Web Accessibility a priority over the next two years." Microsoft, Adobe, and Macromedia currently offer online accessibility support links on *www.section508.gov*.

An ongoing collaboration among organizations affected by Section 508, including industry, government, and other communities, is *The Accessibility Forum*, which began in the spring of 2001. Participants at the February 2003 meeting, hosted by Apple Computer, Inc., included Adobe Systems, Freedom Scientific, Sun Microsystems, the Department of Justice, SAP, Oracle, Macromedia, and the Social Security Administration, among many others.[4]

In December 2002, the World Wide Consortium (W3C) issued User Agent Accessibility Guidelines 1.0. This is the third in a series of Web Accessibility Initiative guidelines. "For the past five years," noted Tim Berners-Lee, W3C director, "the technical and disability experts in the Web Accessibility Initiative have provided definitive guidelines for making accessible Web content and designing authoring software that does the same, automatically. Today with the announcement of the UAAG, developers have the specific guidance they need to make Web browsers and media players more useful to more people."[5]

Access for people with disabilities is now up to designers and developers—and those who pay for their services—to choose accessible design over inaccessible design. And, increasingly, they will be required to make the better choice.

Access for the Disadvantaged

In many ways this is the more difficult problem. It may seem that Web design has no bearing on the lives of people who do not have access to the Web because they have no access to computers. Nothing could be further from the truth. The Web has increasingly become the information and economic backbone of America and much of the rest of the world. There is abundant evidence that the Internet is now the primary means by which people get information that is essential to their participation in society. And the more they participate the better it is for everyone.

A Pew Research Center report at the end of last year said, "When they are thinking about health care information, services from government agencies, news, and commerce, about two thirds of all Americans say they expect to be able to find such information on the Web."[6] The most interesting part of the report is that "even 40 percent of people who are not Internet users say they expect the Web to have information and services in these essential online arenas."

The more we design and build out this information infrastructure without thinking of the disadvantaged, the higher the barrier becomes between the haves and have-nots. The knowledge-based network economy requires people with education and ideas. At the same time, the automation of manufacturing and distribution often driven by the Web eliminates jobs traditionally filled by unskilled laborers. If we do not provide access to those who may have filled these jobs, we are effectively closing the door on their future. And we are limiting our own potential because we are limiting the network.

There are three areas that need to be addressed:
- Access to computers and to the Internet;
- Education about the use of computers and the benefits of the Web; and
- Employment technology literacy required to survive in the new economy.

In one form or another these have been agenda items for policy makers, think tank leaders, and many corporations for years. Companies such as Apple, IBM, Microsoft, and others have contributed computers and software to schools and other nonprofit organizations. In some instances they have provided free training or personnel to assist in setting up networks. As the network grows, more of this will occur. But the real glimmer of hope comes from the bottom, not the top. In true Internet fashion, grassroots initiatives have sprung up all around the country driven by the vision, energy, and dedication of individuals. Individuals such as "Toni" Stone, Rey Ramsey, David Prendergast, Jessica Zucker, Rajeswari Pingali, and many others, are committed to making the Web work for everyone. As the network continues to grow, and costs continue to come down, these few examples will multiply many times over.

Antonia "Toni" Stone—CTCNet
At least a decade before anyone began talking about the "digital divide," Toni Stone, a former public school teacher, started a computer technology

center in the basement of a housing development in Harlem, New York. Stone founded Playing to Win and the Harlem Community Computing Center in 1983 because she realized, "In an increasingly technologically dominated society, people who are socially and/or economically disadvantaged will become further disadvantaged if they lack access to computers and computer-related technologies."

Stone was a leading advocate for equitable access. Mobilizing public and private support for the PTW Network, she turned her personal commitment into a national network of neighborhood technology learning. In 1994, she founded the Community Technology Centers' Network, connecting community centers in the United States and abroad to promote equitable empowerment through technology skills and usage. The CTCNet brings together agencies and programs that provide opportunities to people of all ages to explore and discover technologies, and to develop personal skills and confidence. It offers resources to enhance each affiliated agency's ability to provide technology access and education to its members and to nurture other like-minded programs.

Toni Stone died in November of 2002. She left behind a legacy of dedication to leveling the playing field. She also left behind a growing CTCNet, a network of more than one thousand community technology centers where people in low-income communities gain access to computers and computer-related technology such as the Web.[7]

Rey Ramsey—One Economy
Rey Ramsey opened the doors of One Economy in July 2000. His goal was to maximize the potential of technology to help low-income people build assets and raise their standard of living. His vision, however, did not start with computers. It started with housing. "Once you put something in the home," Ramsey says, "it has a better chance of becoming part of the culture. And, if it's part of the culture, it can lead to real change."[8]

Less than 30 percent of the lowest-income households have Internet access, so One Economy partners with government housing authorities, community-based nonprofit organizations, and affordable-housing owners, to "wire" more low-income households for access. One Economy lobbies for new affordable housing to include Internet access, and works with the private sector to figure out the best ways to get the job done.

Access is only part of the story however, appropriate content is equally important. A survey of one thousand Web sites found less than 10 percent appropriate for adults with limited literacy. In response, One Economy launched the Beehive (*www.thebeehive.org*) in October 2001, with consultants provided by Cisco, and funding support from the Ford Foundation, Washington Mutual, and the Fannie Mae Foundation. The site provides information people can use to improve their lives and join the economic mainstream. It is structured around five basic areas—money, health, school, jobs, and family—and is written specifically for low-income people, at a literacy level they can understand.

In the year and a half since the site was launched, traffic has increased from eight thousand visitors per month to more than 54,000 visitors per month. And over the last year visitors have spent an average of fifteen minutes on the site each visit. This sounds like the beginnings of a real change.

David Prendergast—America's Second Harvest

Through a network of over two hundred food banks and food-rescue programs, America's Second Harvest, the largest domestic hunger-relief organization in the United States, provides emergency food assistance to more than 23 million hungry Americans each year. It serves all fifty states and Puerto Rico by distributing food and grocery products to approximately 50,000 local hunger-relief organizations including food pantries, soup kitchens, women's shelters, and community kitchens.

The food comes from what would otherwise be waste—surplus from manufacturers and food processors like Kraft, Hormel, General Mills, Nabisco, and ConAgra—as well as from distributors and retailers. In 2001, Second Harvest distributed more than 2 billion pounds of packaged food, 50 percent more than distributed the year before. The increase, according to David Prendergast, vice president of technology for Second Harvest, is due to the implementation of ResourceLink, a new online tool that allows suppliers of food products to report surpluses directly from their plants to the network. This reduces delivery time and adds valuable shelf life for the food banks. There will certainly be additional efficiencies in the future, as Prendergast says, "We're barely scratching the surface of what technology will enable us to do."[9]

Jessica Zucker—Global Reproductive Health Forum
The Web is not just an American phenomenon. The Gateway for Total
Youth Empowerment (GATYE) is an invaluable Web resource designed
for adolescents in Nigeria. Begun in 1999 with a grant from the
Packard Foundation to the Center for Health Sciences, Training
Research, and Development (CHESTRAD)—a nonprofit Nigerian non-
government organization—the GATYE is accessible from cyber cafés
strategically located in Ibadan and Lagos where the highest percentage
of Nigerians live.

The GATYE has collaborated with the Global Reproductive Health
Forum (GRHF)—an internet-based project from the School of Public
Health at Harvard—on Web training, on-going technical support,
proposal development, and occasional visits to Nigeria for face-to-face
brainstorming. The site provides health education, referral information
for health services, educational support, and vocational training in an
interactive manner appealing to the youth of Nigeria. "By incorporat-
ing all of these various aspects of a teenager's life, we act as a support
and advocate for these young people," said Jessica Zucker, the project
director of GRHF. "The GATYE is a resource," she added, "that is vital
to this country and many others."[10]

Rajeswari Pingali—Mobile Telecenter
Spreading literacy to villagers in the remote countryside of India via a
custom-designed Honda off-road motorcycle, carrying a solar-powered
laptop computer, may sound like a pipe dream. In fact, it was the dream
of Rajeswari Pingali, one of twelve fellows participating in the Digital
Vision Fellowship program at Stanford University.

Digital Vision, funded by the Reuters Foundation, began in October
of 2001 to address technology accessibility issues. The small program
(twelve fellows in 2002) encourages participants, using the vast resources
at Stanford, to develop their own initiatives for feasible, small-scale
solutions to making information technology accessible and relevant to
people living in remote regions of developing nations.

Stuart Gannes, the program's director, said the primary focus is on
promoting information technology use in areas such as literacy, agricul-
ture, commerce, and health care. The fellows work with their own
companies, and other nonprofit foundations, for funding the projects

they propose, such as increasing wireless phone access in rural Brazil and enabling e-government in Mexico. They also work with foundations or organizations with expertise in the targeted regions to help implement the final project.

Fellow Arnon Kohavi is working with the San Francisco–based Jhai Foundation, which has worked with five rural villages in the Hin Heup district of Laos since 1998. Kohavi addressed voice and data communication projects during his year at Stanford, and is developing a wireless network to link the five Laotian villages sometime next year.

The "mobile telecenter" developed by Pingali gained the support of two foundations and a state government in India. This kind of support, critical to long-term success, is helping turn Pingali's vision into reality.[11]

Pingali, like Zucker, Prendergast, and Ramsey are doing what Toni Stone started years earlier. They are all expanding the network, and as the network expands, the benefits, the possibilities, the social and economic returns expand. Remember that the usefulness of a network equals the square of the number of its users. The more we design to include everyone, the more everyone will gain.

6

The Growth Continues

Although the speculative frenzy has subsided, all researchers agree that the number of Internet users will continue to climb steadily over the next several years. New tools and technologies discussed in this chapter are already having a substantial impact, and numerous industries and institutions will be affected. Even more important, as the Web becomes deeply integrated into more and more daily activities, the time spent online will also continue to increase. In the past year, in ten out of twelve global markets measured by Nielson/Netratings, total time spent online grew significantly. The growth is attributed to higher speed connectivity and increased familiarity and dependence on the Internet.

Between May and October of 2002, time spent online in Germany and Sweden rose 22 percent over the previous year. In Hong Kong, Web time usage increased by more than 10 percent for the same six-month period, and the United States showed a 7.7 percent increase.

Costs Come Down

Meanwhile, according to a Direct Marketing Association (DMA) report from October 2002, a major shift in Web site development and promotional spending has occurred. The overall average cost for Web site development (excluding promotional costs), went from $535,480 in 2000 to $159,150 in 2001. Both my own experience and my discussions with numerous Web designers suggest that the average has slipped well below $100,000 for 2003. Of course this all depends on the size of company and the complexity of the site. Larger companies are more likely to spend upwards of $80,000 while smaller companies often produce "brochure" sites for no more than $5,000–10,000.

Marketing budgets, according to the DMA survey, shifted from an average of over $750,000 in 2000 to about $325,000 in 2001. Some of this certainly may be attributed to the limp economy. More of it can be attributed to a realization of where real business value resides on the Web. "As marketers gain a better understanding of their Return On Investment (ROI), they have begun to allocate more resources to online site development than promoting their Web sites as the way to increase profitability. Improving the customers' experience online is now a priority."[1] This means greater opportunities for Web designers in nearly all industries.

New Tools, Products, and Trends

It is the nature of the Web that new technologies spawn new products and new trends, which increase the use of the Web and in turn spawn newer technologies, products, and trends. Almost daily now, there are announcements of new network-based tools, new languages which allow the tools to work, new products connected to the Web, and new information gathering and distributing trends. Three in particular are currently accelerating Web growth: Wi-Fi, IM, and Blogs:

1. *Wi-Fi.* The hottest thing in the United States in 2003 was wireless hot spots. Wi-Fi is the branded name for these wireless LANs— areas wired for high-speed wireless Internet access such as coffee shops, airports, city parks, and in a few cases, entire small towns. Bryant Park in the middle of Manhattan is wireless and sees a lot of laptops at lunchtime as soon as the weather turns warm. Many college campuses are at least partially wireless so students lounging on the lawn can access the Web. Warehouses are using wireless for real-time inventory checks, and hospitals are using wireless to provide bedside access to patient records. Gartner Research says the Wi-Fi market doubled in 2002 and should show another 60 percent increase this year. There is currently still some confusion between competing standards—802.11b and 802.11a—which have to do with speed and possible interference from a noisy spectrum. But, by the time you are reading this, these issues should all be resolved

with the introduction of a third standard, 802.11g, or a convergence of all of the standards into a single wireless product. There are currently security issues with Wi-Fi, but this is not dampening its growth.[2]

2. *IM.* Instant messaging is not new. Teenagers have been using AOL's IM or Yahoo!'s Messenger for sometime. It's faster than e-mail, pops up on their screen no matter what they may be working on, and lets them know who else may be online. Developers or "coders," who often work with earphones tuned to their favorite music so they can concentrate, frequently use IM to talk with other developers sitting no more than a few feet away. It's easier and less interruptive than stopping to take off the earphones to speak out loud. Many business users have also logged onto consumer applications of IM to provide customer support or to deliver messages to large audiences simultaneously. The difficulty with these consumer applications is security. The unencrypted messages are sent through public networks. What's new is IM software tailored to business to minimize the security issue. Goldman Sachs, Merrill Lynch, Salomon Smith Barney, and Sanford Bernstein are using Hub IM software from Communicator. This connects their businesses without the use of a common e-mail server such as used by AOL or Microsoft IM. Communicator is one of several companies now targeting IM to the business market. Yahoo! will ship their business-oriented IM offering sometime this year.[3]

3. *Blogs.* Fulfilling the promise of participation media, Weblogs or "blogs," are personal diaries, opinions, or journals offering commentary on current events with links to other articles, comments or musings of a similar nature from other "bloggers." Like instant messaging, blogs are not new. Blogmania began late in 1999 with the introduction of tools such as Edit This Page and Blogger.com. These are free services that allow individuals to design and publish their own Weblogs without having to know HTML. Blogs are as diverse as the personalities that produce them, ranging from fierce to funny to frightening. Some have been around for years, are frequently updated, and have quite a following; others are short-lived. Personal blogs have led to blog lists, and to community and portal blogs such as MetaFilter and Blogroots. Blog culture has also

led to protocols, which automatically link comments on one blog to a "source" on another blog.

Other protocols allow bloggers' computers to receive updates through "news feeders" and other sites such as Weblogs.com are tracking blogs and making "blog trends" available. No one seems to know exactly how many blogs are out there. "More than half a million" was the phrase used by the *Wall Street Journal* on November 18, 2002, in an article that referred to blogs as "one of the twenty-first century's burgeoning media."[4] By May 18, 2003, the *New York Times* had the number up to "an estimated three million active blogs online."

With blogs getting the attention of mainstream media such as the *Journal* and the *Times*, companies have now begun to realize that the concept of blogs—the combination of personal opinion and news commentary—has marketing potential. When Macromedia launched three new software products on the Web last year, it added a set of blogs to its site. Each blog has a community manager who communicates directly with customers, answering questions and directing them to other relevant information. "Within the space of a couple of days we had hundreds of thousands of posts,"[5] said Tom Hale, Macromedia vice president in charge of developer relations. Traditional online feedback forms do not allow the same kind of quick multi-voice information sharing as blogs. Through the provision of useful information and open discussion between managers and members of the community, Macromedia gains the trust of its user community.

Industry Growth and Change

The Web has affected nearly all businesses, large or small. Most have struggled with balancing their old business methods with the new. Three of the most changed industries are highlighted below.

Self-service Travel

Travel is the number one activity among Internet consumers. More than 60 million households in the United States booked travel online in 2002. According to Forrester Research, they spent approximately

$20 billion on those bookings, or 10 percent of the travel industry total. Airline bookings were the largest share, but hotel bookings are growing faster. Forrester expects hotel bookings online to more than double over the next four years.

Online bookings are generally good for the consumer. By serving themselves online, they get lower prices. By waiting until the last moment, they get even lower prices. This is both good and bad for the airlines, hotels, and car rental companies. They have spent heavily on technology to build online services, meanwhile consumers comparison shop for the lowest possible fares. The good news for the industry, according to PhoCusWright, a travel industry consulting firm, is "that airlines will save $200 million in travel agent commissions and other fees by selling tickets directly from their Web sites, while car rental companies and hotels will save another $200 million combined by doing so."[6]

Analysts expect travel companies will increase their use of the Web in the future and consumers can expect to see a host of other online changes. "Used to be, airlines differentiated themselves with service, but technology will now be the big differentiator," said Henry Harteveldt, an analyst at Forrester. "Airlines and other sites will offer many more online options, like flight alerts, and trip reminders."

Entertaining Entertainment

A late 2001 report from PricewaterhouseCoopers on the entertainment industry projected strong growth for the industry through 2005, driven primarily by the importance of the Internet as a distribution medium. The study suggested growing demand for online books, music, newspapers and magazines, and predicted that the online distribution of filmed entertainment would soon become a reality. It also suggested that the industry would develop new business models that would help drive the Internet toward a paid-subscription model for content.

As mentioned earlier, the *Wall Street Journal*'s pay-for-subscription model has thus far been very successful. In the film distribution arena a young company that went public last spring is also doing well. Netflix, the largest online entertainment subscription service in the United States, provides more than one million subscribers access to a library of over 13,500 movie, television, and other film properties. For $20 a month subscribers can rent as many DVDs as they wish with no return dates and no late fees. The DVDs are delivered free-of-charge by first class mail. Following the Amazon model, Netflix uses personalization technology that provides recommendations based on a member's tastes and preferences, and allows members to post movie reviews.

The more entertaining aspect of the entertainment industry is listening to the lawyers, lobbyists, public relations people, and politicians as they jump through hoops trying to preserve the old world. Ever since Napster, they have been threatening to sue anyone who questions the "established" order. Media conglomerates are in merger frenzy as they look for ways to control the use of digital entertainment. Suffice it to say, that strict command and control will only waste time and money as people, and increasing digital power, continue to drive the Web forward. In the near future, look for Netflix and similar companies to provide downloadable movies for even less than they now charge for DVDs.

Banking on the Banks

Online bill payment in 2003 was growing in popularity, according to Gartner research; it expected the market to grow by about 38 percent, to 40 million users. A separate study by the Pew Research Center in November of 2002 found that the number of Americans who have done some of their banking online grew by 164 percent since 2000. And a third report, from Celent Communications, looking at American online banking against the global picture, put United States penetration at 22 percent in 2002.

"While the dot.com party may be over, U.S. retail bankers are just beginning to celebrate their online banking accomplishments," said Alenka Grealish, retail-banking analyst at Celent. "With national adoption rates reaching 20 percent in North America, online banking is becoming a mainstream phenomenon. Twenty percent, however, is just the tip of the iceberg. Banks in Nordic countries and South Korea have pushed adoption beyond 35 percent."[7]

Banks should not celebrate too fast, however. Most still have a long way to go in terms of offering "value-added" features such as customer self-service, bundling payment plans, automatic enrollment, and developing interfaces that are focused on customer need, rather than on bank services. All of this is good news for Web designers serving the banking industry.

Invisible Wings

After the attacks of 9/11, Americans realized how unconnected many of our government agencies were. The FBI, CIA, NSA, as well as regional and local security and law enforcement organizations were still holding information in silos, protecting their turfs, hoarding knowledge rather than sharing. The harm caused by this was certainly not intentional. It's just the way things had always been done. A decade of rapid technological, communication, and social change and we were still slogging our way forward "with one foot stuck in the mud of our past." Overnight the world had gotten much smaller, a lot faster, and more open than we ever thought possible.

Watching television newscasts of the Iraqi war in March 2003, I was struck by the awesome connectivity of it all. Command central set up in containers in Doha, Qatar, was jammed with personnel working on laptops, scrolling Web pages, linking to databases, sending e-mails. The missiles, we were told, using multiple digital guidance systems, were orders of magnitude smarter than they were just ten years earlier. We were shown a missile being fired from a battleship in the Persian Gulf—a video clip, e-mailed from the ship just moments before. Saddam Hussein's palace complex, airfields, and oil wells were all visually available via DigitalGlobe imagery from Earthviewer.com, and four talking heads simultaneously delivered their opinions from different parts of the world. We had the cell phone numbers and e-mail addresses for most of the leading Iraqi commanders and government officials. And we listened to the "chatter"—looking for changes in the patterns of communication.

The week before the Iraqi war began, George Packer told the following story in an article for the *New York Times Magazine*:

> On the day after September 11, antiwar activist Eli Pariser sent an e-mail to a number of friends urging them to press their politicians to respond to the 9/11 attacks with restraint. His friends passed the letter to their friends who passed it on to more friends and it replicated exponentially. A few days later, he joined forces with David Pickering, a recent graduate from the University of Chicago, who had posted a petition with a similar message on a campus Web site. Pariser posted Pickering's petition to his own site and on September 18, 120,000 people from 190 countries signed the petition. By

•

October 9, less than 30 days after he had begun, Pariser mailed the petition to George Bush. It was over 3,000 pages, with more than 500,000 signatures. The White House did not respond, but Pariser discovered the tremendous power of the Web. "It was word of mouth," he says. "This is why this system of organizing works." Later he commented, "It's not the Internet that's cool—it's what it allows people to do."[8]

He's right. He's also wrong. The Internet is cool. It's cool because it's a meta-idea—an idea that supports the creation, production and proliferation of other ideas.

Like the seeds of a dandelion blown by the wind, the promise of the Web continues to spread, with each new site containing the germ of many more.

The Practice

*T*he practice of Web design is just that. Something we practice—and practice, and practice, and practice. If we ever get it 100 percent right we will all be out of business. There is no 100 percent right. There are far too many variables, too many "ifs," too many possibilities for change—new information, methodologies, and technologies; new needs, desires, and capabilities; old needs, practices, and habits—that must be accommodated.

From the time I first thought about this book, in early 2002, to the time it will be available from the publisher, in early 2004, the total amount of information in the world will have doubled. It will double again in the next two to three years. This will certainly impact how and what we continue to communicate, and the language we use to do so. Somewhere in all that new information will be at least one new thing, maybe a dozen or many more that will bear on the Web site you are now planning.

As we will discover, the design of Web sites is an imprecise process. Peoples' incredibly variable reaction to the growing abundance of information, how they understand it, manage it, and share it, is a challenge for even *the most competent designers. There are, however, many useful tools and methodologies, which we will explore, that can help identify and satisfy the site visitor, and satisfy business objectives. There are simple methods that may be used to help structure and organize information and then test that organization. There is a lengthy discussion on the meaning of "brand" on the Web, how it is conveyed and interpreted. And finally, there are some basic standards, and systems guidelines to be followed for developing practical, intuitive, scalable, and accessible sites.*

It is important to remember that none of these suggestions is hard and fast, cast in concrete. That does not mean the ideas are whimsical or unreliable. They are based on substantial evidence gained over ten years of Web design experience. But things change, and that is the point. The methods and tools suggested are flexible and should be adapted to current needs. That is why the practice of Web design is just that. It will never be perfect, but it will continue to get better as all of us continue to practice.

7

The Information Age Is History

Sirens are screeching, car horns are blaring, and a bullhorn is bellowing for people to clear the street just outside my open window. It is the passage to summer—the first day of spring madness in New York. But this riotous noise is music compared to the continuing cacophony of mass media that assaults me from different directions—the chaos of "information," "news," and "marketing messages" boiling out of radios, televisions, newspapers, magazines, films, billboards, telephones, paging devices, and the Internet.

There was a time when information was precious, when news was important. We collected and stored the facts in our heads. But something began to happen around the middle of the last century. Information got ahead of us. It started to grow at a rate we were unprepared to handle. Throughout the sixties and seventies, information abundance made collecting and recalling more selective and more difficult. During the eighties, real angst set in. We suffered from "Information Anxiety," as Richard Wurman explained in his classic book by the same name. In the nineties, information became the currency of business—the preferred medium of exchange, and the information managers became information officers. Today, we have rounded the Metcalfe curve, and this currency has become a commodity, another mass-produced, unspecialized, overdeveloped product. And we are nearly drowning in it.

An Ancient Currency
Information has always been our currency. Since the beginning of cellular life when one cell exchanged data with another and then others,

until by some stroke of ingenuity, the neuron emerged enabling two cells to communicate over distance. "With that single enabling innovation, the variety of life boomed. With neurons, life no longer had to remain bounded in a blob. It was possible to arrange cells into almost any shape, size, and function. Butterflies, orchids, and kangaroos all became possible. Life quickly exploded in a million different unexpected ways . . . "[1]

Humans emerged and developed languages. They told their stories to one another and the stickiness of the information became the foundation of social glue. They bartered cloth for clay pots and for shoes for their horses, but the real currency was knowledge—how to weave the fabric, or craft the pots, or shoe the horse. From the earliest Sumerian pictographers scratching events on clay tablets to the revolution of Gutenberg's printing press, and the innovations in publishing that followed, information was the light on every path to power. With the inventions of Morse's telegraph, Bell's telephone, Marconi's radio, and thousands of lesser-known "data distributors," information became the oil in all the engines of commerce.

Many of the business "change programs" during the past century, which were mentioned earlier, were not uniformly beneficial, but the total effect has certainly given us more stuff. Yes, there is still an enormous gap between the haves and the have-nots, but today, there are more products and services—increasingly information-based—available at higher quality, in less time, and at less cost than at any time in history. The problem is not scarcity of supply; it is scarcity of demand. Who wants all of this stuff? No one.

But this is the wrong question. The question should be: Who wants some of this stuff? And the answer is: everyone. People want what *they* want. They want what will fulfill *their* desires, what will satisfy *their* particular needs. Rich or poor, they want the things that will make their lives easier, richer, more meaningful and more fun. And the Web, following the rules of openness and "plenitude," is increasingly making this possible.

Information as currency is not new. Without it, we would have no history. What has changed—continuously—is the way we exchange it. And with each major change a new information revolution begins. Each bringing with it another set of concerns about the implications of such a change. "What hath God wrought?" was the first message Samuel Morse sent from Washington to Baltimore with his telegraph in 1844.

The creation of information space brought about by the Internet and the Web is only the latest in an ongoing procession of innovations that allow humankind to continue exploring new paths, and creating new engines for growth—creative, economic, and humanitarian. The practice of Web design is fundamentally about understanding this latest change, what it means to be informed, the enormity of the spaces in which information resides, the multitude of channels through which it flows, and the methods and tools for accessing, evaluating, storing, sharing, navigating, and governing what is available.

One Cannot, Not Communicate

Virtually all activity, even lack of activity, can be considered communication. Yet clarity in communications is one of our most difficult problems. What does it mean to be informed? Most people who study this question agree that to be informed requires more than just data. The data must be meaningful or useful to the recipient. Before undergoing any physical operation in a hospital today, you must give your "informed" consent. This means you must understand (often nearly an impossible task) the information being presented. Numerous court cases have established that simply putting information before a patient is not sufficient to assure that the person understands the gravity of the situation. Questions must be answered, discussions held, to determine the level of understanding.

"Informed" compliance with local, state, and government laws requires that we understand the laws. No one seems to know if we really do, since governments are not sued as often as doctors and hospitals. But somehow we manage to muddle our way through, grasping the essence of the things most relevant to our lives, and ignoring or keeping a weary eye on the balance.

Today, we are an "informed" citizenry that makes "informed" decisions about a host of incredibly complex issues. Many things influence the degree to which we are *truly* informed, but two areas deserve special attention from Web designers.

First, our primary language is "fuzzy" by its nature. Words, no matter how precise we try to make them refuse consistent definition. The standards for interpretation, for meaning on which we can agree, are not precise. At the code level of individual characters, we can all agree at least in our primary tongue, that an *A* is an *A*, a *B* is a *B*, and so on. But, as soon as we gather several of these characters together to form a word our agreement crumbles. The word "peace" has been in the global spotlight for decades, yet we cannot agree on its meaning. Place any word into a line-up with other words to form a sentence, even a simple sentence, and the problem of interpretation escalates. This is obvious in the following two sentences. "This is part of the peace process." "We are on the road to peace." Is the peace in these sentences an activity or a location—a series of events or a place we will recognize when we get there?

The fuzziness of language is also reflected in its ambiguity. For example, the ambiguity found in the following real newspaper headlines taken from Steven Pinker's *The Language Instinct: How the Mind Creates Language*:[2]

- Child's Stool Great for Use in Garden
- Stiff Opposition Expected to Casketless Funeral Plan
- Drunk Gets Nine Months in Violin Case
- Queen Mary Having Bottom Scraped

This difficulty—the lack of precision and the ambiguity in our language that causes all this trouble—is also what makes language so wonderful. It allows us to continually add words, delete words, shift the meaning of words, and in this process of reinventing our language, extend our creative options—our capacity for knowing in unknown ways.

Second, by relying too heavily on our primary language—words—we may miss the deeper meaning often conveyed by the context in which the words are wrapped. The ability to communicate complex ideas is said to be the most distinguishing characteristic of the human species. But it is not restricted to reading, writing, and arithmetic. And we are not alone in our ability to communicate without words.

Nature is filled with amazing examples of complex non-verbal communication; from the red spot on a herring gull's bill that needs only to be pecked for a baby gull to receive food; to the extravagant dance of the honey bee that conveys the precise location and approximate yield of a new-found field of pollen; to the mysterious exchange of navigational information among Monarch butterflies that passes through four generations before leading the great-grand children hundreds of miles back to a home they have never seen.

Like the rest of nature, we are informed, even on the Web in its primitive state, by all of our senses. Content cannot exist without a context. The speed with which a site downloads; the amount of "god-awful" clutter, or lack of clutter; the impact of color and sound; the amount, character, and direction of motion, all make an impression—convey information—before we can read the first three words. The context of any message is equally as important, often more important, than the content.

On the Web, like everywhere else, communication is not just a ping-pong volley of data exchanges, it is a dance; with kicks and jumps and twist and turns, and it can be as rhythmic, raucous, or ridiculous as the dancing partners desire. Meaning will be determined by the minds involved.

No More Best Practices

Businesses love to manage. Traditionally that is how tasks were accomplished. Business managed the process and measured the outcome. This worked well for businesses in the early part of the last century, but with the explosion of information availability, new "management" processes—driven by technology requirements—often do more harm than good. They are still linear, controlling, fixed in a word-built world, oriented to practice not purpose, and too focused on system requirements instead of peoples' needs. There must be thousands of best practices, processes, and software tools for managing information. There are thousands more for managing knowledge. Recently, knowledge management has become "knowledge engineering." There is now even software for managing or "engineering" ideas. Most of these things do not yet work. And it is easy to see why.

The following paragraph is taken unedited from the homepage of KMNetwork:

"What Is Knowledge Management? From a business-technology perspective, *"Knowledge Management caters to the critical issues of organizational adoption, survival, and competence in face of increasingly discontinuous environmental change . . . Essentially, it embodies organizational*

processes that seek synergistic combination of data and information processing
capacity of information technologies, and the creative and innovative capacity
of human beings."3

This sounds worse than the car horns and sirens outside my window.
Compare the above paragraph with the following one from Richard
Lederer on the value of short words:

"Short words are bright like sparks that glow in the night, prompt
like the dawn that greets the day, sharp like the blade of a knife, hot
like salt tears that scald the cheek, quick like moths that flit from
flame to flame, and terse like the dart and sting of a bee."4

You may think this has nothing to do with knowledge management. In
fact, it is all about information clarity. Knowledge management, if it is
to mean anything, must be about information value, and the first step
toward value is clarity. Every writer and designer should follow
Lederer's rule: "Use small, old words where you can." Here is another
sound rule: Use visual metaphors from life, where possible. At the risk
of overstating the position, here's a third rule: Stop using the same
techno-talk and best practices that everyone else is using.

In the practice of Web design, there are no best practices. Every
site is different and every user brings his idiosyncrasies to the
experience. That's one of the beauties of the Web. Yes, there are some
rules that may be followed. Of course, you can learn from the successes
and failures of others. Certainly, there are guidelines that must be considered and growing standards to which we must adhere. There are
numerous procedures and methodologies and technologies that can
help save time, money, and headaches. There are also "long-shots,"
weird ideas, and infinite possibilities based on purpose. They should
all be considered rather than following an automatic prescription of
best practices.

Many businesses love best practices. They follow the path of reason.
They are orderly, rational, and logical. They have been tested and
proved. They can be used to make sure everyone is "on-board," "in
sync," and "on track." They are great "justifiers" for decisions. However,
they cannot be used—at least not effectively—to explore new terrain or
to find new ideas. Ideas are nearly always found beyond the borders of
reason, on the fringe, when one is informed but out-of-sync or off-track.
And most good ideas are hard to justify. They require taking risks.

A comprehensive, logical, step-by-step process for Web development is recommended. But, in reality, the process is not so clear-cut. It is rarely completely logical, and often depends on simultaneously searching for the solution and defining the problem. Design, by its nature, is filled with conflict; it struggles with opposites and thrives on tension. Particularly today, when companies, institutions, even countries advocate shorter development time, a continuous flow of new ideas, increased quality, reduced costs, broader distribution, and higher returns. And technology is providing a host of new tools for both design and implementation.

Today, input and ideas may come at any point in the process, functional details for a variety of tools must be considered as part of the initial input, and they may change at any point. And contributing writers, designers, illustrators, programmers, lawyers, and accountants may be located anywhere in the world.

As we have seen, information, our primary currency, has become a commodity. Language, our social glue, risks losing its stickiness from excessive complexity. And the current practice of Web design is often without purpose. In order to succeed, to prosper, to fulfill the promise of the Web, the information and language related to the practice of Web design must be simple. It must balance the natural and sometimes explosive change of a living system with the same systems' need for continuity. Above all, the practice of Web design must contribute to making people's lives easier, richer, more meaningful, and more fun.

8

Mission-Driven Design

The first question that must be asked of anyone who wants a Web site or wants to change his or her existing Web strategy is: Why? What is the motivation? What do you hope to accomplish? For a "blogger" the answer may be simple: I want to express myself in public. I want to put my opinions out there and see what others have to say. I want to start a discussion—verbal or visual—on a particular topic, or multiple topics. Many businesses in the early days of the Web just wanted a presence. They wanted to show their wares to the world. Others moved rapidly to e-business, providing online services and commerce, while still others focused on making an emotional "splash" with their brand—encouraging visitors to explore, play games, and participate in brand-based activities. Major corporations often have fifty to one hundred different sites, each for a separate line of business, product, or service, and most deliver confused, mixed, even incoherent messages and wasteful visitor experiences without useful transactions.

Today all companies realize that a Web presence is not enough, publicly or internally, and many who invested heavily in proprietary software for e-business are still waiting for the returns. They need to transform their Web and IT expense into an asset. Organizations are looking for ways to reduce operating costs, improve customer service, increase revenues, enhance partner and supplier relationships, increase new business opportunities, and strengthen "emotional attachments" to their brands. The Web may help in all of these areas. It only requires a clear sense of direction, some inspiration, and then a lot of hard work.

The Process

The successful Web initiative begins with a plan that addresses the goals of at least two and sometimes three groups of people, and the activities and technologies that will support the achievement of each of their goals. The first and most important group is the visitor to the site—the customers, suppliers, employees, partners, or information and entertainment seekers. They are the primary drivers of success. Second is the business organization or publisher of the site—including product development, marketing, sales, accounting, service, or investor relations. They are the ones who often think they are the drivers. Third are the sponsors of the site, usually advertisers.

Planning documents often grow beyond comprehension. They should be short and to the point. But that does not mean PowerPoint. This is not a strategy "deck" with bulleted items. It should be a brief story— *Here's where we came from and where we are, this is what we think we want to change and why, and here is where we are going and when we want to be there.* The plan should outline specific—very specific—objectives for each group of people mentioned above, how the site, or sites, might meet these objectives, the metrics that might be used to determine if the goals have been met, what the broad technology parameters are, and what the budget and time-frames are for development. Once this is agreed to, it should be shared, relentlessly, with all of the parties involved. When it changes, as it gets more detailed, it must be shared again.

Even huge, complex, global businesses can learn from the bloggers. Think of your site as the beginning of a discussion, a dialog with different people from the groups above. At this point, what you want to discuss and what you hope will come from the discussion is far more important than how it will be achieved. Forget about technology. Forget about the Web. And most important, forget all the acronyms: SCM, CMS, CRM, E-CRM, ERP, and ESS. (This corporate techno-quick-speak causes enormous problems for those who do not know what the acronyms mean. And there are many who do not. Does CRM stand for Customer Relationship Management, Customer Resource Management, or Customer Retention Management? What do each of these really mean?)

Imagine yourself riding around town in a car with four other ordinary people. They may be your customers, suppliers, or partners. What do you want to talk with them about? What do you want to ask them? Let them tell you what's on their minds—their stories, their wants, and needs. As they do, pay attention not only to what is said, but also to the dynamics of the conversation, the total exchange from one person to another and another. The elements of this exchange are like the steering wheel and gearshift of your car. They are what help you, and the others, get to where you are going, and enjoy the ride along the way.

Sometimes businesses will prepare a strategic plan in-house before approaching a design company. Others will outline the overall objectives of the Web initiative in a request for proposal, and work with a design firm on developing the plan. In either case, most design groups follow a four- or five-phase development process. In all cases, the first phase is the most important. Following is a very brief outline of the four phases Waters International has used and refined over time for Web development and integrated communications programs. Each phase will unfold on the following pages of this section and some specific tools will be elaborated on.

Phase I: Analyze

If, as Einstein said, "The intuitive mind is a sacred gift and the rational mind is a faithful servant," the objective of our analysis phase is to have the "servant" prepare an enormous feast for the "gift." Data gathering and analysis are vitally important, but the intent is to reveal the intuitive notions lurking nearby.

The goal of this phase is to collect and assess information that may impact the development and success of the site. Depending on the scope of the initiative, this may include analysis of business needs, audience needs, sponsor needs, the competition, and the market. Through interviews, a review of existing materials, and workshops, the objectives for the site are clarified, the desired experience for various audiences is clearly defined, and activities to support the experience are outlined. The results are summarized in a short *strategic plan* that encapsulates the business objectives and the methods by which they will be met and measured. Also, a *project brief* confirms the current business situation, the primary, secondary, and tertiary audiences and their goals, and preliminary functional and technical specifications. The project brief becomes the foundation for all of the work that follows.

Phase II: Organize

In an over-communicated world, information architecture is essential. For business communications, the information hierarchy with its various signals, signs, and paths should allow different people to easily find what they are looking for. It must also provide enough serendipity to keep them awake.

During the organization phase, the Web site is fully defined by establishing an information structure that incorporates the company's online business objectives, the audience's needs and experience possibilities, third-party goals, and other strategies determined in Phase I. The creative and technical teams work collaboratively with the client team to design the site architecture, and detailed functional specifications and technical specifications are written. Using the project brief as a guide, the creative team will design and test the user interactions, while the technical team designs software application interactions, or structures for the integration of existing applications that will be used on the site.

Phase III: Humanize

Today business is personal. Who we are as people and who we are as businesses are intimately connected. In business communications, the languages of form, color, typography, and texture are like the language of love. They may break the bounds of reason, but they can make the spirit soar.

Based on the approval of the elements developed in Phase II, the creative team begins to transform the information structure into visual design. They will develop and present the conceptual and visual approach to the Web site. This usually begins with something we call a *mood board*, a presentation that uses imagery, texture and color palettes to convey the overall look and feel of the site. This is then extended through key pages in each level of the site. It is critical to show second, third, and fourth levels in relation to the prior levels to assure consistent usability.

Phase IV: Energize

A "Bias for Action" is the first principle of excellence in Tom Peters' now classic book: In Search of Excellence. *New ideas may drive business, but new ideas are meaningless without the action that brings about their effective implementation and dissemination.*

The objective of the energize phase is to use the information from the previous phases to rapidly build out the site. During this phase, three activities take place. The client-side code for the site is built, the databases and functionality for searches and other dynamic components are built, and all maintenance pieces are created or implemented. Quality assurance testing is ongoing throughout the build.

Looking back on this, it all sounds so orderly and easy; it is no wonder that clients think it is also inexpensive. As I mentioned, an orderly process is required. But in reality, the details of the process—the six to ten steps taken in each phase, and the multiple tasks in each of those—are never exactly the same. There is often overlap from one phase to another. And, the work is not complete when the site is launched at the conclusion of phase four. It has just begun. Now the site must be monitored, assessed, evaluated, and measured for success against the original criteria. Continuous adjustments and additions will need to be made. Resources—human and economic—will need to be committed to the maintenance of the site. Planning for this post-launch activity is often overlooked. It is a crucial component of the planning in phase one.

One of the most important aspects of this process to remember is that the first two phases, which are a fair amount of work, are all about establishing goals, and structuring information and visitor experiences to meet these goals. They are not about color, typefont, and logo size.

Identifying the Visitor

Over the past ten years, we have developed or adopted a number of design process tools. One of our favorites, and most critical, is the *discovery workshop,* where we develop, in collaboration with our clients, "personas" or individual profiles that represent visitors to the site. The concept is one we adopted from software designer Alan Cooper of Cooper Interaction Design. He has used personas in his software development work for years as a method of clarifying the users' goals. It is a process that has become common in the last few years with many user interface design groups. The idea is simple: develop a precise description of the Web site visitor and what he or she wishes to accomplish. Then develop multiple scenarios through which the visitor may experience the site. It is important that interaction designers, functional designers, and the client be involved in this process.

Typically, companies conduct surveys or run focus groups to learn about users. The results of these methods tend to be given in percentages. Some companies develop single profiles to represent the average user in the target market. These methods may be useful but they do not capture the specific needs, interests, or habits of the individual user.

We develop many personas and we develop them with our client. Our goal is twofold: to help clients thoroughly understand that markets are people not numbers, and to find the one most important person they need to please. Not one who represents a common denominator, but one about whom we can say, *If we truly satisfy this person—if he or she is delighted—then we may satisfy these others as well.*

What is difficult for some clients to understand is why we focus on one persona when the client wants to reach a mass of people. It defies logic. But it is precisely this focus, and how we arrive at the one persona, that makes the process work.

Our workshop is typically divided into two sessions. The first session is persona development. The activity includes group and team exercises with a mixture of designers, developers, and client members on each team. As a group, we list all of the types of people we think would be seriously interested in the site. This may result in thirty to forty different types. As we discuss the goals of the site, the business, and the visitors, we identify similarities in personas and overlap in their objectives; and the list is culled to eight to twelve most-likely candidates. We then separate into smaller groups and each group defines the character of two to three of our imaginary visitors.

Character definition must be very explicit including such things as: name, age, location, professional experience, Web knowledge, personal interest or habits, history, personality traits, likes or dislikes. The idea is to make this person as real and believable as possible. Each group is provided a large selection of photos of people to choose from to visually identify their persona. Each persona is also given one primary goal to achieve on the Web site. As each persona is defined by the small teams, a photo and critical characteristics of this persona are posted to a wall. Then the entire group reviews and refines further.

During the second workshop session, using a variety of scenarios based on information gathered during initial investigations, each persona is given specific tasks to accomplish on the site. For instance: "Uncle Bob" may be searching for a gift for his teenage niece. He is a savvy Web user but he is also an overworked investor relations vice president who has just put out an earnings release for his company. He has little patience with technology, and a hot temper. His wife reminded him, just this morning, that they are having dinner this weekend with his niece, and he promised her a gift "surprise." How will he reach our Web site? What are the specific steps he will take on the site? What does he need to see when he first arrives? How many options is he presented with? When he makes the first click, what does he want to see next? The questions are infinite. All discussion regarding Uncle Bob's activity must be from his perspective, using his name and characteristics to make decisions. Although developers are involved in these discussions along with designers and client representatives, the focus is strictly on "front-end"—customer facing—issues. There is little to no talk about how this will be accomplished. We are concerned here with *what* needs to be accomplished.

Technology groups frequently go through a similar process called *use-case scenarios* to determine "back-end" functionality. They ask similar questions of a typical user: What happens when he presses, "purchase now"? Their concern is how and where the information gets distributed; through the middleware, the database, the merchant bank, etc. These are vitally important questions that will determine how well the site works, and we will address them later. For now, they are only important to developers and programmers. Uncle Bob doesn't care.

Case Study: NMWA

In 2001, the National Museum of Women in the Arts (NMWA) came to us with an exciting assignment. As the only museum in the world dedicated exclusively to recognizing the contribution of women artists, NMWA sought to maximize its position by enhancing its Web presence to: increase membership (particularly with a younger audience), to improve relationships with current members, state committees, other organizations and artists, and to extend its reach with the general public and arts benefactors.

NMWA had been on the Web with a basic site for about four years. It now wanted a "world-class" Web presence—a transaction-oriented site that would integrate with its collections database, its Library and Research Center, offer e-commerce capability through the museum shop, and provide extensive information on its educational programs, special exhibitions, state programs, and online membership acquisition and support.

The task for us was to provide NMWA with the tools to ensure that the way the museum was perceived when seen through its Web site would consistently support and project the best possible picture of what the "physical" museum does and how it does it. Initial meetings with NMWA staff revealed a disconnect between their emotional perceptions of the museum—reflected in colors like taupe, mauve, and burgundy—and their ideas about the museum—reflected in words like exciting, fun, and innovative. The Web site needed to fall in between these poles; sophisticated, yet accessible; professional, yet entertaining. It would certainly have to move away from the somber and static, and toward the dynamic in appearance and communications function.

Virtually any visitor to NMWA's Web site could be considered a potential supporter or member, whether in a personal or professional capacity. Broadly speaking, anyone who loves art, who promotes "women's" causes, or who believes in the nexus between art and education could be drawn to the museum. The major targets in this broad group of people were individual art lovers, corporate and foundation donors, collectors, and state committee members. Working with representatives from each of NMWA's internal departments, we identified an initial list of some forty visitors. This list was narrowed to twelve using the criteria: "If we satisfy the needs of this person, we may satisfy these other people." The culled list included:

- **Prospective Member** (including present, past, Charter, Board members)
- **Prospective Donor** (including corporations, major donors, foundations)
- **Researcher** (including academics, college students, historians)
- **Art Buyers** (including collectors, gallery owners, other museums)
- Potential Employees (including student interns, volunteers, museum professionals)

- **Shoppers** (including vendors of goods)
- Media
- Event Planners (including hosts, vendors of services, consultants)
- Affiliates (including community groups, government officials, international offices)
- **Educators** (including teachers, administrators, group leaders)
- **Students K–12**
- **State Committees**

Using the same criteria and considering the initial objectives for the site, we narrowed the list further to seven priority users (appearing in bold). Of the seven, we determined that Milagros Cogan, the *prospective member* would ultimately be the most difficult to please, and should therefore serve as the basis for developing the functionality, and the look and feel of the site. Milagros Cogan is a young, single, professional woman living in California who has never visited the museum. Knowing that Milagros likes art—she visits local galleries regularly—and knowing that she is very Web savvy—she uses the Web frequently in her work—a friend has recommended her to the NMWA Web site. Our challenge, once Milagros arrives to "check out" the site, is to convince her to become a member (either now or later) by appealing to her love of art and concern for women's issues; and by making her online experience—including applying for membership—easy and enjoyable.

Focusing on Milagros does not mean that the others are not cared for. The needs of all are considered and ultimately will be met. But features are not added to the site for the benefit of other characters if the feature may get in the way of satisfying our primary persona.

The runner-up for primary position was Ann Johnson, a prospective donor, director of development for the GE Fund. Ann will be scrutinizing the site for professionalism and analyzing the organization for worthiness. Milagros was chosen as the toughest customer over Ann only because it is Ann's job to evaluate nonprofit institutions, and thus she might have more patience and purpose in clicking through the site.

Following are brief profiles of the seven personas developed for NMWA.

Prospective Member

Milagros Cogan
Age: 28
Residence: San Francisco

Professional Profile:
Although Cogan studied Comparative Literature and Women's Studies
in college, she veered into the corporate world where she is now
a well-paid Technology Recruiter for PricewaterhouseCoopers. It
is a fast-paced profession requiring quick analytical skills and
communication dexterity. She is good at it, and loves it.

Personal Profile:
Cogan has an active single life that includes going to galleries,
traveling, and socializing. She is bilingual, having been born in
Argentina.

Skills:
Using the Web is second nature to Cogan, who possesses good
communications and computer skills.

Motivation and Achievements:
Cogan wants financial security, but she also wants to enjoy life. She
is proud of running the Golden Gate marathon.

Quote: "Just do it."

Goal on NMWA's Web site:
To "check it out" as per a friend's recommendation.

Prospective Donor

Ann Johnson
Age: 50
Residence: New York City

Professional Profile:
Director of Development for the GE Fund, earning $200K.

Personal Profile:
Johnson had been married for a while to her banker husband before having their two children, aged twelve and fifteen. The family enjoys a Riverside Drive apartment in New York City, household help, private school for the kids, and personal training for the parents. She is an empathetic person.

Skills:
A good manager with a firm grasp of budgets, Johnson knows how to be a team player.

Motivation and Achievements:
To make a difference in the causes that matter to her, namely social injustice and equity for women and people of color.

Quote: "Get to the heart of the matter."

Goal on NMWA's Web site:
To evaluate the museum as a potential recipient of GE funding. Besides the exhibits and educational programs, she is most interested in the museum's financial statements, including a list of other contributors.

Researcher

Jeffrey Hammberg
Age: 50
Residence: Toronto, Canada

Professional Profile:
Professor of Art History at Toronto University, previously taught at Oberlin. Hammberg is a good scholar who has published two books. His special interest is renaissance painting.

Personal Profile:
A widower, Hammberg has one son in college and one in high school. His least-pleasant trait is impatience.

Skills:
Writing, lecturing, critical thinking, and fluency in foreign languages, among others.

Motivation and Achievements:
Hammberg aims to be recognized as an expert in his field. To that end, he received an award for excellence on his latest book from the Canadian Critics Circle.

Quote: "Cogito ergo sum."

Goal on NMWA's Web site:
To seek information about a woman artist who lived during medieval times.

State Committee Member

Evelyn Webb
Age: 60
Residence: Baltimore and Colorado Springs

Professional Profile:
Coming from a wealthy background and marrying young, Webb has never worked for money. However, she has dedicated much time to the arts, serving on the Board of Directors of the Baltimore Symphony and the Baltimore Museum of Arts.

Personal Profile:
Happily married for 30 years and the mother of two grown children, Webb is a natural leader—the downside being that she is quite demanding.

Skills:
Networking and organizing come naturally. She has picked up reasonably good computer skills from her kids.

Motivation and Achievements:
Webb is a passionate advocate for the arts, but she considers her greatest achievement to be raising her children.

Quote: "My way or the highway."

Goal on NMWA's Web site:
To access up-to-date information about the museum, including any materials or forms she might need in her role as a committee member. She wants to also use the site to communicate with NMWA staff and other committee members.

Shopper

Susie Kaufman
Age: 35
Residence: Chicago

Professional Profile:
Kaufman earns $110K as a media executive for an NBC affiliate, meaning she sells time. She received her MBA from Northwestern University.

Personal Profile:
Like many MBAs, Kaufman is aggressive and organized while being a "people person." She is used to multi-tasking, which helps in dealing with her professional husband and four-year-old daughter.

Skills:
Kaufman is highly computer-savvy and knowledgeable about the latest cultural trends. She's a good salesperson.

Motivation and Achievements:
Kaufman wants it all—money, respect, and the sense of being part of what's happening. Her biggest coup was making vice president this year.

Quote: "Time is money."

Goal on NMWA's Web site:
To buy an original gift for her client at Oxygen.

Student K–12

Tanika Cooper
Age: 12
Residence: Washington, DC

Professional Profile:
Full-time student in the public school system.

Personal Profile:
Cooper is the eldest daughter of civil employees. She's a good student and an outgoing child.

Skills:
Cooper plays clarinet in the school band.

Motivation and Achievements:
Going to college is Cooper's long-term goal; for now, she's happy to participate in the science fair and earn Girl Scout badges.

Quote: "You go girl!"

Goal on NMWA's Web site:
To research African-American women photographers for a class assignment. She's also interested in field trip opportunities for her Girl Scout Troupe.

Educator K–12

Kathy Burns
Age: 42
Residence: Fairfax, VA

Professional Profile:
A fourth-grade teacher at Robinson public school, Burns is dedicated
to children and is particularly interested in multidisciplinary
programs. She earns $50K and receives good benefits.

Personal Profile:
Burn's first marriage ended in divorce, with two children. Several
years ago she married again to a coach at the school, who also has two
children.

Skills:
Burns paints and makes ceramics at home. She's also a big fan of AOL
and sending e-mail to friends and co-workers.

Motivation and Achievements:
Burns believes in new ideas, and in making a difference. She was
gratified to be named Teacher of the Year.

Quote: "Knowledge is power."

Goal on NMWA's Web site:
To discover ways of integrating art into her curriculum.

Fewer Features, More Benefits

There are three things that happen during the discovery workshops that are important to the development of a successful site. First, by discussing the activity on the site from the perspective of the persona, the egos of client, designer, and developer are taken out of the equation. This minimizes personality and departmental conflicts that can unravel Web planning. Second, by experiencing the potential site through the eyes of the explicitly defined persona, we are able to clarify the needs of a real visitor in a real life situation, rather than speculating on what we think the needs are. And third, by focusing on meeting the specific needs of one particular visitor, the tendency to add unnecessary features and functionality is controlled.

Feature creep and *data creep* are the biggest problems on most business sites. Every department has multiple "things" they want seen and multiple functions they want accessible, and they want them all on the homepage. As a result, the visitors are hit with such a barrage of confusing labels, messages, signs and signals they don't know where to click, and often click off. Focus on one visitor, delight him or her—without forgetting your other visitors—and you have the beginning of a successful site.

9

Organizing the Trip

In 1990 while working with GE Financial Services on the design of its annual report, Gary Wendt, then president and chief operating officer of GEFS, suggested we have an organization chart to accompany the introductory letter which mentioned the twenty-two different businesses that comprised the company. This sounded like a reasonable idea to me so I asked from whom I might get this chart. Taking a pen and piece of paper, Wendt said, "I'm sure you can draw it up. It goes like this. One big circle in the middle, and twenty-two smaller circles around the big one. Each small circle is connected with a direct line to the center circle." At the time this sounded like an awful organization chart. Where was the hierarchy? Where was the reporting structure? How did anyone know what he or she was supposed to do?

I soon realized that this was in fact the way the company was organized. GEFS was a true reflection of Jack Welch's "boundaryless organization." Nearly everyone had direct access to the core management team and to one another. This is very much like the connectivity available today on the Web. It is the opposite, however, of the hierarchical organization required to organize, design, and build a commercial Web site. As we will discover in this chapter, without carefully planned information structure and navigation in the early stages of Web development, visitors to the completed site will not be able to move freely from one area to another without wasting time on questions they should never have to ask: Where am I? How did I get here? Where can I go? How do I find what I want?

Information Architecture

There are at least two information structures required for the development of any site. Depending on the complexity of transactions available there may be many more. The *site map*, also referred to as the *information map* or *information architecture*, provides the global structure, while the *page map*, representing the individual pages of a site provides guidance on a "local level." These might be compared to state road maps, which show interstate and secondary highways, while city maps show main thruways, city streets and alleys.

Anyone who has driven in Los Angeles realizes how important the freeways are to moving quickly from community to community. If you have ever taken the wrong exit, you also realize how important directional signs are at the local level for getting back on the freeway.

The Site Map

Even a small business may have hundreds of pages of information it wants to make available on its Web site. A large company site may have thousands of pages: product or service information, online demos, brochures, specification pages, order forms, personalization forms, information on management, marketing, finance, press relations. How should all of this be organized?

This begins with the strategy and the goals of the three audiences mentioned before: the visitors, the business or publisher, and the sponsors. (Sponsors are generally advertisers and do not require information structure. But they do require "real estate" on pages, and this will influence the presentation of information, so they should be considered from the beginning.) Balancing the goals of the other two groups is the challenge.

Card sorting is a method we have used with great success. Using 4 x 6 cards labeled to represent various pieces of information, we group cards into categories that make the most sense from our visitor's perspective. They are labeled with simple language that the visitor will understand. They should not be labeled by business unit or division. This is a frequent mistake made by many companies because the people within the company spend all their waking hours seeing the company from the inside, rather than the way a customer sees it, from the outside.

Working from the goals established for our primary persona, the categories are then grouped into larger sections that become the main

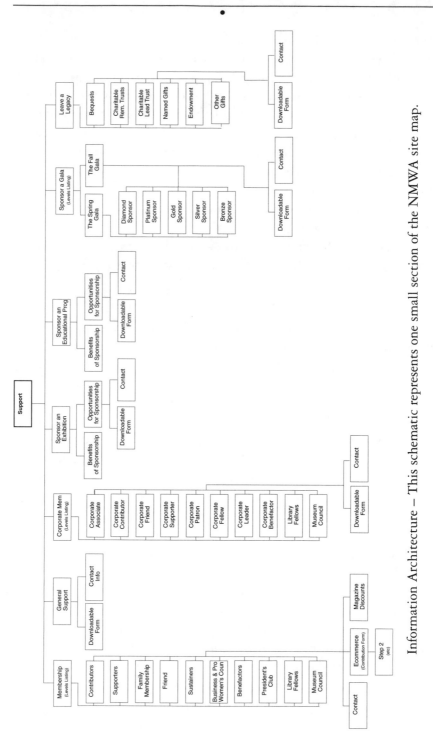

Information Architecture – This schematic represents one small section of the NMWA site map.

navigation sections for the site. Each of these sections may have several subcategories, or second level navigation, and each of the second level categories may have several other groupings, and so on. The number of main and secondary sections will vary depending on the scope of the site. The idea is to get the main navigation to as few labels as possible, yet provide the visitor with clear direction and a sense of what will be found in different directions. This is more easily said than done.

The advantage of cards is the ease with which they can be shuffled around to explore how successfully a particular approach meets the goals in different visitor scenarios. This is often done on a large table or with cards pinned to a wall, and should be done with client, designer, and developer involvement. When they are involved in the map-making process, it is easier to reach consensus, meaning fewer disagreements later.

The site map, or information architecture, is the primary organization and development tool on which many decisions will be based. Although nearly identical, the site map should not be confused with the table-of-contents-type site maps shown on many current sites. When the navigation is well designed, the table of contents is not required, although it may have some value for a site visitor because of their familiarity with tables of contents from magazines and books. It is less valuable, however, for Web designers than schematic renderings. A schematic with labels representing main categories of information, boxes representing specific pages, and connecting lines showing potential paths from one area to another, provides a more complete view of the site and is easier to annotate for coding or special activity directives (see schematic on page 84). Once the map has been agreed upon, it will be used by the client, designer, content developers, site builders, and database programmers throughout the development process.

If you were building a house, this would be the structural blueprint. It shows each of the floors, all of the rooms on each floor, and the passageways that connect the rooms and the floors. It is important that this blueprint be first, and correct, because many other plans are based on it: the electrical plan, the plumbing plan, the HVAC and telecommunications plans. And additional detail plans such as molding or cabinetry will be based on these.

Like the structural blueprint for your house, the site map shows categories of information (often called "wells" or "buckets"), pages within the categories, and passageways from one to another. It should also be designed first because there may be many other plans, or specific flowcharts, which connect at some point to the site map: the database plans, an e-commerce plan, personalization and customer relationship plans, or content management plans.

The blueprint for your house would also show the points of entry and exit—front door, back door, side door, and the location of all windows to the outside.

Although the Web site map usually begins its hierarchy with the front door—the homepage, here is an important difference from the blueprint for your house. Your Web site has no walls. People may come and go at any point. Yes, they may enter through the homepage on their first visit. Thereafter they are more likely to go directly to the second story bedroom, or a comfortable chair in the den, which they enjoyed so much on their first visit.

This is where page maps become important. No matter what page your visitor enters on, she should always know where she is, be able to easily see her way to the home page, or into other main areas of the site, and have a sense of what may be found in each of these areas. Unless, of course, your objective is to add intrigue, mystery, and adventure to your visitors' site experience. Then you may want to think about a haunted house, with trap doors, partially legible signs, secret passageways and other elements of surprise.

The Page Map

A house without walls, haunted or not, presents another problem. It cannot be seen. People visiting your Web site don't know how big it is. Without spending some time on the site it is hard to tell how deep or wide the information is. This is usually not so important to the visitor who is most likely on a specific mission. It is more important to the site owner who wants to exhibit the full breadth and depth of services, products, or knowledge.

When you pick up a magazine or book, you immediately have a sense of the "heft" or "weight" of its contents. A Web site, though it may have more depth than Webster's College Dictionary, has no weight. When a visitor shows up, whether on the front stoop or on a page five levels down, he or she will see only one page. So it is important that this

Second Level Navigation

Call outs

Home Button

System text

Secondary Main Navigation

Primary Main Navigation

Logo/home

Search
Register
Shopping Cart
Calendar

The Collection

Exhibitions

Public Programs

Library

Support NMWA

Publications

Museum Shop

About NMWA

News

Resources

Membership	General Support	Corporate Membership	Sponsor an Exhibition	Sponsor an Edu. Prog.	Sponsor a Gala	Leave a Legacy

Your participation always has been — and always will be — a crucial part of our success. It's only through the loyal support of members that we've been able to present exhibitions, educational programs, and publications dedicated to celebrating the creativity of women artists. To learn more about membership — or to join today — select one of the levels below.

Individual ($40) - Free admission to the museum, our award-winning magazine, beautiful postcards featuring images from our collection, and discounts on purchases and events

Supporter ($50) - Individual membership benefits plus a complimentary guest pass

Dual ($70) - Supporter membership benefits for two adults

Family ($75) - Supporter membership benefits for two adults and children under 18 plus our Exploring Art book and priority reservations for education and family programs

Friend ($100) - Dual membership benefits plus a special gift from the Museum Shop, two guest admission passes, and reciprocal membership privileges at 80 museums

Sustainer ($250) - Friend membership benefits plus a full-color mini catalogue of our collection, four guest admission passes, and invitations to our Fall Benefit and an exhibition opening reception

JOIN NOW
Become a member now to enjoy discounts on tours, the Museum Shop, and more!

LIVE OUTSIDE THE U.S.?
Please call Member Services at 1-202-783-5000,
Monday-Friday, 9 am-5 pm EST to join, renew, or give a gift membership.

CURRENT MEMBERS
Renew or upgrade your membership online today.

THE GIFT OF ART
Membership makes a great gift for friends, family, and associates. Purchase a gift membership in minutes.

Page Map – This does not represent the final page layout but does include all information elements that need to appear.

page—every page—be organized for optimum efficiency and effect. The objective is to provide obvious leads to the most needed information, and clear indicators to what's contained in other areas, without creating such visual clutter that the visitor is overwhelmed.

Regardless of where they show up, there are three things they should be able to determine immediately: who you are, where they are, and what they can do. How you answer these questions is determined on the page map. Often called a *wire frame* or a *page schematic*, this map provides a rough structure for all of the elements that need to appear on every page (see schematic on page 87). Those elements can include: The company identifier (usually logo and tag line), the page identifier (a title e.g., News Releases), the main navigation (prominent clickable labels and search box), secondary navigation (less prominent clickable elements), main text, main graphic, "sidebar" text and graphic, footer information, and advertising space allotments, if necessary.

For publishers in the print world or graphic designers familiar with magazine and newspaper standards, the page map is like a grid. It is a black and white line presentation. It is not about color and images. It is about structuring the space of the page, or the "real estate," as Web designers or information architects are more apt to say. It shows the hierarchy of information and the approximate space and position of various elements. Starting with the homepage, page maps should be created for each main section of the site; this usually includes secondary and tertiary levels, and any special sections such as the checkout process for an e-commerce section.

Like the card sorting process, with a completed site map and a set of page maps, visitor scenarios can be tested again. Clicking through this rough "paper site" and then making adjustments on the maps is less expensive than making changes once visual design has been established, and far less expensive than making changes after programming has begun.

Once the page map has been structured this should stay more or less the same throughout the site. This does not mean that every page has to be exactly the same. As in magazine design, tremendous variation can be achieved by manipulating certain elements—such as type, graphics, color in size, style and position—while maintaining continuity by preserving other elements such as page size, masthead, page numbers, etc. The benefit for the Web visitor is structural integrity.

Test users may not always be able to verbalize this but they can feel it. It provides them with a sense of place and continuity, a sense of stability, in what many still see as a chaotic space.

For savvy Web users, of course, all of this may only provide them with a sense of *same ol', same ol' . . . I've seen it all before and unless you have something new to offer or something valuable for me, I'm outta' here.*

Understanding Usability

The primary goal of your Web site is usefulness. This should not be confused with usability. Usefulness means there is something here of practical worth, something applicable to me at this time—the experience, information, product, service, entertainment, price, I have been looking for. Usability, on the other hand, means this thing works. It works well. I can accomplish what I set out to do without wasting time or getting frustrated. Both are vitally important and intimately connected to the success of any site.

Usefulness should drive the planning stages of any Web initiative. It will be determined when answering the "mission" questions asked in the last chapter. Usability is related to how the site is organized and presented. There are numerous usability "experts" who have issued vast proclamations of dos and don'ts through their books and Web sites. Any Web designer should be familiar with these rules. They should also ignore at least 50 percent of them. The difficulty, of course, is determining which 50 percent. Thoughtful common sense is usually the best guide.

Common sense means being courteous to your visitor. If you are presenting the visitor with a wealth of text, make an outline, headlines, or highlights available to give a sense of what's included. If your visitors may have to wait two seconds or longer for something to download, let them know. Put up a sign that indicates that activity is taking place and the approximate time to finish. If they have already visited an area let them know by changing the color of the link, so time is not wasted repeating steps. Think of how an elevator talks to you. When you push the up button, it lights up to say, *I got your message and I'm working on it.* You enter the car and push the floor button. It lights up, repeating the message. A bell often rings for those who may not see the light. The door closes and you see the floor numbers light one by one as the car ascends, showing you where you are.

Jacob Nielsen, the "godfather" of usability and most outspoken of the experts, says people do not read on the Web. Jerry McGovern, another leading and vocal usability expert says, "Remember that the reader is king of the Web. . . ." Both focus on stripping sites of needless graphics and emphasize the importance of structuring content. Both, like the rest of humankind, bring their personal prejudices to the subject. They are most at ease in a word-built, language-biased, publishing-based world of information, where the word "content" refers to text as if it were our only means of information exchange. Yes, information needs to be structured. It should be broken into manageable pieces that are easy to access, and the language used will make a huge difference. Today, everyone has more to read than they have time for, but they will read what they want to read, or need to read, both on the Web and off.

"Don't make me think," is the first law of usability for Steve Krug. It is also the title of his book. If you read only one book on usability this should be it. Although the title seems to be a contradiction to what is "usefulness" on the Web, it is dead-on about usability. *Don't make me think about what I should not have to think about*. Krug's approach is far less heavy-handed than others and many of his recommendations are based on common sense. He also suggests useful ways to conduct usability testing without spending a fortune.

All of the experts tend to push for accepting site elements as standards based on familiarity through current use. The dimensionalized button and rounded tabs for navigation are two such examples. The physical metaphor of a 3D button is a hangover from the early days of industrial fabrication. When I see these I think of the instrument panels in the cockpit of an airplane from the forties. And manila-colored tab dividers recall the files in the upright wooden file cabinet behind Sam Spade's desk. Or when presented in multiple colors they are like the dividers in my high school notebook. Our recognition of these things makes it easy to understand their function on the Web, but if we made all such things standards, humans would never have emerged from caves.

The difficulty with standards is getting everyone to agree on what they should be. All communication media, like all industries, organizations, and social activities have standards. If we did not agree to the standard metrics of an 8 oz. cup, 32 oz. quart, or the size of a teaspoon

•

versus a tablespoon we would never be able to exchange recipes. On the other hand, if we never experimented with the amount and mix of different ingredients, think how bland our meals might be.

As important as visual experimentation is to design, and as critical as the individual elements on the screen are to the success of any site, they do not come first. The overall site architecture—the site map—is first. The page maps come next, followed by the elements on each page. Each of these and all of them together should be continuously reviewed from the visitor's perspective. Many designers cannot help thinking in visual terms from the very beginning. This can be great if it ultimately works to provide the visitors what they came to the site for. A large part of the success of your site is determined in this organization phase of design. When carefully planned information structure and navigation come first, everything else gets easier.

10

Developing the Look and Feel

Many designers begin to develop the look and feel of business Web sites or product sites based on "brand" guidelines. Using the appropriate logo, corporate colors, typefonts, words and pictures to establish the tone of the site. This chapter reveals how the Web has a stronger influence on the brand than the brand has on the Web. The following pages review the meaning of brand, the relationship of the brand to the Web, and outline a critical tool that may be used for developing image standards in multiple media.

Logomania

I made a big mistake a few years ago when speaking at a design management conference in Montreal. "Look at all these logos sitting on top of the buildings all over this town," I said, "They all look the same—red or green or orange squares and circles or triangles with arrows and different letterforms. Looking at the skyline of this city I am amazed at the amount of money that must have been spent erecting these signs which don't really mean anything." My point, which I continued to expound on, was that logos are not brands. A logo may be thought of as a signature for a brand, a brief visual representation of a brand, but it is not "the brand."

A brand manifests itself in hundreds or even thousands of ways within a company, through the actions, voices, practices, and promises of each employee and groups of employees to their customers and to one another. It is not about advertising, a marketing slogan, or an image

•

campaign. It is not about packaging, displays or events. And it is certainly not about oversized neon logos on the tops of buildings. It reveals itself in each and all of these things together. Brand is encapsulated in the multitude of experiences someone has with a company through its people, products, and services. The bloated logo, and its rapid proliferation encouraged by rigid standards for reproduction, says more about greed and pomposity than it does about customer value provided by the brand.

Although some design members of the audience disagreed with my discrediting the value of logos, and the rigid graphic standards that have preserved their monumental stature, this was not the big problem. My mistake was sounding like a crass American criticizing the landscape of Montreal, laying the blame for "logomania" on the people who live there. I apologize to all who may have taken offense. Logomania is not a Montreal problem, it is a global problem.

The Brand Parade

The logo's benign beginnings, which accompanied the mass production of products toward the end of the nineteenth century, could not foretell the explosion that would occur in the eighties. The initial icons were meant to be symbols of trust. As design historians Ellen Lupton and J. Abbott Miller state, "Familiar personalities such as Dr. Brown, Uncle Ben, Aunt Jemima, and old Grand-Dad came to replace the shopkeeper, who was traditionally responsible for measuring bulk foods for customers and acting as an advocate for products . . . ."[1] As production expanded and communications quickened, "a nationwide vocabulary of brand names replaced the small local shopkeeper as the interface between consumer and product." This is similar to the "Super Store" retail outlets such as Wal-Mart, Home Depot, and Target that have replaced the local hardware or corner drug store.

Following the information explosion of the seventies, our brand vocabulary went global, on every channel available. We wore the logos on our feet, our pants, our shirts, hats, jackets, umbrellas, and underpants. We lived with brands in the kitchen, living room, dining room, bathroom, and the bedroom. We worked at brands, traveled on brands, were entertained by brands, and stopped for dinner at brands. We talked about, listened to, invested in, watched, argued with, and screamed at brands. And in 1988, when Phillip Morris acquired Kraft for $12.6 billion, the value of the brand was firmly established—over $10 billion more than what the company was worth on paper.

Brands were no longer about products or services. They were about an attitude, a set of values, a lifestyle, and a history of emotional ties. Starbucks, Gap, The Body Shop, and Nike epitomized the new meaning of brand. The images in advertising—the primary means of conveying brand in the past—no longer showed the product. They attempted to capture the attitude. As journalist Naomi Klein noted, "What the success of both The Body Shop and Starbucks showed was how far the branding project had come in moving beyond splashing one's logo on a billboard. Here were two companies that had fostered powerful identities by making the brand concept into a virus and sending it out into the culture via a variety of channels: cultural sponsorship, political controversy, the consumer experience, and brand extensions. Direct advertising, in this context, was viewed as a rather clumsy intrusion into a much more organic approach to image building."[2]

Today we have come full circle. All of the channels, the methods, the nuances, the disparities of brand impression, come home to rest on the company Web site—the new, small local shop. All of the talk about increasing brand loyalty, strengthening brand relationship, intensifying the emotional bond, and sharing community concerns proves itself at the company site—in the shopkeeper's voice. The company Web site is not the central point of information dissemination. It is the most important single point of brand confirmation, the nerve center of all business communications. The place where customers, employees, partners, and politicians now gather to participate in the give and take of business life.

Brand Central

Although the functionality and look and feel of the business Web site should visually and verbally convey the essence of the brand, the site cannot be thought of as just another medium for broadcasting brand messages. If the "brand message" and "brand image" take precedence over good functionality and useful information, they do more harm than good. The information and tools provided and the ease with which they may be used is what the "brand" is about, not the words and images that "talk" about brand. The site should function as an easy to use communications hub through which a multitude of internal and external voices may be heard, proving the value of the brand. It should also be a branding hub, to which all other media drive traffic—not just to "get the message," but also to interact in a meaningful way with the company. When this is done correctly, the site becomes one of your most valuable brand assets. There are at least three reasons it should not be thought of like other communications media:

1. *The Web site, even as the new small local store, is deeper and wider than all other media.* While television or print advertising may convey exciting messages, catalogs or brochures might contain a broad array of product or service information, and annual reports or financial "road shows" can help delineate the corporate mission and move the stock market needle, the Web site can contain all of these elements—do all of these things—and more. This does not mean it will replace advertising or all printed materials, but increasingly advertising and other media will be used to drive customers to your Web site for more information, customized services, and to make purchases or interact in other ways with the company.

   The Ford Motor Company site contains all of the things mentioned above plus connecting sites for each of its brands, multiple sites for parts and service, sites for vehicle financing, and links to a variety of owners' sites or clubs. Under an area labeled innovation, it has large sections on safety—Family Safety, Seat Belts, Air Bags, Driver Distraction Lab—and a section on design where you can meet the designers and explore design features of different vehicles. Another section labeled dedication leads to a wealth of information on Ford's commitment to the environment, community, corporate citizenship, and other programs. Recently, in preparation for its 100-year anniversary, Ford has added a rich section on the history of the company. There are few limits to how deep or wide your site might become. The depth and breath, however, do not matter if the information, tools, and points of contact are not easily accessible and useful to the visitor.

2. *The Web is not a broadcast medium; it is an interactive experience.* It should provide for visitor involvement in simple and multichannel communications. FedEx allows visitors to specify the time for pick-ups,

print labels for packages, and track the location of shipments. Dell lets you select the components you want in your computer, the services and support you require, and a flexible payment method including a Quick Lease or Quick Loan. The site provides a payment calculator to help you determine what's best. Disney has such an array of games, puzzles, movie clips, and tools for creating your own videos, books, and letter exchanges with Disney characters, you could spend a week and not begin to experience them all. The Ford site, although not great at encouraging participation, has added interactive features to its history section. A visitor can register for the anniversary event, read stories about individuals' experiences with Ford products or services, or submit his or her own story.

Harley-Davidson, long recognized for its customers' allegiance to the brand, offers numerous possibilities for interaction on its homepage: the ability to create an online photo album; to use the Ride Planner to build, save, and share a trip; to rent a Harley or search the Dealer Used Inventory base. It also provides a link that provides numerous online services for dealers. These types of company interactions are what a brand is all about. This is not about broadcasting company messages, it is about making company promises come true.

3. *The Web is a personalized experience.* Visitors come to your Web site one at a time. They chose their own path in their own time. They select their area of interest, what tools they may use or not use, and to whom they may send an e-mail. And this is before they register. Once registered they may let you customize more of their experience. You may allow them to save profiles, wish lists, and product specifications and when they return, you present what they saved plus additional personalized recommendations that meet their criteria. They might have access to account information, special tools, customized information, internal databases, and their own Web pages on your site. And they may choose to participate in online chats, or forums, or collaborative product idea development.

This kind of personalized experience just cannot be had with other media. Companies like Amazon, Gap, Banana Republic, Charles Schwab, Dell, Disney, and many others are continuing to add features that further embrace their customers, suppliers, and employees online. Surprisingly many industries—in particular the pharmaceutical industry—are not. With the exception of Merck, all of the major pharmaceuticals as of this writing are continuing to push product and provide little if any opportunity for interaction or personalized experience. With the growing awareness of health issues and the graying of America, they are missing a huge opportunity.

Visualizing the Brand

A design process tool that we have found very useful for Web development and for integrated communications programs is the "mood board." This is derived from the kind of presentation board often used by interior designers or architects to convey the "mood" of a room or other interior space.

An architect designing your offices or home will at some point accompany the floor plans with an interior "scheme." This usually consists of swatches of carpet or tile for the floor; fabric for various pieces of furniture and other fabric for the window treatments; different paint chips for the walls, moldings and doors; and any special finishes in glass, wood or metal. This is often presented in a composition meant to capture the overall feel for the room. It may also reflect certain aspects of the budget, the cost of fabric for window drapes, or the price of furniture covering.

Our mood boards are very similar. They are composed of visual and verbal swatches representing various elements that convey the essence of the brand. We use a mood board or multiple mood boards to help us define, express, and share the mood of a brand or complex of brands, a Web site, or a specific communications initiative, without the limitations of a particular media framework. The board is then used to test and guide the interpretation of the mood in different environments; including print, TV, Web, mobile devices, and physical environments (see page 98). There are three to five key components included on a single presentation board:

1. *The image window.* The largest visual on the presentation is an abstract composition of colors, textures, images, words or letterforms. It is made from photographs, graphics, illustrations, and text; and although it may contain representational imagery, it is never intended

Unique
Women-Focused
Exciting
Progressive
Historical
Inclusive
Fun
Meaningful
Respected
Accessible
Beautiful
Current

Mood Board – The combination of images, textures, color palette, logo, and key words represents the overall mood that should be conveyed by the Web site and supplemental communication materials.

to be a literal depiction of anything. It is intended only to convey a mood. It may contain infinite detail, but it cannot rely on the detail, because some of the details will be lost in different media frameworks. Typefonts are the most obvious example. They may change substantially from Macs to PCs to PDAs or from one browser to another.

2. *Mood guidewords*. During our interview process in the analysis phase we always ask individuals to provide us with a list of adjectives that describe their company or this particular Web initiative. We suggest they start by writing down the first words that come to mind, and continue until they feel like they have covered everything important. Then they must whittle the list down to no more than the seven most important adjectives. We collect the lists, and compare and compile a final list that is put on the board. This list of words should convey the same mood as the image window.

3. *The color palette*. The color palette is usually composed of four to six core colors with another four to ten supplemental colors. The total palette of eight to sixteen colors should be a cohesive unit, yet allow a particular implementation to shift from lighter to darker hues or

from cooler to warmer without leaving the palette. With a well-constructed palette, special areas of a site may have their own coloration or personality, assuring visitors of where they are, yet remain clearly connected to the whole site.

4. *The texture palette.* The interpretation of words and pictures, even when seen in fragments, is often so literal that people overlook their emotional response. We find it useful on occasion to prepare a palette of six to eight textures to help capture the mood of a site. Textures can also be interpreted literally, mostly through recognition of the source of the texture, but it takes a little longer for this interpretation to take place, and during that gap, the viewers' emotions can grasp the mood.

5. *The motion guide.* This is not about Flash or video, although it could be. It is about breaking out of the up, down, left, right, document view of the Web. We occasionally use schematic gestures to indicate sweeping or circular or perspective motion in areas of a site. After all, gestures in any face-to-face conversation are a critical part of the communication.

The specific visual elements or words presented on the mood board may never appear on the final Web site. Although some things might appear, the objective of the mood board is to serve as a strong guide to all of the writers and designers who may be working on the site. In some ways this is similar to the graphic standards of brand identity programs of the past. They are meant to provide brand cohesion and consistency regardless of the environment in which they appear. The old programs, however, were narrow and focused on controls of the logo, a limited color palette, and typefonts. The mood board provides little control, yet it can provide a much broader, richer, and deeper interpretation of the brand essence.

Designers use mood boards to help establish the visual design of the Web site. This should not be confused with a *style guide.* The style guide is often prepared around the time a site is nearing completion, and is used primarily as a tool for maintenance and up-dates to the site. A style guide contains some of the elements of the mood board, such as the palette, image window, and mood guidewords. It will also include specific templates for key page types and detailed information such as page size, logo treatment, preferred sizes and typefonts, and special treatments for buttons, call-outs, dingbats, or other critical elements.

The Brand Reservoir

Graphic Standards programs of the past were encapsulated in large three-ring binders. They spelled out the do's and don'ts of logo and corporate color usage and included numerous examples of the correct way to present information. There are many companies still using these manuals today, though they are far too limited, time consuming, and expensive to be effective. It is much easier to shoot an e-mail to a prospective supplier, including the URL and passwords necessary to access a separate site with the standards online, than to ship off an expensive manual.

The online Brand Standards, like the company Web site, can be much deeper and broader than the printed manuals. They will have more to do with the underlying values of the brand than the details of reproduction. They may include such things as the different roles played by members of a communications team and how they support and interact with one another. They can show the company's communications development process, including naming and branding strategy, different customers' needs, and writing and design strategy to meet those needs. They may also include image and factual databases that can be used in the company's communications. And to be truly effective, they might let various advertising agencies, design groups, or public relations personnel working with the brand share examples of their most successful communications efforts in print and interactive form, and share feedback from customers interacting with the company.

Like the Web itself, the company brand or product brand grows in depth and complexity through experience with its customers. It gains a rich patina through its use over time. The look and feel of the company Web site or product site will certainly be influenced by the established brand guidelines. More importantly, the brand will be influenced, tested, proved or disproved, by the site itself—by what it offers and how it works. The visitor's experience of your brand on the Web is more than the colors, logos, words and pictures you put on the site. It will be heavily influenced by how fast the visitor can find what is needed, get more information, or complete the transaction and move on.

·

11

Building the Site

There are as many different ways to build a site—and different tools that may be used—as there are to build a house. And each site builder or coder, just like a carpenter, has his or her own bag of tricks. But the relationship of two essential ingredients of Web site development is important for everyone involved to understand: The difference between *functional specifications* and *technical specifications* must be clear. This chapter will briefly review these, and then touch on the value of building a prototype site and the use of the Web as a collaborative tool.

Functional Specifications

As mentioned earlier, detailed functional specifications and technical specifications should be part of the organization phase (II) on any Web project. They are also very separate reports. Many companies write a technical spec, which includes the required systems functionality and the server platform or configuration needed to support the site. This is only half of the job. The other half, the functional spec, must come first. This outlines the specific functionality that will be available on the site from a visitor's perspective. The technical specs then detail what technology will be used to accomplish these functions.

Functionality certainly occurs within the system—inside the computer or various computers or the network—and this is where confusion often arises. System functionality, often referred to as "back-end" functions, is totally different from "front-end" or customer-facing functions. The two are intimately connected but the front-end customer-facing functionality should always drive the back-end.

During the site architecture design phase, much of the discussion and thinking is about what functions a visitor to the site might be able to perform. Writing the functional spec on a simple site includes the number and name of options presented to the visitor when they arrive on the site, what happens when one of those options is clicked, and what new options will be presented. On a more complex site with various tools for searching, calculating, purchasing, or saving information, the function in each area needs to be spelled out. This should be written from the visitor's point of view. Using the NMWA site example discussed earlier, the functional spec may look like this: Milagros Cogan may choose to search the collections database (db) or the library and research db. If she clicks on the collections db, she will be presented with the option to browse the db or to type in a specific request by date, artist's name, country, etc. When Cogan chooses to browse the eighteenth century, she will be presented with several items, etc.

The scenarios used during the development of architecture provide the basis for writing the functional spec from the visitor's perspective. Once these are clear it is much easier, and often less expensive, to determine what technologies are required to make them work. If system functionality comes first, invariably the visitor will be slighted, more often confused and frustrated, and the results will not be as successful.

Technical Specifications

This is where the hardware and software that will be used to accomplish the site's functionality gets specified. It is also where a number of people make a big mistake. Although new developments in technology capability may prompt new ideas, the technologies to be deployed should never be specified without a thorough understanding of the visitor functions to be accomplished. The effective Web site is driven by technology meeting the needs of people, not people responding to the demands of technology.

Before specifying the servers and software to be used on the NMWA site, it was necessary to know what database systems and software were being used in different departments within the museum and outside support organizations that needed to connect with the new site, i.e., the library and research database, the collections database, the existing membership system, etc. If the Web site could not easily integrate with these systems, the purpose of the site—meeting the expectations of Milagros Cogan—would not be fulfilled.

The rapid business and technology changes of the last two decades have left most companies and institutions with a mixed bag of systems and software designed for departmental need, not enterprise need. Although Enterprise Resource Planning (ERP) has been a marketing catch phrase used by technology companies for years (ERP is essentially an attempt to integrate all departmental functions within an organization to create a single software program that runs off one database), it is much easier to say than to accomplish.

Today there are huge numbers of servers, operating platforms, software programs, programming languages, and protocols available to help people accomplish a vast range of tasks on the Web without the time-consuming costs of ERP. Of course each situation is different, but there are a few basics that designers need to keep in mind when specifying and building a Web site.

Compatibility

The beauty of the URL and HTTP standards is that they allow any networked computer to find and communicate with another. The barrier— even though the Open Systems Interconnection (OSI) model has been around for twenty years—is that the different application programs with which documents were created are still *different*. With new languages, the differences become less formidable each year, but one question should still be asked of any hardware/software configuration: Is this an open system? If it is not, find one that is.

Specifications often begin with the Web server. This is the software that interacts directly with the visitor's Web browser by receiving request for documents such as HTML or Microsoft Active Server Pages (ASP). HTML documents are static pages that display content whereas ASP documents are dynamic pages that act as a live page interpreter. These ASP files retrieve information from a source such as a database, and then manipulate the raw data from the source into a page that is viewable by the visitor. Web servers and other back-end components often work much like families, in that certain groupings of these components communicate together better than others. The Web server often plays an important role in choosing other back-end components, such as database servers and programming languages.

Speed

The importance of a Web site's speed is clear. The visitor does not want to wait for pages to load or results to be produced. To ensure that a site runs quickly, hardware and software specifications must be scaled to accommodate the anticipated traffic to the site. Hardware factors that influence a Web site's speed include the server and its connection to the Internet. The speed of the server can vary depending on the megahertz (MHz) of its processor(s), amount of RAM, speed/configuration of hard drives, and motherboard. The speed of its connection to the Internet determines how much data it is able to send to users in a given amount of time.

Scalability

It is difficult to predict the future usage of any Web site. However, if a site should outgrow its initial configuration, "scaling-up" to meet new usage requirements will be less difficult if this has been taken into consideration from the beginning. Basic questions should be asked: Can additional servers be added to provide greater capacity? Should the databases be expanded to accommodate additional cells? If we need to switch hosts or if we decide to host this internal, what will the difficulties be? Who owns the source code for this site? Files should be structured, and code written and commented on as standard procedure, so it is easily understandable for others not involved in the development of the site.

Efficiency

The efficiency of programming promotes greater speed, greater flexibility, and lower complexity. This can be achieved by both using as few different technologies as possible—and using them well. In the interest of lessening development time, it is often wise to use third-party components for certain features of a site. This should be done only when necessary, and when custom development of a feature is impractical. The more separate components that are used, the more complex the server interaction becomes. This may lead to greater maintenance requirements, lower speed, and reliability issues.

Building the Prototype

Testing a visitor's ability to use a site cannot be overemphasized. You may have developed personas to clearly define your audience, run through scenarios at the card-sorting stage, and more scenarios with the "paper site" to determine the final architecture. But for any site of more than a few pages, you should now build an HTML prototype. This should include the homepage, major section pages, some second level pages and special transaction sequences such as the checkout process in an e-commerce site. It does not need to have final content but should use what content is available to make this as real as possible. It does not require extensive programming. Flat HTML and possibly some simple scripting will provide enough of a working site that you and your clients can click through the navigation to assure that it all makes sense.

A development site, or staging area, should be established on a server that matches the configuration of the server on which the final site will reside. Programmers will work on the development server to prepare the prototype and to develop the real site before it is moved to its final home. It is a good idea to share the URL for the prototype with friends, or coworkers that are not involved with the development. Ask your clients to do the same, and give them some specific questions to ask the visitors to the prototype: Did you understand the options provided on the homepage? When you clicked on (—) did it take you where you thought it would? Did you have any problems finding your way to (—)?

This is not about getting opinions on the "design," although you will certainly get them. It is about finding out how well the site is working for the uninitiated visitor. Again, it is much easier and less expensive to make adjustments now rather than after the final coding is done.

After the review and adjustments are made, the prototype site may be used as the framework on which the real site is built, although it is often easier to put this aside and build the real site from scratch. At various points along the process of building, the clients should be notified and asked to review sections completed or near completion. It is critical that they understand what is now working and can be tested, and what is still in development. Testing as you build will shorten the quality assurance testing when the site is finalized.

After the site is built, each page, every action, and all transactions must be tested on a variety of computers. Purchases should be made through the purchase mechanism. Credit cards should be used. (They can always be backed out of the system.) Databases must be queried, profiles filled out, e-mails sent, administrative tools for uploading databases or making changes tested, and all auto responders and error messages checked. This always takes longer than you think and more time than you have, but it is preferable to delay the launch by a few days rather than risk having a site live with errors.

When testing is complete, the site is ported to the final servers and made live. The heavy work is done, but monitoring, measuring, and making adjustments will go on, and on, and on.

Case Study: Kimco Realty

When Kimco Realty Corporation approached us with an exciting opportunity, it had been on the Web for about five years with an attractive site that included a database listing its real estate properties. It wanted to redesign the site to make it a more useful business tool for its customers and for its employees. Kimco is America's largest publicly traded owner and operator of neighborhood and community shopping centers, with over six hundred properties of leasable space in forty-one states, Canada, and Mexico.

We conducted interviews with key members of management. In a persona development discovery workshop, which included representatives from Kimco's Information Technology group, Investor Relations, Property Development, Leasing Agents, and the Acquisitions Group, we all came to a few decisions that drove the site development.

1. The property database was central to all business activity with customers and most internal activity as well, and should therefore be the prominent focus of the site.
2. Different types of property information in the database were important to different people, so they should have separate paths for access.
3. Existing customers as well as unknown prospects should be able to easily search for properties along the lines of their particular interest.
4. Property activity in a portfolio this size happens frequently so the property database needed to be updated easily, quickly, and often.

5. Maintenance of the site, although centrally coordinated, would be spread over a number of people from different departments within Kimco.

The first decision led to the development of one of the primary visual and functional features of the site: a dynamic map that indicates the location of all properties in the Kimco portfolio based on the latitude and longitude of each property. Visitors may browse the properties through the map or they may search through a variety of specific criteria such as location, square footage, demographics, ID number, or co-tenants in a property.

The primary navigation available throughout the site is divided by visitor interest such as leasing, development, acquisitions, property services, and investor relations. The same dynamic map appears on leasing, development, and acquisitions but it appears in the color of that section and includes only the properties that relate to that area of activity. This is controlled by identification tags in the database. When visitors select a property by the map or a search, they are shown: a site plan, an aerial view of the property, a property photo, a demographic chart, specific property information, area maps and directions, and the name and direct contact information for the agent responsible for this property.

The secondary navigation, also available throughout the site, includes a My Kimco section that allows registered visitors to save their search criteria and be automatically notified when new properties that match their criteria are added to the database. The criteria are also made available to appropriate Kimco leasing representatives who may contact a registered visitor to suggest property alternatives. Kimco tenants may also make a lease renewal request or a property repair request through the site.

The revised Web site, which has been "live" for about two years at this writing, has become integral to the way Kimco carries out much of its business. The public however, does not see the most interesting aspect. The administrative side to this site is as large, if not larger than the site itself. The administrative tools are available through a unique URL and each user has his or her own password that allows access to specific portions of the site. Depending on an administrator's area of expertise, the administrator may review and respond to a tenant's request, property inquiries, or submitted acquisition or development projects. They upload news releases and financial data, download resumes for Human Resources, upload the core property database, and review and communicate directly with customers based on search activity.

Although this site is about marketing and brand image, there is very little marketing fluff. There is a wealth of information available on the business areas of Kimco, and the people and principles of Kimco, but the site is designed to provide many options for making the visitors experience as rich, easy, and meaningful as possible. No extraneous content, just the information and the connections that the visitors—external and internal—need to get the most benefit from their business transactions with Kimco.

By the time you read this, the look and feel of the site may be redesigned again. But the strategy and the scalability that was considered from the beginning should allow the basic structure to stay in place for some time. We keep the development site alive (on separate but matching servers) and regularly share and test new things with Kimco, making modifications and adjustments as new business issues emerge.

The Sandbox

The development site, or staging area, for a Web site is often referred to as a sandbox. I'm not sure where this term originates, but it seems appropriate for continuing the promise of Web development. It suggests an adult playpen where designers, writers, and developers come with their shovels and rakes and buckets to dig holes, make tunnels, and create castles. Yes, there are tasks to be accomplished, deadlines to be met, codes to be followed, but the more we play—experiment, test, try new ideas—the better we get. Playing together in the sandbox is what the practice of Web design is all about.

There are numerous "collaborative" products on the market. Software programs that are intended to provide "shared online workspace" for designers, developers, their clients—or anyone for that matter—working together on a project. I have not found one yet that makes a contribution worthy of its cost. Yes, they are used, but most are cumbersome, clunky, and too rule-based to work the way people work. People doodle, make margin notes, scribble, draw arrows, and even write down phone numbers or mental reminders that have nothing to do with the task at hand.

People can also be cumbersome and clunky, but they have managed for millennia to work with, or around other people. We seem to have built-in adjustment gauges that modulate the rational and emotional give and take of working with one another. The gauges don't always work. There are flare-ups and burnouts, but for the most part we adjust and keep going. Using the telephone, fax, instant messaging, legal pads, whiteboards, text editors, and Web servers for development sites, people manage to do amazing things—playing in the sandbox. Collaborative online tools may be getting better, but they have a long, long way to go before approaching the efficiency of the chicken wire and gum approach that humans usually take.

I was involved very briefly with a company developing a "knowledgeware" Web-based product. The concept was to use a gardening metaphor. There were to be "planters," the people who brought ideas to "the knowledge garden." There would be "gardeners," the people who tended to the garden. They were the ones who made sure that the ideas provided by the planters were presented clearly and were well organized. And there would be "harvesters" who would, of course, harvest the ideas. The concept was interesting, but you can see the problem right away. People don't work that way. In the real world, planters are also gardeners and harvesters, or they are harvesters first and then planters or gardeners. Or, there are some who just want to be weeds. If I were planting a "knowledge-garden," I would make a special allowance for the weeds because I'd bet that that's where the best ideas would come from.

Building a Web site may seem contrary to creative thinking. It requires clear functional and technical specifications and strict adherence to authoring standards and Web protocols. It is based on highly detailed organizational schematics that require thorough understanding of the systems involved, and an understanding and sympathy for the visitor to the site and the business goals. This demands ideas at every turn. Living systems—human or otherwise—continuously change and adjustments must be made.

The practice of Web design can certainly improve by developing personas to walk through site activity, card-sorting to help organize the site architecture, mood boards to guide the visual interpretation, and a prototype site for testing before the final build. But building castles in the sandbox is where it all comes together, and this, like all of the other areas, requires imagination, invention, inspiration, and continuous practice.

The Players

In the early days of the Web there was only one principle player: the Webmaster. The knowledge and skills of this person tended to be all over the lot. The only real requirements were comfort and familiarity with computers and some basic knowledge of HTML and Internet protocols.

Today, in the second decade of Web design, the knowledge and skills required for any business transaction Web site have grown substantially beyond the capacity of a single individual. In most cases, there are multiple teams with many members each contributing their particular expertise. The number and types of people involved is often the single most confusing area of site design. Who does what? When do they do it? And how do they all "play nice" together to achieve great results?

The following pages discuss the roles and responsibilities of critical participants in the site design and development process. This is presented from the perspective of the design objectives of a site. It begins with a discussion on the meaning of "design," then looks at three particular objectives that must be considered for any business Web site. First is the site's form—how does it look and feel? Second is the site's function—*does it work? And third is its* feasibility—*is it a viable business initiative?*

Although form, function, and feasibility are presented in this order, they are of equal importance, and the design teams responsible for each should be tightly integrated with one another. As we will see in the discussion on individual teams, the primary responsibilities for each team, its members, and its culture are substantially different, but when the roles of each are clearly understood by the others, the process of development can be smoother and the results greater.

This section concludes with a brief review of a fourth group of "players" that is becoming increasingly important: governing organizations, and the creators and keepers of law. Thus far, management of the Web has been remarkably loose and free, following the principles of self-regulation. There are strong reasons to continue in this fashion, but as the Web grows in importance the need for freedom and the need for law increase. This will become a constant balancing act.

12

Form, Function, and Feasibility

"Hey there young fellow, what do you do?" I heard a voice say one morning years ago as I was walking down Fifth Avenue. It was coming from a cartoon character on a large screen on the side of a truck parked at the curb. "That's right, I'm talking to you," the character said as I looked around. "What do you do for a living?"

"I'm a designer," I replied, feeling just a little foolish speaking to an animated cartoon.

"Oh, what do you design, hats?" he said, taking off his illustrated hat with a flourish.

What is he talking about, I thought. "No, I don't design hats, I'm a graphic designer."

"Ah ha, you design graphics—like charts and maps, right?" The animated character spoke loudly as he bounced around the screen. He was drawing a small crowd.

"No, I don't design maps—well, yes I do but . . ." I stumbled, thought for a second and continued. "I design corporate communications materials. I help companies solve communications . . ."

"Whoaaa! That's impressive." The cartoon interrupted me, "You mean things like phone systems and fax machines, right?"

I knew I was in trouble. This could only get worse. "I have to go," I said. "It's been nice talking with you." And I quickly pushed my way through the crowd.

"Hey, wait a minute," I heard the cartoon calling after me as I hurried down the street. "I still don't know what you do."

Defining Design

In nearly all professions today there can be a number of specialized areas. For the most part, however, if someone says he is a dentist, you know—more or less—what he does. Likewise for a librarian, a lawyer, a plumber, or a doctor. A designer, on the other hand, may do things related to each of these professions as well as a world of others.

There are orthodontic designers and library systems designers. There are people who design legal documents, and legal processes; people who design plumbing fixtures, fittings, and flow distribution systems; and others who design medical instruments, medicines, operating procedures, and health care methodologies. There is a designer somewhere involved in nearly all aspects of your business and your life. Someone or some group designed the chair you are sitting on, the table you are using, the accounting system, layout program, or word processing tool you work in, the pen you write with, the phone you speak into, the television you watch and all of the information presentations pumped through it, the bed you sleep on, the blankets you're covered with, the house you live in, the laws you live by, and the book you are now reading.

Since design is so pervasive, before beginning to talk about the different players involved in Web design, it might be useful to attempt to clarify what design means. The word is both verb and noun. It is used to represent both process and product. Clients of consultant design firms always ask for nouns. They want Web sites, videos, logos, books, posters, chairs, watches, but what designers do is the verb—the process, "the making," that results in the product. The difficulty is that no matter how well we try to define the process, it defies rational definition. We may reasonably discuss the results, but how we actually arrived at this result is often a complete mystery. This has created tremendous problems for the design professional as well as society as a whole. Graphic as well as product designers have complained for years that even their mothers do not understand what they do.

Many people think design is just about making something look pretty. Certainly aesthetics is a major component. So are intelligence, wit, practicality, intuition, and inspiration. The emphasis on "beauty" is perpetuated by the way we talk about design. We use the verb to help us describe nouns. We say things like, "What an exquisitely designed chair,"

"This is a beautifully designed annual report," or "We have a system designed for efficiency." We may be responding to the color, the relationship of forms, or an emotional nerve that has just been touched, but what we mean is, "This is an exquisite chair, a beautiful annual report, an efficient system," and design is the activity that made them so.

Design is about intent. It is the plan, the method, the plot, the often wandering path that will be followed to accomplish something. We may say, "This is a great design." The reference is to the plan, not the product. Design is all the planning activity that brings the product to life. It is the process that imbues products and services with value. To design is to plan—to think and to act on the thinking, to feel and to express the feeling. At the highest level, regardless of the practice area, design is a process of distilling information to achieve understanding, connecting various elements to create experience, and shaping matter to a purpose.

Commercial design is the vital activity between request and response. It is often collaborative but always subjective. It occurs somewhere between perception and language, between what we see and what we say, what is envisioned and the way it is expressed. It is a dialogue between people and things, about what we want to do and how we may do it, where we want to go and how we may get there. Design involves observation, analysis, perception, reasoning, dreaming, and opinion. It deals with isolation, juxtaposition, multiplicity, spontaneity, change, and control. And it results in grace, beauty, distinction, impact, and value.

Design is an age-old affair between ideas and their realization. It is the heart of strategy and the hand of craft, the synthesis of desire and satisfaction, the single seam of form, function, and feasibility. It is the subtle collusion of emotion and reason as data is transformed to information, information to knowledge, knowledge to understanding, and understanding—with a little luck—is transformed to extended lives of expanding value. Design is the multi-faceted voice of the cultural conversation that continues to push us forward as it preserves the best of our past.

Creatives, Geeks, and Suits

If design can be so sweeping, so pervasive, so grand, who can possibly be the designers? This is the fun part. We are all designers. Everyone. We are all born with tremendous creative capability. Design is how we choose to use that potential. This does not take importance away from professional designers—those who may be trained in the subtleties of perception and cognition, the influence of color, form and motion, or the intricacies of code and calculations. Their experience and training should bring special insight to the tasks at hand. But in all of these areas, design is about selection—exploring choices and making decisions. We all do that every day in a multitude of ways. From the clothes we choose to put on in the morning to the route we take to work, from the way we organize our desktop to the people we choose to work or live with, or the way we choose to spend our time—for the most part, we can not help but design our lives. How good we are at it is another question.

Just as we design our lives we may also design our Web sites. Many individuals conceive their own sites, write the copy, structure the information, create the graphics, do the programming necessary to make their site work, and monitor the results. For any transaction-oriented business site, however, the process of design and production has grown so important and complex that a wide spectrum of design specialists may be needed. Like the colors of a rainbow, each brings his or her own hue to the project. And, each usually belongs to one of three larger groups of participants.

The groups are most often labeled Design, Technology, and Business. They are frequently referred to as the "creatives," the "geeks," and the "suits." This labeling highlights the different focus that each group brings to the process. Unfortunately it also emphasizes the differences rather than the commonalities. Complex Web sites demand collaboration. Often Web designers, convinced that their concept is just what is needed, get frustrated when the technology team says it can't be done, and the business team says they don't get it, or is caught in the middle not knowing whom to believe. Occasionally the technology group may come up with what they think is a terrific architecture that meets the business needs, but the designers say no one will use this, because it's not intuitive. And the business group, not knowing enough about design or technology, is caught in the middle again. When the businessperson suggests that the site must be organized around product groups and have specific "sell" copy for each, the designer and technologist look knowingly at one another, but because the businessperson is paying the bill they are reluctant to say that it is dumb and won't work.

One of the primary difficulties here is that each group has worked in the past, with different tools, in different environments, with different outcome expectations. Each has a different specialized history and in that history used different languages. In the very broadest and simplest of terms—omitting huge areas of overlap in the interest of highlighting the problem—the differences may be seen as follows: Business people have a history of command and control; a language of finance, titles and departments; a bottom-line orientation; and work primarily with spreadsheets and calculators. Technologists have a history of "tinkering;" are trained in complex computation; use the languages of science and math; and love computers and gadgets. Visual designers have a history of non-conformism; use the language of line, form and color; are trained in creative play; and use a combination of words and images as their primary tool.

The decade-old connected world brought about by the Web has shoved us all closer together. But we are still learning one another's language and need to look for the similarities, not the differences. We are all beginning to use the same tools, to work in the same environment, and are seeking the same outcome. A more beneficial way of looking at these groups and discussing the Web development process, is to stop segmenting the players into teams by old standards.

A Three-Strand Rope

Since we are all designers, the groups can be seen as three design groups: interaction designers, functional designers, and business designers. The roles do not radically change. I am not suggesting that we all start doing one another's jobs, or that any one group should forego their primary concerns, or any individual should sacrifice his or her personal aesthetic. This is simply a semantic change. One that may help shift the perception away from the adversity often provoked by traditional boundaries towards the goals of a larger group. Interaction designers focus on the desires of the user, functional designers focus on the workability of the system, and business designers focus on producing financial value. And all three collaborate on a common goal: to produce a unique, usable, and valuable Web site.

These three groups—interaction design, functional design, and business design—correspond to a conceptual model often used to discuss three essential qualities needed when developing products in the high-tech industry. The development of a customer-facing, transaction-oriented Web site, in any industry, requires the same three qualities:

1. *Desirability*. This is the primary focus of the interaction designers. What is it that people really want? What do they have a burning desire for? What will they respond to? Interaction designers must know how to create and satisfy desire. They must make the visitors experience intriguing, meaningful, exciting, memorable, and satisfying.

2. *Capability*. What are we capable of producing? What is it possible for us to make? Can this functionality be accomplished? These are the questions that must be answered by the functional design group. They must know that the tools and technology can be built or assembled to deliver the goods. They need to have the capability to assure that the system will work.

3. *Viability*. Is this site a viable business option? Will our customers—or suppliers and partners—find it easier to do business with us? Can we reduce our cost or improve our profit margins? Does this benefit our brand? These are the issues that must be resolved by the business designers. They must determine that this site, like any other new product or service initiative, will be an asset rather than a liability for the company.[1]

These qualities—desirability, capability, viability—are the primary responsibility of the corresponding group of interaction designers, functional designers, business designers; they are also the joint responsibility of all of the players. And, depending on the scope of the initiative, there may be many.

In the interactive design group there are often communications strategists, cultural anthropologists, information architects, graphic designers, writers, and animation or streaming media specialist. The functional design group may have systems analysts, HTML or XML (Extensible Markup Language) coders, scripting programmers, database designers, and certified systems engineers. And in the business design group there is usually a business strategist, business developer or marketing representative, communications director, information technology representative, and someone from investor relations or human resources.

A three-strand rope is a convenient metaphor to help visualize how these people fit together. The individual players are like the single fibers within a rope. Based on their training, experience or special skills, they twist together in one direction—around one primary goal. The interaction designers, all concerned with various aspects of satisfying the visitor's desires, form one strand. The functional designers, assembling components and code that will meet the visitor's demands, form another strand. And business designers, working together to assure that satisfying the visitor's goals will also satisfy the business goals, form the third strand. These three strands then twist tightly together to form a strong rope. This organizational metaphor reveals multiple individual talents performing a variety of tasks while working in unison, with no single leader, yet providing simultaneous strength and flexibility.

Although there will be overlap in some activities and specific roles, disputes over who is responsible for what are easier to settle when each person is aware of his or her group's primary focus, and of the vital importance of the other two groups. The old design discussions around which comes first, form or function, no longer apply. One does not constantly follow while the other leads. In fact they never dance alone. Form and function must be joined by feasibility. Then pushing, pulling, tugging one another, the three progress as one. There will continue to be disagreements. There may be fierce arguments. This is the combustible nature of design and human relationships. It is a large part of what drives us forward—creating, reviewing, arguing about, and making choices based on numerous options and opinions. But by working together as designers—with intent, sharing a common goal, respecting one another's design abilities and design goals—disagreements just may be easier to overcome.

The Fourth Strand

The three essential qualities of desirability, capability, and viability will undoubtedly be joined with increasing frequency in the future by a fourth: *permissibility*. Thus far, the Web and most of the innovations resulting from its influence have been relatively free of government interference. But as Web use increases, new tools appear, and existing organizations feel more threatened; regulations and laws to protect our rights to think, speak, create, and share ideas using the Web will become essential.

This will require that all of the designers above work hand-in-hand with "government designers" to assure that the basic rights of freedom of speech and free expression that exist offline will be preserved online.

We generally do not think of legislators and lawmakers as designers. Maybe we should. That is, after all, what they do. Legislators review information, analyze situations, distill meaning, combine what they think and feel with what they have learned, and craft new plans or bills. They then work with other legislators to turn their bills into laws in hopes that their new "designs" will improve the quality of all our lives. Thinking of lawmakers as designers, as crazy as this may sound, may help shift our focus—and theirs—from the politics of law to the purpose of law—from enforcing the letter of the law to invoking the spirit of the law.

Speaking of the language of law in his book *The Eagle Bird*, lawyer Charles Wilkinson, a leading legal authority on natural resources and public land, says, "why is it that the words of our laws do not carry the high pitch so evident in the arts and literature, why is it that laws do not speak of the wonder and majesty of the bald eagle?" According to Wilkinson, lawyers say "that statutes must be absolutely precise." Yet Wilkinson adds, "why is it that a word like majesty does not help us a great deal in measuring something? How is it possible to be precise about eagles without knowing of majesty?"[2]

Eagles, of course, have nothing to do with the Web. Wilkinson is speaking on behalf of the natural resources of the western United States, and the need for "an ethic of place," based on "the recognition that our species thrives on the subtle, intangible, but soul-deep mix of landscape, smells, sounds, history, neighbors, and friends that constitute a place, a homeland."

The Web is vastly different from the natural land that Wilkinson speaks so eloquently of, but laws governing its future will also need an "ethic of place" or an ethic of space, based on an "intangible, but soul-deep" mix of very similar elements. Among the factors that must not be overlooked when decisions need to be made are "beauty, inspiration, and wonder," which are fundamental to its—and our—survival.

When lawyers and lawmakers spend time in this new space, meeting distant neighbors and making new friends, and choose to represent the multitude of voices with a common plea—for freedom of speech and the right to privacy—we'll have a four-strand rope even stronger than three.

13

Interaction Designers

"I think in pictures. Words are like a second language to me. I translate both spoken and written words into full-color movies, complete with sound, which run like a VCR tape in my head. When somebody speaks to me, his words are instantly translated to pictures. Language-based thinkers often find this phenomenon difficult to understand, but in my job as an equipment designer for the livestock industry, visual thinking is a tremendous advantage."

Temple Grandin, *Thinking in Pictures*

Temple Grandin has a Ph.D. in animal science, teaches at Colorado State University, and is a renowned designer of systems for animal management. She has designed a third of the livestock-handling facilities in the United States. She is also autistic. At the age of three, with a total absence of speech, a tendency to violence and fixation, and a complete inaccessibility to others, Grandin was taken to a neurologist who diagnosed her with autism and the possibility of lifelong institutionalization. Her book is a fascinating report of her life with autism—her gradual awakening to the differences in the world she perceived, and the one others seemed to live in; her struggle to understand autism and the power of images and words; and her lifetime, passionate commitment to the humane treatment of animals.

A Cow's Eye View[1]
As a leading designer of farms, feeding installations, and slaughterhouses, Grandin is the quintessential interaction designer. Her work is at the apex

•

of animal life. Her concerns are with the interaction between livestock and the variety of mechanical and electronic devices with which they live and by which they die. Her greater concerns have to do with the interaction between farmers or other animal handlers, the animals, and the devices used to control them. These concerns extend to the activity between the animal handlers, industry associations, and state and government regulatory agencies that establish policies regarding the management of livestock.

Although the artifacts of her work—the feeding chute, slaughter-house, or corral—are different than the artifacts of a Web designer—the site and its various tools—the spectrum of interactivity is comparable. The primary focus of the Web interaction designer, or design team, is the reciprocal action between the visitor and the "electronic tool" (the site) being visited. The objective is to provide a desirable—easy, useful, fun, intelligent, valuable—experience. The extended concerns include the activity between other people working on the interaction design team, mutual work with the other teams—the functional designers and business designers—and the interaction of this site with other sites or organizations that may affect the visitor's experience.

Grandin's approach to design is always from the animal's point of view. "When I put myself in a cow's place, I really have to be that cow and not a person in a cow costume. I use my visual thinking skills to simulate what an animal would see and hear in a given situation. I place myself inside its body and imagine what it experiences."[2] This may seem a far cry from the design of Web sites, but just as Grandin is sympathetic to the needs of the cow, good Web designers must be sympathetic first to the nature and needs of the human being who will use the site. Listen to the language she uses. "I have to follow the cattle's rules of behavior. I also have to imagine what experiencing the world through the cow's sensory system is like." This sounds like a Web designer talking about the behavior of users and the activities of a persona visiting a site.

Of course people visiting a Web site are different from cows entering a barn. Cattle are animals of prey. They live with fear as a primary moti-vation to avoid predators, and they use their wide-angle vision—nearly 360 degrees—to protect themselves. Humans are considered a predatory species. We have eyes in the front of our heads that enable us to perceive depth and distances much better than cattle. Yet we share similarities. "It is the little things that make them balk and refuse to move," Grandin says when asked if cattle are frightened of death, "such as seeing a small piece of chain hanging down from an alley fence. For instance, a lead animal will stop to look at a moving chain and move his head back and forth in rhythm with its swing. He isn't concerned about being slaughtered; he's afraid of a small piece of chain that jiggles and looks out of place."

Grandin's solutions are often simple and straightforward. "Cattle and hogs will not walk into a dark place," she says, "so installing a lamp to illuminate the entrance to an alley will entice them to enter. Animals, like people, want to see where they are going." People, like animals, also get bothered by small jiggly things that seem out of place. On the Web, they may not be so frightened, they just get confused, frustrated, and leave.

Visual Thinking

Grandin's visualization skills are reminiscent of Nikola Tesla, another great visual thinker. Tesla, the inventor and electrical engineer who gave us alternating-current power transmission, the coil transformer, wireless communication, and hundreds of other inventions, designed and tested his complex turbine engines in his head. He could "see" the entire system and said it did not matter if it was tested in the lab, if he tested it in his vision, it would work. Most of us do not have such powerful pictures in our minds, yet visual thinking is one of the most important skills required of interaction designers.

Although image has become an increasingly important part of global communications over the last quarter century, visual thinking—outside of the visual professions and the relatively new field of cognitive science—remains one of the least-understood areas of knowledge manipulation. Visual thinking has to do with seeing, not only the reality in front of us, but what could be there—the reality we can imagine. Seeing on both fronts is always an active engagement. "One does not see, or sense, or perceive, in isolation—perception is always linked to behavior and movement, to reaching out and exploring the world. It is insufficient to see; one must look as well."[3]

It is also insufficient to just look. In undergraduate school I took a course in hand lettering taught by Zen Buddhist Timothy Whitehead. He had a very unique—Zen-like—approach to lettering. Each class began with an exercise in listening. In a very methodical manner, the students, following Whiteheads careful instructions, placed a piece of paper squarely on the table in front of them, positioned their pen neatly aligned with the paper, and placed an ink well on the table slightly above the paper. On Whitehead's count, we would pick up our pens, dip them in the ink well, close our eyes, tilt one ear to the paper, and stroke the nib across the surface. "Listen to the lettering," he would say in a soft voice. "Now dip . . . Now hold . . . Now stroke. Listen to the sound of lettering."

The class of thirty or so students was unbelievably quiet, as everyone closed their eyes, stroked, and listened together. It took me years to understand what this was all about. Learning to draw letterforms, like all other drawing and all other learning, is not just about eye-hand coordination or seeing the form or looking or memorizing. It involves all of the senses: seeing, hearing, touching, tasting, smelling, and thinking— exploring the vast combinatorial possibilities of these experiences.

It is also something we learn at a very young age. Give a piece of paper to a six-month-old baby and watch what she does. She will look at it, wave it in the air, wrinkle it up, and try to throw it. She will pick it up, look at it again, smash it into her face, put it in her mouth, tear it in half, clap it with both hands, and wrinkle it more. If the paper is the kind that makes some noise, this can go on for some time. What is happening here, of course, is learning. She is exploring, testing, and discovering the possibilities of interacting with paper. She is also adding to her database of experiential possibilities.

Unfortunately, most of our formal education does not continue this kind of exercise. Our education system has been for years—and for the most part, continues to be—heavily biased toward a limited range of learning tools. Reading, writing and arithmetic are unquestionably important. The emphasis we place on them, however, has been so stringent that some people still believe that we think only with words. Since the early days of cognitive research this idea has been repeatedly refuted. Steven Pinker, professor of psychology and director of the Center of Cognitive Neuroscience at MIT, provides one of the best and most direct explanations:

"The idea that thought is the same thing as language is an example of what can be called a conventional absurdity: a statement that goes against all common sense but that everyone believes because they dimly recall having heard it somewhere and because it is so pregnant with implications. (The *fact* that we use only five percent of our brains, that lemmings commit mass suicide, that the Boy Scout Manual annually outsells all other books, and that we can be coerced into buying by subliminal messages are other examples.) Think about it. We have all had the experience of uttering or writing a sentence, then stopping and realizing that it wasn't exactly what we meant to say. To have that feeling, there has to be a "what we meant to say" that is different from what we actually said. Sometimes it is not easy to find any words that convey a thought. When we hear or read, we usually remember the gist, not the exact words, so there has to be such a thing as a gist that is not the same as a bunch of words. And if thoughts depended on words, how could a new word ever be coined? How could a child learn a word to begin with? How could translation from one language to another be possible?"[4]

I am often asked what education is required for today's Web designer. The first and most important training is in how to see (translation: how to think). This is not just visual thinking, strategic thinking, linear thinking, lateral thinking, or creative thinking. It is a combination of all of them, and most good designers acquire this ability in a combination of ways. A broad liberal arts degree is important, but not always essential. A degree in the visual arts—with emphasis on line, form, color, pattern recognition and information organization and manipulation—such as graphic design, architecture, or industrial design, is vitally important; but again, not always essential. Training in music, math, biology or psychology is important but not a requirement. The most important requirement for an interaction designer is an active, restless, relentless curiosity about the world, and keen observation of people's often fuzzy interaction with every aspect of it.

Why Interaction Design?

Currently there seems to be confusion in general—and within the design industry in particular—over the role and title differences between an interaction designer, an interface designer, and an experience designer. These can be, and often are, used interchangeably. Any one of these may also be an information architect, a graphic designer, communications designer, software designer, or a designer of way-finding systems. Though there are subtle semantic differences, and each carries its own historical baggage, the emphasis on distinctive labels sometimes causes more confusion than clarity.

I use "interaction" design because it suggests a two-way street, action and reaction—a mutual or reciprocal influence. "Interface" on the other hand, is a surface or boundary between two areas. On first thought, "interface" may seem to be more appropriate to Web design because the surface of the screen appears as a boundary between the visitor to a site and the inner workings of the computer or the owners of the site. But that is precisely the problem. The surface should not be a boundary. It should not draw a line. It is a space for interaction like the front door to your house. Many current Web sites keep the door closed but have a couple of mail slots for communication. For human interaction to occur, the door must be opened. "Interaction" design puts emphasis on opening the door.

"Experience" design may be closer to "interaction" than it is to "interface" design, but it has another problem. Although the experience of the visitor is a primary concern, it is not in the designers' control. It only exists in the mind of the visitor. We may develop mental models to help shape our interactive tools, signs and symbols, and hope that they will make for a good experience, but how they are perceived will be determined by what the individual visitor brings to the perception.

Graphic design, industrial design, and communications design, as descriptive titles, all suffer similar problems: they are strongly associated with specific practices and areas of business from early to mid-twentieth century which tend to limit their interpretation today. Each have broad, rich, and often overlapping professional practices, but the term "graphic" is closely tied to the "beautification" of the products of printing and publishing, while "industrial" is hooked to the "streamlining" of industrial products and automation, and "communications" is mistakenly associated with the telecom industry. Communications design may seem to be the best general term for much of this activity. After all, everything relates to communication. But business communications in the past were primarily one-way statements. For communication to happen, information must be flowing both ways. Communication is not a one-way street. It is the most interactive of all processes.

The practical aspect of the label "interaction design" is that it provides a more definitive and communicable term for something graphic designers, communications designers, and industrial designers have done for years. That is to design things that affect the intersection of humans, products, and information: chairs, hammers, eyeglasses, pencils, posters, books, or software programs. How people interact—act and react—with these things is the arena of the interaction designer. By having a term on which we all agree, we may more cogently discuss the pros and cons of a suggested design.

The Interaction Design Team

As mentioned earlier, there can be many members of a design team involved on a complex business-transaction Web site. The titles and specific roles may vary from one environment to another, but there are four general roles that are particularly important:

1. *Project leader, manager, or producer.* This person is responsible for the overall planning, coordination, status, deadlines, workload balancing, and if working in a consulting environment, billing of the project. This is a heavy administrative role but requires more than administrative skills. The project leader, manager or producer must be well versed in design principles, information architecture, the basics of HTML and XML coding, and have very good written communication skills. It is not atypical for a producer to have to jump in to make modifications to a site map or page map, edit copy, or even do a little programming. The primary role however is to keep everyone—on all of the teams—abreast of where the project stands, what needs to happen next, and when to changes to the schedule or specific deliverables need to be made.

2. *Information architect.* The architect is responsible for the underlying organizational structure and navigation of the site. The primary concern is to make the structures that support the site content explicit for the visitor. This requires a thorough understanding of the behavioral traits of the visitor, the breadth and depth of the site content, experience with scenario development, tremendous organizational and visualization skills, and familiarity with visual design principles. The information architect is a critical member of the discovery phase and persona development. He also serves a key liaison role with the functional designers and business designers to assure that the technologies will support the architecture, and that the site architecture will meet the business needs.

3. *Creative director or design leader.* This person assists in understanding and defining the necessary market trends and business strategy. The person

is responsible for the design staffing of the project; articulating the brand strategy to the team; ensuring the creation of a compelling, consistent and intuitive visual strategy for the project; and ensuring the quality of the deliverables. This requires graphic communications training or experience with visual thinking, brain storming, information structuring, brand design, good practices in business communications, and the ability to "feel" when things are right or not.

4. *Content coordinator or writer.* The principle writer or coordinator is involved in establishing the business strategy, but more importantly establishing the voice of the site. This will involve establishing and monitoring writers' guidelines for other contributors. This person is also responsible for reviewing and editing other writers' materials, coordinating sources and schedules for third-party content feeds, and proofing copy before it goes live. This, of course, requires good written communications skills. It also demands knowledge of information structuring, Web site structuring, and good negotiating skills.

Key Points for Interaction Designers

The primary focus of the interaction design team is *desirability*—creating a visitor experience that is desirable—useful, fun, meaningful, and memorable. Creating a site that delights the visitor is the obligation and responsibility of the interaction team. This is best accomplished when the designer "becomes" the persona or prototypical visitor, imagining what the visitor desires, seeing things through the eyes of the visitor and feeling what the visitor feels.

Be sure that the information architecture at the highest level of the site and at the page level makes good common sense for the visitor. This can be accomplished by using scenarios frequently to test the usability of the architecture. Use color, space, words, type, texture, and online tools to encourage the visitor's interaction with the site and enhance the overall experience. But do not add features unless they can be justified through the visitor's eyes. Beware of small, jiggly, unnecessary things.

Above all, remember that successful interaction design cannot be handed off to the production team and forgotten. Staying in constant and close contact with the functional designers and business designers throughout the complete development process will minimize headaches and heartaches when the site is finally launched.

14

Functional Designers

This is the technology group—the programmers—most often referred to as geeks. The programmers create, assemble, compile, and test the software code that permits a Web site to work. One reason they are called geeks is that most people do not have a clue what they really do. This chapter attempts to shed some light on what functional designers do, their relationship to interaction designers, and the real value they bring to any Web initiative. It will also touch on the relative newness of Web programming and the importance of programming standards. Without the functional designers and their code, nothing on the Web would happen. A visitor to your site would click a button and nothing would move. Or worse, something does happen, but it is the wrong thing.

From Engineers to Printers to Accountants

Functional designers are often compared to engineers and building contractors in the world of architecture. Architects envision the building then collaborate with engineers and builders to make the vision a reality. Architects typically work with a variety of different engineers: electrical, plumbing, HVAC, telecommunications, and sound. They may also work with a variety of builders, from those who pour the concrete and erect the steel to those who provide the finishing detail.

Like building engineers, functional designers for Web sites tend to have areas of specialty: systems analysts, information architects, database designers, scriptwriters, and high-level programmers. In each of these areas, designers may have particular skills or knowledge: XML, JavaScripting, C coding, using ASP on an SQL Server, or PHP in Linux or Unix. Good functional designers, however, have a broad knowledge of systems and coding, and can move, if required, from one environment or language to another without terrible difficulty. The power of this knowledge is knowing when to use what to accomplish specific functions in the most efficient manner.

Since software is directly connected to information, a more useful metaphor for functional designers in the Web world may be printers in the graphic design world. Printers are responsible for putting all those little dots, which can barely be seen by the naked eye in four basic ink colors onto multiple pieces of paper so they all look like the same spectacular, continuous-tone multi-colored photograph. It's like magic. They know things like ink tack and viscosity, dot formation, paper strength and brightness levels, press speeds, running ability, and finishing, folding and binding techniques. Graphic designers who work in the print world know many of these things too, but they are not printers. Based on their knowledge, graphic designers usually working with a business client, specify what they want to achieve, and then work with a printer to accomplish the goal.

In the Web world, functional designers are responsible for putting all that multi-colored code, which looks like gibberish to most people, into a space that most of us do not understand, make it link to more code in other spaces we understand even less, so that amazing pictures and words, sound and motion, may appear in different but appropriate form on a variety of media simultaneously all around the world. It's even more magical than printing. They know things like how to define functions, describe field types, query databases, execute transactions, and work within or around language biases, browser constraints, and system and platform limitations and compatibilities. Interaction designers who work in the Web world know many of these things too, but most are not functional designers. Based on their knowledge, interaction designers, working closely with their clients (the business designers) specify what they want to achieve from the site visitor's point of view, and then work with functional designers to accomplish the goal.

Although these analogies may help us understand the roles and relationships of functional designers, they do not begin to suggest the degree of difficulty involved in software design. The levels of complexity that Web engineers may be required to deal with are orders of magnitude beyond the complexities of printing or of erecting a building. The difference is that buildings and printing belong primarily to the physical world of atoms while Web sites belong to the digital world of bits. We often forget that software is substantially different from hardware. What functional designers do has little bearing on the plastic, metal, and glass machine sitting on your desk, or in the palm of your hand. Functional designers (software engineers) build the other machine—the virtual one made of abstract symbols—that resides somewhere inside of the actual one, or even inside a number of other ones.

Though we don't usually think of it as such, accounting is a type of software. I'm not referring to a particular accounting software package. I mean the very process of accounting is software. And accountants are the "financial engineers." Think about what accounting is, and what accountants do. Accounting is a system of recording, adjusting, and summarizing business and financial transactions and analyzing, verifying, and reporting the results. It is the entire set of procedures, and related documentation associated with business finance. Accountants work with data and detail. They perform calculations, run routines, and follow set courses and standards based on accepted principles of accounting.

Compared to the steel and concrete of buildings or the paper and ink of printing, the hardest thing accountants work with is a calculator, which they use to move abstract symbols around in space according to established rules. The work is complex, has many variables, and is vitally important to any business. Accounting might be thought of as the virtual machine—the inner works—of business. Without it, even in its simplest form, business management cannot know what it's doing.

Functional designers are much like accountants. They follow rules of logic; establishing structures, fields and tables; making assumptions and determining variance; aggregating records and allocating value. The code they write is like accounting. It is abstract, it must be written to standards, it is all inside the machines, and without it a Web site cannot function.

There Is Function and Then There Is Function

The functional specification document mentioned earlier, a requirement of early stage Web development, should always be written from the visitor's point of view. It outlines the activities that the visitor can accomplish on the site. The visitor should be able to see these actions. If this button is pushed, the visitor goes to this area. If that item is clicked, then greater detail is given. And if "purchase now" is selected, the visitor will be shown the three- to five-step checkout process. These are the responsibility of the interaction designer because they all have to do with the user interaction.

Behind this scene there are many other functions that need to happen within the system that the visitor never needs to know. These are the responsibility of the functional designer. As a very simple example: When the visitor clicks on "purchase now," a programming function needs to request the buyer's data and the shopping cart data from the appropriate Web forms. A function may then insert the data into a buyer table and start the order process by creating a row in the order table, assigning an order ID for each item, and checking the inventory table. If inventory is available, the inventory table must be decreased as the item is written to the order table. If inventory is unavailable, a message must be sent to the visitor and the initial process rolled back. On the Web, with the possibility of multiple purchases occurring at the same time, this activity must be simultaneous and protected, so there will never be a point during a transaction when data is partially processed. Otherwise we would not know the real state of inventory.

Each action that a user takes on a transaction-oriented Web site may initiate multiple functions similar to this one, on the back-end or inside any number of computers. These functions require a separate architectural map, a database schema, that shows the content and connection of various tables: the product table, inventory table, order table, buyer table. This may also show the relationship of numerous databases such as customer profiles, business rules, account management, credit checking, monetary conversion, etc. This is the responsibility of the information architect or database designer on the functional design team.

In some cases a programmer who lays out the architecture and writes the code for the system internals and for the user interaction may do all this. In other cases this will be developed by numerous programmers in different cities working on various parts of the system that all need to work together. For this reason, it is important when tossing around terms like information architecture and functionality that everyone understands what specific information and what specific functions are being discussed.

Visitor functionality and systems functionality are totally different animals and require different mind-sets for development. "To be a good programmer," Alan Cooper says in *The Inmates Are Running the Asylum*, "one must be sympathetic to the nature and needs of the computer. But the nature and needs of the computer are utterly alien from the nature and needs of the human being who will eventually use it." Most people cannot serve two masters, or switch back and forth from one to the other without compromising both.

Standards and Controls

One difference between accountants and Web software engineers is history, and that means standards. Accountants have been around for thousands of years. The earliest tax accounting records go back to Egypt and Mesopotamia around 3000 B.C. The American Association of Public Accountants, the first national accounting society in the United States was formed in 1887. By contrast, software engineering for computers is barely over fifty years old. The first contract software engineering firm was only begun in 1959. And of course the Web, by the time this is published, will have just become a teenager.

The first half a dozen years on the Web were wild. They have often been compared to the Wild West. Most people think this had to do with the dot.com explosion, which it did, but it had more to do with the functional aspects of the Web. There were no standards. There was no real law and order regarding the building of Web sites. The simple HTML coding provided by Berners-Lee was just too simple. Maverick designers and developers bent and twisted HTML to accomplish all sorts of things it was never intended to do. And browser companies such as Netscape and Microsoft fought to capture market share by introducing their own proprietary tools.

In the last few years, through the efforts of the W3C and grassroots organizations such as the Web Standards Project, designers and business leaders have begun to realize that new tools, languages, and methodologies have more value, gain greater use, and require less work if we all agree to a few basic standards. The guidelines that exist today are still new and will certainly continue to evolve, but one fundamental principle should be remembered. The Web is based on interoperability. This was critical to Berners-Lee from the beginning. It means that the Web should operate independent of any particular platform or device. It should be accessible on every computer operating system as well as all handheld devices, and in the future, all kinds of other appliances.

This is the beauty of the Web. It is also the nightmare of most designers. The flexibility of presentation required for interoperability is diametrically opposed to the control that designers have demanded in the past— particularly ones who have come from the world of print. Viewers may access a Web site through multiple devices with a variety of visual formats. They may change the size of their screen, alter the size and font of text, and decide if they want pictures or not, even alter the colors they see. This is why many experienced print designers would have nothing to do with the Web in the early years. Many still have not adjusted, although tools such as Cascading Style Sheets (CSS) provide "built-in" design flexibility. CSS allows designers to specify more than one font, detail size relationships rather than specific sizes, and use percentages or relative values for layout features such as margins or widths and depths.

Critical to the use of tools such as CSS is the support of browsers for the standards on which the new tools are based. And the browsers continue to get better—supporting the standards—with each new version. Which means that functional designers need to know the browsers and other devices being used by a site's audience, and should work as close as possible to the standards recommended by W3C and supported by browser and device manufacturers.

Today, the very basic standards include: JavaScript as the most popular scripting language; HTML 4.1 which supports tables and forms that are easier to read; CSS for templates that clearly separate format from content; XML 1.0 for structured data such as spreadsheets and financial transactions; and the Document Object Model (DOM), which allows objects on a page to respond to JavaScript instructions to edit or reformat a page.

The Functional Design Team

As with the interaction design team, there can be many members involved on a complex business-transaction Web site. And the titles and specific roles will vary from one environment to another, but there are three general roles that are particularly important:

1. *Project leader* or *team manager*. This person is almost always trained as a software programmer. He is responsible for coordinating the activities of all other members of the team and the communication and interaction between teams. Without a thorough knowledge of programming methods and standards, and familiarity with a variety of platforms and languages, he will have trouble gaining the respect of other team participants. He should also be well versed in the comparative strengths, weaknesses, and costs of various operating systems and third-party components. The project leader's primary role is to assure everyone else that the tools and technologies chosen for a Web site will work within the parameters outlined for the project. He must then be sure he has the people and skill sets required to produce the site.

2. *Information architect*. The architect is responsible for the internal organizational structure and navigation of the site. The primary concern is to assure that the internal functions match the user's request, without adding needless complication to the user's experience. This requires a thorough understanding of a variety of back-end functions, different applications, relational databases, and how they relate to one another. It also requires tremendous organizational skills and the ability to see the order of multiple connections at once. The information architect must work closely with the interaction designers and with the business team to assure that all needs are being met.

3. *Programmer* or *coder*. This is the person who will ultimately make the site work. Every programmer I have ever known has his or her own set of special tricks, short cuts, and preferences for one tool or methodology over another. This is true for interaction designers and business designers as well, but it seems particularly true with programmers. This is not a problem as long as they remember that many other people may have to work with the code in the future. The code structure, naming conventions, and file structures must follow accepted standards as closely as possible.

Key Points for Functional Designers

The primary focus of the functional design team is the *workability* of the site. It must work to produce the results a visitor expects under the conditions specified. It should work as quickly and as efficiently as possible within the budget limitations. This is best accomplished by understanding first the functional requirements of the visitor, and then the business requirements of the site, thereby selecting the technologies, structure, and languages that will meet these requirements in the simplest, most direct manner.

Interoperability—cross-browser, cross-platform, cross-device—is the objective. All functional technologies, tools, and programming should meet the standards recommended by the W3C. It is the functional designer's responsibility to stay abreast of these recommendations. Remember that other programmers may have to add to or modify your code in the future; therefore, code should be written and commented to standards. Also keep scalability in mind; and wherever possible, leave room for future additions.

The underlying principle of functional design is that it is only successful if the user can use it. The functional designers must work closely with the interaction designers to assure that the "needs of the computer" are not driving the development process.

15

Business Designers

Indians in South America use a simple but ingenious handmade trap to catch monkeys. They cut a small hole into the side of a coconut, scrape out the interior, and lash the coconut shell to a tree with leather cord or vine. They place a small amount of rice in the coconut as bait and leave the trap overnight. A monkey comes swinging along, spies the rice and reaches into the coconut to grab it. The trick to this trap is the size of the hole. The monkey can get his hand in, but once he grabs the rice, his fist will not go back through the opening. He is trapped.

Letting Go of the Rice
Freedom appears to be very simple. If the monkey would just let go of the rice, he could remove his hand. But, like many of us, when we have our hands on something we are familiar with, it is very hard to let go. In the jungles of South America, if the trapper fails to return to check his trap, as they sometimes do, monkeys have been known to starve to death, clinging to the rice. Fortunately, people are smarter than monkeys—most of the time.

If we were to anthropomorphize the monkey we might say that the real trap was the monkey's prevailing vision; precisely what traps people. As Dee Hock, founder and CEO emeritus of Visa, says, "The problem is never how to get new, innovative thoughts into your mind, but how to get the old thoughts out." Although radical changes have occurred in the structure, culture, marketing and the decision-making process within companies over the past two decades, many of the old thoughts about business are still strongly embedded.

Switching Metaphors

This problem is addressed in design education by an exercise called switching metaphors. It requires some concentration and then prolonged observation, and it must be done by the designer facing the problem. I will give you a brief example. The first step is to identify the popular analogies—the images, words, figures of speech—that need to be replaced. Then create a list of new analogies—words, images, numbers, phrases, sounds—that will be used each time the old ones pop into mind. The following example is a starting point:

For at least the last one hundred years, the primary metaphor for business organizations has been the "machine." It is composed of interchangeable parts. We have used the linear, repetitive interlocking of gears to represent the mechanisms of commerce—the separate parts that grind or click or tick together to produce goods and services. From the control of Henry Ford's assembly line for mass production to the orderly punching of time clocks to record our efforts, images of the Industrial Age have governed our perception of business.

The new metaphor for business organizations in the network world is a living organism—a plant, a tree, an animal or human. Business as a living organism does not have separate parts but rather integrated systems—a complex structure of interdependent people, departments, and even other businesses, that combine activities to determine the shape and function of the whole. The mutually dependent systems continuously ebb and flow, dynamically adjusting to changes in the business climate. This new coalition of people is as flexible as the branches of a willow tree, but as strong as an old oak.

Old words	New words
Machine	Tree
interchangeable	integrated
linear	ebb and flow
repetitive	variable
interlocking	interdependent

•

mechanism	organism
grind	fluid
assembly line	coalition
orderly	dynamic

Now you have the idea. Certainly you can add much more to this. And once you have the broad business metaphors replaced, think on about the department-specific metaphors. Why does marketing continue to use "war"—with the "troops" in the field "killing" the "competition"—as its primary metaphor? Marketing is not war. Business is not war. The words conquer, capture, and control could be replaced with unite, cooperate, and agree. With a little thought I'm sure you can come up with even better ones.

The point to remember is that acknowledgement of the old metaphors must happen before new ones can take their place. It is best to write the current metaphors down, and then as you find a new one, scratch the old one off the list.

Business has moved steadily from manual labor to cerebral labor for over forty years now, but for the most part, we have not changed our language because we have not acknowledged its influence. Language influences our thinking as much as thinking influences our language. "Words are the bugles of change." Charles Handy wrote in *The Age of Unreason*. "When our language changes, behavior will not be far behind."[1] Letting go of phrases like the "well-oiled machine" allows us to grasp the amazing growth possibilities of a "dynamic organism."

But Is It Viable?

Now that we have gotten rid of all the old metaphors, we can discuss the role of business designers in developing the Web site. Without you there is no site. You provide the vision, the direction, and the raison d'etre for the site. But, who are you?

Five years ago, senior people in many companies had administrative assistants "do things" for them on the Web. Today there is no excuse for anyone in business to not be familiar and active with Web communications. Senior management in particular needs to be involved. Say what you want about the dot.com bubble, but the technological changes it ushered in are affecting every business. And the CEO must be involved—actively involved, using the Web—to understand what's happening.

There are many business sites from product specific to supplier nets to employee knowledge channels. Certainly the CEO or COO cannot be actively involved in all of these. But the company site, to which all others link, is like the old company store it sets the tone and establishes the voice for the company. This is much too important to turn over to the IT group or to the marketing people because it's not about technology or telling and selling. Yes, these groups will need to be involved, but so will legal, finance, sales, product development, and human resources.

A successful model that has been used by many companies, large and small, is to establish a separate Internet group, central to the company, with representatives from each of the other groups contributing. The advantage is that the Internet group is charged with more than building a Web site. They are designing a broad information architecture for the business. The goal: interoperability of systems and people—no more "turf wars," no more proprietary databases. Everything must link.

This is not a "task force" or the bureaucratic interdepartmental committee that Alvin Toffler referred to as a "camelephant." This is not a quick fix for which no one will admit responsibility. This is a long-term engagement that is tied directly to the core strategy of your business. A business strategist who has direct access to the CEO usually leads this group. Remember, the site is the nerve center of all business communications. You may visualize this as the trunk of a tree. It will have many and deep roots extending throughout the organization and connecting internally to other organizations. It will also have numerous limbs and branches extending outward to link to your various publics.

Financial viability should be looked at from the perspective of each of the groups involved internally and externally. Each group has customers. Sales and service meet the needs of external customers; human resources serve the needs of internal employees; investor relations serves the investor and analyst communities; legal serves many groups, internal and some external; likewise for purchasing, facilities management, and so on. Each group should think of how to become a better value supplier in their area of expertise by using the Web.

The Ride Planner and the Dealer Used Inventory, on the Harley-Davidson site mentioned in chapter 10, are examples sales and marketing should find useful. Kimco's Property Management group encouraging both tenants to request repairs and renew contracts through the Web, and developers and property owners to submit projects is another good example. Human Resources should think about making all of the employee benefits policies and records available online, whether assembled internally or provided by a third party. Corporate communications and investor relations should completely rethink the tired old annual report. Why do companies continue to spend hundreds of thousands of dollars producing paper reports that no one reads, and then spend another few thousand to put the same thing on the Web in a form that is even harder to read? This can certainly be done in a more informative, entertaining, meaningful, and less expensive way if thought about as a Web initiative from the beginning. Maybe it should be thought of as a blog, or a movie, or a combination of both.

The idea is to generate better ways of providing the current services—quicker, more clearly, more flexibly, more thorough, more fun, less expensive—then go on to generate value-added services. Once each group has all of its ideas down on paper this is submitted to the new Internet group—the business designers—who have the joyful task of making sense of it all and then determining what is financially doable.

It is best to start with a master plan, the dream plan, and then cut back or hold off on elements that cannot be financially justified. It helps to do preliminary site architecture, even multiple architectures, based on the wish list. This makes estimating of technology costs easier and more accurate. Determining the return on investment requires different criteria for each department or value-added service. If there are e-commerce components, then increased revenue needs a real projection. But the other factors are often more important: reduced costs, increased productivity, improved customer service, enhanced partner, supplier and employee relationships, or increased business opportunities.

Keep in mind that each of these offerings may change existing internal support structures. Departmental disruption and ongoing support of Web initiatives are two costs that are often overlooked or underestimated. Putting up a useful business Web site is not like producing a brochure or catalog that is essentially done when it comes off press or goes into the mail. The transaction-oriented business site is a living organism. It needs to be regularly fed and cared for.

There will undoubtedly be trade offs when determining departmental priorities, but with a master architectural plan in hand, and all associated costs and possible returns segmented by area, decisions can be made on what to build first and target dates can be set for future development.

The Business Design Team

As with the other teams, there can be many members involved and the titles and specific roles will vary from one company to another, but there is one role that is critical, although this person may not serve as an active member of the team.

Today it is imperative in any business that the chief executive officer is involved in the initiation, planning, and ongoing support of the primary company Web site and Web strategy. The CEO articulates the vision for the company, a sense of community, the principles to which people adhere, the practices by which the company lives. The CEO is the living symbol for the shared values of the people within the company. These principles and values need to resonate throughout the site.

Yet many CEOs seem to be in hiding. A study in the fall of 2002 conducted by Burson-Marstella disclosed that only 12 percent of large global companies dedicate an area of their Web sites to the chief executive. Most sites that had any information limited it to a brief biographical sketch accompanied by a photograph. Less than a third of the sites included speeches or statements that spoke to the company's core values or articulated a personal vision for the company.

Now, more than ever, people are turning to the Web to find out about companies and their management. "In 1997, five percent of business influentials—investors, regulators, analysts, journalists, and other executives—revealed that they learned about CEOs online. Today, that number has quadrupled." According to the study, 22 percent of executives, 23 percent of analysts, and 38 percent of the media access corporate information on the Web. These numbers will certainly continue to escalate. That's why it is important that your site be a reliable source of corporate management information.

Information on your company, its practices, and its people is out there. In chat rooms, discussion groups, and blogs, the employees are talking, the managers are talking, the suppliers and partners are talking, and your customers are talking. It's time for CEOs to talk—to put their views, opinions, and feelings online. This, above all else, can make your company Web site viable.

Key Points for Business Designers

The primary focus of the business design team is the *viability* of the site. Does it make financial sense? Is it financially sustainable? Is it reliable and believable? Will it enhance our brand? Will it strengthen our relationships with customers, employees, suppliers, and partners?

When answering these questions it is best to eliminate all the old metaphors in your corporate and departmental language, and replace them with meaningful expressions that you believe. Trust is the single most important ingredient of your site. And the CEO should be the single most important spokesperson. A good place to begin is by establishing a high-level Internet group composed of representatives from key departments. This may include corporate communications, IR, IT, marketing, procurement, finance, service, legal, and HR. The goal of interoperability between systems and people should be made clear to everyone. Establish clear business objectives for each department's value-added services on the site, and different criteria by which each can be judged, early in the planning stage. Then be sure that each group has the support structure they need to satisfy their customers' demands.

The single most important point to remember is that successful business Web design cannot be handed-off to the technology group or the marketing group. Senior management must be involved and should be in constant and close contact with the interaction designers and functional designers throughout the complete development process.

16

Governing the Web

At the heart of the Web is the freedom to share information and opinion. At the heart of America is freedom of speech. This country is over two hundred years old and we are still defending and defining what freedom of speech means. The Web is only twelve and we have barely begun to define its freedoms. The issue of governance will undoubtedly grow in intensity and complexity in the coming years and designers will need to be aware at least of the trends and of the resources for guidance. The following pages briefly review the current large issues and provide some indication of the types of questions and opportunities that may be coming in the near future.

Freedom of Speech

I'm sure you have heard the story of Jonathan Lebed. It made the network news, the *New York Times Magazine*, and was a major part of Michael Lewis's 2001 book, *Next*. Even with all of that, the highlights are worth repeating. The story says something about the underlying power and influence that the Web has on our lives, and the continuing potential for disruption of long-standing systems, mores, and beliefs, in unexpected ways.

In 1999, when Lebed was only fifteen years old and living with his mom and dad in Cedar Grove, New Jersey, he made almost $800,000 in six months by trading stock through the Internet. The Securities and Exchange Commission (SEC) investigated, accused him of stock manipulation and fraud—"the first minor ever charged with stock market fraud"—and demanded he give up all the money. In September of 2000, the case was settled and Lebed was allowed to walk away with over half a million dollars.

It all began shortly after Jonathan turned eleven and opened an account with America Online. Around the same time he became an avid fan of CNBC, getting up at five in the morning to watch the market news before leaving for school. On his twelfth birthday he used $8,000, which came from a savings bond his parents had given him at birth, to invest in the market. Inside of a year he had turned his $8,000 into $28,000. He started his own Web site, stock-dogs.com, and began to plug the stocks of small capitalization companies he found interesting. In a matter of months, as an amateur stock analyst, he was drawing thousands of people to his site, receiving letters from officers wanting him to plug their companies, and being asked by his school teachers and friends for stock tips.

By the time he was thirteen, Michael Lewis says, "He had glimpsed the essential truth of the market—that even people who call themselves professionals were often incapable of independent thought, and that most people, though obsessed with money, had little ability to make decisions about it. . . ."[1]

After a grueling interrogation by the SEC, Lebed's lawyer, Kevin Marino, asked Lebed and his parents to each write a few paragraphs describing their feelings about the SEC's treatment of the boy. Neither of his parents really understood the details of what he had done, or what the SEC was doing, but Lebed wrote a four-page document making it abundantly clear that he knew precisely what he was doing and that he had done nothing wrong.

In his document, after reviewing a press release on Qualcomm's stock performance and comments by a Paine Weber analyst, Lebed said, "People who trade stocks, trade based on what they feel will move and they can trade for profit. Nobody makes investment decisions based on reading financial filings. Whether a company is making millions or losing millions, it has no impact on the price of the stock. Whether it is analysts, brokers, advisors, Internet traders, or the companies, everybody is manipulating the market. If it wasn't for everybody manipulating the market, there wouldn't be a stock market at all. . . ."[2]

A fifteen-year-old kid, using the Internet, was making mince meat out of professional analysts and the SEC. His activities and his perception of the activities cut to the very heart of one of America's most cherished institutions. Granted, this all occurred at the height of the Internet bubble. But after the bubble burst we all became aware of the professional shams. As Lewis said, "The system was rigged, the Internet had exposed the rigging, which meant that the system couldn't survive for long, at least not in its present form. Capitalism was eating the capitalist."

Lewis tells another story about another fifteen-year-old, Marcus Arnold from Perris, California. During the spring and summer of 2000, Arnold became the leading expert on criminal law on AskMe.com, one of the most heavily used knowledge exchanges on the Web. He lied about his age, his name, and his legal credentials online, although he did admit that he was not accredited by the state bar association. He spent six hours a day in school and another four hours doing homework but still managed to answer hundreds of questions; in one two-week stretch he answered 939.

AskMe had a system of ranking those who provided answers to questions, based on the quality and speed of the answer provided, as judged by the person who asked the question. During the time Arnold was working his way up through the rankings from ten to number three, there were about one hundred and fifty other experts in the criminal law section, many of them professional lawyers. Arnold, who ranked number one by the end of the summer, learned all he knew about the law from watching Court TV and browsing Web sites.

Putting all other implications of these stories aside—the ability to create new identities in a new environment, the social disruption of speeded up information, the market force of adolescence, the knowledge gap between professionals and amateurs, and the undermining of status based on privileged access to information—the core of both stories is about the freedom to share information and opinion. Regardless of subject, age, time, knowledge, experience, or even truth, these kids using the Web were practicing their inalienable right to free speech.

No Freedom of Spam

"I just want my inbox. It belongs to me, and I want it back,"[3] James Gleick said in his article, "Tangled Up in Spam," in the *New York Times Magazine*. Well, it looks like he may get it—eventually.

Congress is currently reviewing a bill called the CAN-SPAM Act (Controlling the Assault of Non-Solicited Pornography and Marketing Act) introduced to protect consumers from unsolicited commercial e-mail. If passed, this will require all unsolicited marketing e-mail to have a valid return e-mail address so recipients could ask to be removed from lists.

Once notified, marketers would be prohibited from sending additional messages under penalty of civil fines from the Federal Trade Commission.

Twenty-six states have already passed laws prohibiting spam. Most involve civil statutes designed to give citizens and businesses the right to sue spammers and collect statutory and actual damages. In April 2003, however, Virginia governor Mark Warner signed two bills that will raise the penalty for spam to a Class 6 state felony. This could carry a prison term of five years plus a fine. It is the toughest such anti-spam law in the United States. And since the law covers e-mail passing through Internet Service Providers located in Virginia, it allows prosecutors to go after spammers who may be located in other states.[4]

Penalties under the Virginia law could be sought for: sending huge volumes of bulk e-mail, generating substantial monetary proceeds from spamming, employing a minor in the spamming process, and forging e-mail header and routing information. This last item is one of the most important. The Internet system depends on accurate information about servers, routing, and relays. There is no reason to falsify these unless you are up to no good.

Contrary to what many people believe, these laws are not a violation of free speech. In fact, spam is a blatant violation of privacy. "Nothing in the Constitution compels us to listen to or view any unwanted communication, whatever its merit," Chief Justice Warren Burger wrote in a 1970 decision. "We therefore categorically reject the argument that a vendor has a right under the Constitution or otherwise to send unwanted material into the home of another."[5]

So why do we continue to receive so much junk mail—online and off? Because industry and the marketers of industry have lobbied hard for self-regulation. This principle is also fundamental to the culture of the Web. "Time and again, the online world has behaved like a self-healing organism," James Gleick said, "outwitting authorities who tried to impose structure from above. But cyberspace belongs to the world of human beings who rely on laws to discourage the worst behavior and protect the powerless."

Increasing Use of Law

There is a growing trend in some industries to use their power in combination with existing law to suppress the rights of people's use of technology. The most obvious case is the music industry's targeted attacks against the creators of peer-to-peer (P2P) technologies. Following the court's decision to shut down Napster, the industry has vowed to sue other P2P systems. Fortunately, the Electronic Frontier Foundation (EFF) has already begun meetings with P2P developers to discuss the legal challenges, and is prepared to defend them if necessary.

The EFF—begun in 1990 by Mitch Kapor, former president of Lotus Development Corporation; John Perry Barlow, lyricist for the Grateful Dead; and John Gilmore, early employee of Sun Microsystems—was the first organization to identify threats to our basic rights online and to advocate on behalf of free expression in the digital age. "The recording industry has targeted the technology," the EFF states, "instead of the users who are actually violating their copyrights. Peer-to-peer technology is a wonderful tool for the mass distribution of all sorts of content."

In March 2001, the EFF along with the American Civil Liberties Union (ACLU), the American Library Association (ALA) and other organizations filed a lawsuit challenging a new federal law know as the Children's Internet Protection Act (CHIPA). This law attempts to force public and private libraries and schools that receive federal funding to install Internet blocking or filtering technology for child and adult Internet users. Studies have shown repeatedly that this technology does not work. The more effectively a filtering program blocks inappropriate materials, the more it blocks appropriate material as well, effectively reducing the amount of any available material. EFF is working with other groups, such as the Online Policy Group and ACLU on a public education campaign to help educators and parents find better ways to protect children without limiting the free exchange of information.

There are numerous other organizations such as the Internet Free Expression Alliance (IFEA), the Global Internet Liberty Campaign (GILC), the Digital Future Coalition (DFC), the Electronic Privacy Information Center (EPIC), and the Free Expression Network (FEN), which are all working with designers, developers, businesses, and government representatives to preserve and strengthen the fundamental benefits of the Internet and the rights of its users.

There are also increasing numbers of lawsuits. During the Internet boom, U.S. courts ruled that business processes could be patented. This led many e-commerce companies to seek patent protection for their services, which in-turn led to patent infringement suits. Amazon.com,

BarnesandNoble.com, and Expedia are three of the larger names that have had to negotiate settlements. In May 2003 a federal jury found eBay guilty of patent infringement. They will contest, and eventually will likely reach a settlement. But this is a needless waste of energy, time and money. "Right now it seems there is this looming problem of not very sensible patents," said Norm Beamer, a partner at Fish & Neave, a law firm specializing in intellectual property, "that are nevertheless being used to threaten and extort people who are in business. . . ."[6]

Harlan Cleveland, former assistant secretary of state and political theorist, wrote of the "folly of refusing to share something that can't be owned." As Cleveland pointed out, "What builds a great company or a great nation is not the protection of what it already knows, but the acquisition and adoption of new knowledge from other companies or nations. How can 'intellectual property' be 'protected'? The question contains the seeds of its own confusion: it's the wrong verb about the wrong noun."[7]

Replacing the verb and noun, the real question is: How can knowledge be shared? This is the problem we designers now face. We must establish the ground rules or guidelines for the interchange of intangibles—ideas, theories, images, cultures, beliefs—that will provide mutually advantageous futures for companies, countries, and individuals.

Mechanisms and Policies

"The Web Consortium tries to define protocols in ways that do not constrain the norms or laws that govern the interaction of people," Tim Berners-Lee said in 1999 in his book *Weaving the Web*, "We define mechanism, not policy. That said, it is essential that policy and technology be designed with a good understanding of the implications of each other." The W3C does not make law or even set standards. It makes recommendations. It is hoped that the recommendations will become standards as industries and individuals creating new tools for the Web adopt them.

This international group, jointly run by the MIT Laboratory for Computer Science in the United States, the European Research Consortium for Informatics and Mathematics in France, and Keio University in Japan, is the guiding force for Web development. Berners-Lee, the current director of the consortium, began it in 1994 to help "lead the Web to its full potential." There are currently over 400 organizations that are members of the Consortium. Many are companies interested in advancing the technology for their own benefit, but many others are interested in preserving the open source, common protocol, and interoperability principles on which the Web is based. Through workshops, work groups and prototype applications, the W3C membership reaches general consensus before issuing a recommendation.

The early years of the W3C were rough as industries and developers, following old-world business rules, fought to create their own standards and dominate the market with proprietary tools. But as the Web has grown, membership in W3C has grown, and awareness of the value of open standards has grown. The overwhelming support for the recent Royalty-Free Patent Policy recommendation is a clear indicator that the W3C has come into its own. The policy premise: it is in the interest of all those who participate in building and using the Web—including patent holders and all others alike—to enable royalty-free implementation of Web standards.

"The Policy affirms and strengthens the basic business model that has driven innovation on the Web from its inception," Berners-Lee said when he announced approval of the policy in May 2003. "The availability of an interoperable, unencumbered Web infrastructure provides an expanding foundation for innovative applications, profitable commerce, and the free flow of information and ideas on a commercial and non-commercial basis . . . By adopting this Patent Policy with its commitment to royalty-free standards for the future, we are laying the foundation for another decade of technical innovation, economic growth, and social advancement."[8]

The next decade on the Web will cover the teenage years. And as any parent who has lived through these years with his or her own children can attest, it will be as different from the first decade as night is to day. But the results can be astounding. Designers now have an opportunity, and an obligation, to help one another craft and preserve the ethic of this new place.

Adoption of the patent policy will certainly speed up the flow of new technologies and intensify market forces as they continue to change. What happened with free music on the Web is already happening with movies, and media companies are struggling to control digital entertainment. Internet Law is becoming a boom industry. This is another opportunity for consultant designers to help make a difference and to grow their business in the process.

Markets and Marketing

The Web is all about information, and information in business cannot be separated from markets and marketing. Defining markets and capturing market-share data have been critical business objectives for at least the last century. But in the last decade of the last century our perception of markets and marketing changed. The widespread concepts of micro-markets, productions of one, and the personalization of one-to-one marketing are representative of the "power shift era" which Toffler introduced in 1990. This is yet to be fully understood.

"A power shift does not merely transfer power," Toffler said. "It transforms it." In marketing as in other business areas, the transformation is by no means complete, but as we will discover, it has certainly begun. A brief history of marketing discloses continuing shifts in our perception of markets over the last fifty years as we moved from a production economy to a consumer economy to the network economy. Creativity has become increasingly important. But it is no longer creative marketing slogans that are important, it is ideas about business—about the products, services, and methodologies of

business that affect people's lives—that are important. We will find that traditional advertising, marketing, and design agencies are all struggling to adjust.

At the heart of this discussion is a value proposition for business sites on the Web. There are numerous examples of companies who are getting it right and others—businesses and consultants—who are missing the point. Many are continuing to use the old language of marketing, not realizing that in "relationship marketing" the emphasis must be on the relationship not the marketing. Pleasing people is what this is all about, and the Web makes it easier than ever when the right approach is taken.

The Web also makes integrated marketing easier and more important than ever. But a transformation is occurring here as well. It is no longer only about integrating messages across multiple broadcast media. It's about integrating real-time, interacting communication systems to serve people. Understanding this difference will have a strong bearing on the success of your Web sites and the results of your marketing efforts.

17

New Basics for Marketing

All that you may have learned in MARKETING 101, or think that you know about marketing from years of experience in the field, is now in question. The "rules" regarding market segmentation; product, price or packaging differentiation; driving home consistent message points; focusing on quality, service, or value, and all the other marketing basics have changed. Many will be thrown out. Some may survive.

This is the dilemma currently facing designers in the world of marketing. It is also their golden opportunity. To take advantage of this chance, to help determine what will go and what may survive, requires understanding the transformation that is occuring, requires going all the way back to the beginning.

To Market, to Market
> To market, to market, to buy a fat pig,
> Home again, home again, jiggety jig.
> To market, to market, to buy a fat hog,
> Home again, home again, jiggety jog.
> To market, to market, to buy a plum bun,
> Home again, home again, market is done.

There's never been a better time for the magic of *Mother Goose*. These silly rhymes remind us of fun, of laughter and delight; feelings nearly lost with childhood. Preserving these emotions is more important than ever in today's world jammed with intense competition, corruption, and deception, where markets are not done—are never done—and you can't go home again.

"Markets are nothing more than conversations," Doc Searls said in *The Cluetrain Manifesto*. Over the last two hundred years the conversation became a one-way message. It turned into information-intense, multi-layered, multi-sourced, time-stamped directives without a voice. *That's a fine looking pig, Jonas*, became, *Grade A, U.S. inspected, 4.35 lbs, calcium added, sell before date, blah, blah, blah*. The Web changes all of this. It turns the one-way street into a community square; it leads us back to the bazaar. "The Net invites your customers in to talk, to laugh with each other, and to learn from each other," Searls states. "Connected, they reclaim their voice in the market, but this time with more reach and wider influence than ever."[1]

As we moved from the buying and selling of pigs, hogs, and buns to the rapid swapping of electronic info-bits signifying hundreds of thousands of derivative values based on millions of derivative products, and on to the multitude of voices on the Web today, one thing has not changed. We still barter in perceptions. We dicker and haggle over impressions. Our appeal is based on appearances. We persuade and trade and traffic in notions.

Perception Is Everything

The following comments were written to his lawyer by Jonathan Lebed, the fifteen-year-old charged with stock-market fraud by the SEC in 2000. (Italics added.)

"A news release just came out today on SPACE.com, the internet media venture founded by former CNN *Moneyline* host Lou Dobbs. The company said it would 'lay off 22 workers, or 20% of its staff.' They explained that the move is taking place, 'in a push to turn profitable sooner than previously planned and achieve Dobbs' goal of diversifying beyond the Web.'

"We both know that the lay offs are being done not as a strategic move, but are taking place because the company is in a financial crisis and may not be around much longer. The comments about turning profitable sooner and diversifying beyond the Web just prove that *the entire business and financial world revolves around perception and nothing else but that*."[2]

I've never met Jonathan Lebed. But I would bet that he, like nearly every American child and many others around the world, remembers the scene from *The Wizard of Oz* in which the Wizard bellows at Dorothy and her friends; "Pay no attention to that man behind the curtain. . . . The great Wizard has spoken!"

Lou Dobbs, like the Wizard, was only trying to keep up appearances. And Jonathan Lebed, like Dorothy and her friends, saw right through him. When will business learn that people, even at a young age, are not dumb? They are not blind. They learn—we all do—to observe and comprehend the world from a variety of perspectives and sensations— including movies.

This story and the statement "keeping up appearances" have the ring of intentionally giving a false impression and of being misleading. The press release may have been an attempt to mislead. It was definitely an attempt to keep up appearances. But that is something we all do. We all wear masks. This does not necessarily mean that we are hiding some "inner self," putting up a "false" front just for others. It merely means that we have an image, an attitude, a set of beliefs about ourselves that we continuously convey to others through our words and actions. The question of believability arises when the image we have of ourselves does not match up with the one that others have, or when what we are "saying" does not confirm what they are "hearing" from other sources.

When you look at a photograph of a group of people of which you are a member, whom do your eyes linger on? To whom do they continue to return? You got it. We look at ourselves. Sometimes we can't stop looking at ourselves. And we make dumb comments like, "Is that really me? I've never looked so bad." Or excuses like, "I never look good in pictures." Why do we linger on the picture of ourselves and make such comments?

We are checking out our image. And the "stranger" we see in the photograph usually does not quite match the "notion" we have in our mind. Some of this can be explained because a photograph is a frozen moment in physical time, whereas our mental picture is a constantly shift-ing abstract notion. As individuals we form our image—or notion of ourselves—and maintain its reputation, not only by the clothes we wear or the cars we drive or the accessories we display, but by the people, books, newspapers, movies, television programs, ceremonies, doctrines, and Web sites we read, learn from, and talk about. These are the things that help us define us for others—and for ourselves. The stranger seen in the photograph comes from seeing ourselves through someone else's eyes. This is a different perspective than the normal reality we hold in our heads.

Business organizations, institutions, and governments use similar accoutrements—buildings, logos, brochures, advertising, Web sites, speeches, and press releases to craft and convey their image or essence. The perceptual difficulty occurs—individually and collectively—when we cross the line of believability or when the image we have of ourselves has no correspondence with the image held by others. When self-perception has lost touch with reality, belief cannot continue. Trust is deleted.

On the Web, perception and marketing are more closely connected than ever. The easy access to multiple channels of information, to different perspectives, and many voices, has altered the perception we once had of those with privileged access to information. It has shifted the power once held by figures of authority—parents, teachers, business leaders, religious and government leaders, financial analysts, and marketers—to people. And their perception matters.

A Brief History of Marketing

During the first half of the twentieth century, nearly every business sent salesmen with their samples out to sell. Once in the door with his prospect, the salesman pitched the benefits of the product; the exquisite craftsmanship, the significant durability, the rich taste, or dependable speed; the available range of sizes, configurations, colors, and smells. It was all there to be seen and touched and talked about. And the salesman closed by taking the order, "Now, how many would you like?" Services were sold in much the same way from banks, insurance companies, and brokerage houses.

Even into the late sixties, life insurance salesmen would sit down with a prospect and review a portfolio of photographs of automobile accidents. Often one of the pictures had recently appeared in the local newspaper. It was the crash that killed the neighbor down the street. "But you know," the salesman spoke softly, but with conviction, "Bob's wife Ann and young daughter Sarah were very lucky, they will be taken care of for a long time, because Bob had just purchased this very same life policy from me two weeks before." True or not, the pictures instilled fear, a prime motivator for life insurance sales.

This was selling in a *production economy*. Many brokers at financial firms continue to sell this way today, "smiling and dialing," calling prospects and pushing the hot product of the day, assuring them that this is their "opportunity to get in on the ground floor." In the production economy, manufacturers made products, the sales staff sold them, and purchasers picked from the available lot.

Then the marketing concept came along and slowly up-ended everything. Somewhere just past the middle of the century, savvy business executives began to distinguish between selling and marketing. Marketing was not about selling products and services to customers. It was about understanding what customers want and need, then figuring out how to satisfy them. "Customers don't buy things," Theodore Levitt, Harvard Business School's guru of marketing said, "they buy solutions to problems. The surviving and thriving business is a business that constantly seeks better ways to help people solve their problems— functionally better, valued better, and available better. To create betterness requires knowing what customers think betterness to be."[3]

Levitt, like Peter Drucker before him, believed that business—any business—has only one primary purpose: to get and keep a customer. "No business can function effectively without a clear view of how to get customers, what its prospective customers want and need, and what options competitors give them, and without explicit strategies and programs focused on what goes on in the marketplace rather than on what's possible in the factory or what is merely assumed at headquarters."[4]

In *Marketing Myopia*, Levitt's now-classic 1960 marketing manifesto, he asserted that all business energies should be channeled into satisfying the consumer, "no matter what." Even last year, a cursory review of mission statements from any dozen or so public corporations attested to the broad adoption of his premise—at least in words, if not in practice:

"Passion for Our Customers: Measuring our success by that of our customers . . ."—General Electric

". . . our worldwide network of IBM solutions and services professionals translates these advanced technologies into business value for our customers."—IBM

"Lucent is organized to best meet the needs of its customers."—
Lucent Technologies
"More than 106,000 P&G people work every day to provide prod-
ucts of superior quality and value to the world's consumers."—
Proctor & Gamble

The marketing concept clearly placed the consumer in the position of
power, and companies tripped over one another verbally "embracing,"
"delighting," "doing whatever it takes" to make customers happy. The
production economy had given way to the consumer economy. Any business that wanted to get ahead, that wanted to win in the long run, had to
constantly study and respond to what people wanted and valued, and make
quick adjustments to competitive offers made by others. "In short, the
organization must learn to think of itself not as producing goods or services but as buying customers, as doing the things that will make people
want to do business with it. Management must think of itself not as producing products but as providing customer-creating value satisfactions."[5]

One problem with the marketing concept is its tendency toward
rigidity. Like most concepts, as they are accepted, they become rule-
bound. The more they are adopted, the narrower and more dogmatic
the rules become. "Solving problems for our customers," has become
such a rule-bound, repetitive mantra, that it is no longer believable in
the marketplace even when it may be deeply believed internally. There
is a perceptual disconnect.

Toward the end of the twentieth century along came Kevin Kelly,
editor of *Wired* magazine, who up-ended everything again. In his
book, *New Rules for the New Economy*, Kelly said, "In the Network
Economy, (you) don't solve problems, (you) seek opportunities. When
you are solving problems you are investing in your weaknesses; when
you are seeking opportunities, you are banking on the network."[6]

As we have seen earlier, the emergence of the Web and ideas like the
network economy came with a multitude of breathless magazine articles
and tremendous hype. Kelly, as the founding editor of *Wired*, sat in the
middle of this maelstrom, adding to the hype and contributing his
unique perspective on the behavior of networks and their effect on our
economic lives. "Economists once thought that the coming age would
bring supreme productivity," Kelly said, "but, in a paradox, increasing
technology has not lead to measurable increases in productivity. This is

because productivity is exactly the wrong thing to care about. The only ones who should worry about productivity are robots."

Our focus on the need to improve productivity began in the Industrial Age—the production economy—when efficiency expert Fredrick Taylor taught the captains of industry how to segment activity and measure each component. With measurement they could streamline individual processes and trim production time. The task for each worker was then to do his job better. "In the Network Economy, where machines do most of the inhumane work of manufacturing, the task for each worker is not 'how to do his job better,' but 'what is the right job to do.'" This is the primary question facing marketers today.

New ideas that lead to new products, new services, and new jobs, are now more important than doing the same old thing better. Over the last decade, enlightened management and marketers have begun to realize that discovering new opportunities is critical. In nearly every industry, everyone can now match the old standards of quality, service, and price. Meeting these basic standards is today's cost of getting into the game. Now you have to improve on them.

Innovation

"Creativity . . . is now the decisive source of competitive advantage," Richard Florida says, in his book *The Rise of the Creative Class*. "In virtually every industry, from automobiles to fashion, food products, and information technology itself, the winners in the long run are those who can create and keep creating."[7] Creativity of course requires risk; and there's the rub. Following the dot.com implosion, terror attacks, exposure of multiple financial frauds, and the recession, many companies large and small—including design agencies and business consultants—are frozen, in a complete state of limbo, uncertain what to do next.

This is precisely the time to look for new ideas, according to Jerry Wind, professor of marketing at the University of Pennsylvania's Wharton School. "Wealth is created during times of uncertainty," Wind says. "Making money depends on identifying opportunities in a turbulent marketplace. But you need to have discipline . . ."[8] Fire, aim, ready is not disciplined. We learned from the dot.com implosion that risks are real and must be managed carefully, but they should not prevent the search for—and careful implementation of—new ideas.

Although public companies have now added the word "innovation" to their mission statement or values list, and talk about encouraging creativity across the enterprise, most are still struggling with how to actually do this. "They know they need creativity in the workplace," says Judith Jedlicka, president of the Business Committee for the Arts (BCA). "They know new ideas are important to continuing their success, but so many don't know how to go about it—how to stimulate it throughout their organization."[9]

One way to start is through a national program BCA launched two years ago called Art@Work. The program assists businesses in recognizing and celebrating the creative abilities of their employees by inviting them to bring personal art they create or perform into the workplace to share with their colleagues. "[It] addresses several key work issues: diversity, understanding one another, communication, and work/life balance. We do believe this is a true integration and celebration of individual and collective creativity," says Jedlicka.

Companies such as Brown-Forman, Fluor, General Mills, Playboy, Pfizer, and many others have participated and the feedback has been positive. As Christopher Forbes, vice chairman of Forbes, Inc. puts it, ". . . we have found that the arts not only make for a more stimulating and creative work environment, but they have a direct and positive impact on the bottom line. By participating in Art@Work and recognizing the creativity of our employees, we evidence our commitment to them and their interests which, in turn, boosts morale and builds team spirit."

This is a great beginning. But it still suggests a separation between creativity and business. The creativity belongs to "artists"— their personal work outside of business—while business shows their commitment and interests, but continues working. Too many executives still see art as the antithesis of work. It is emotional, and business is ruled by reason. There is no doubt that work is an antonym to play, like reason is the opposite of emotion, but everyone will agree that both are required to make sense out of life. Feeling is as essential to thought as thought to feeling, and both are essential to business success.

Creativity needs to become integral to business, to permeate every pore in the organization. This does not mean that business should abandon reason. But most businesses have operated under the tyranny of reason too long. Now, a dynamic balance must be sought between reason and emotion, work and play, chaos and stability, and personal goals and business goals. Creativity is already percolating just beneath the surface of most companies. If leaders listen to their own people—connect on an emotional, human level with their employees, suppliers and customers—they may begin to hear what the problems are, where the delays and dissatisfactions are.

But there is more. Leaders in all organizations need to connect to the voices outside of their business. Connect with family members, with friends, with complete strangers. Most important, connect with children. This is where the off-the-wall ideas are. This is where new opportunities, the new jobs to do, will be found. This is also what designers need to help their clients understand as each of them adapt to the changes that are occurring.

As all designers know, this connectivity is what creativity is all about. The ability to synthesize—what Einstein called "combinatory play"—is where most ideas come from. Putting together familiar things in unfamiliar ways and unfamiliar things in familiar ways, making new connections, moving around bits and pieces of information until something magical happens. But this magical something needs to add value. It needs to ring true. It can no longer be just smoke and mirrors. This is what designers need to focus on and consultants need to keep their clients focused on.

This is what marketing in the network economy is about. It is what designing the Web is about; the ability to create valuable new ideas by connecting people with people, businesses with businesses, resources to needs, possibilities to producers, potentials to realities. Much of this can happen on the Web itself, but much will happen off the Web, and will be fed by information from the Web. "We still live in a world that's filled with opportunity," Seth Godin said in a *Fast Company* article. "In fact, we have more than an opportunity—we have an obligation. An obligation to spend our time doing great things. To find ideas that matter and share them."[10]

18

Making a Difference

Finding new ideas is only half of the equation. Sharing them, championing them, working with others to develop them into real products and services is the other half. Ideas are a dime a dozen. Marketing slogans are even cheaper. Selecting the appropriate ideas and making them real is what's important. Ideas may drive business, but without distribution or implementation, they are useless. This is where and when the ideas begin to make a difference, a difference to individuals, organizations, and industries.

"Creativity is not a differentiating idea,"[1] Jack Trout said in his book *Differentiate or Die, Survival in Our Era of Killer Competition*. He's wrong, of course. And his own book proves he is wrong, because it is filled with creative examples—one after another—of how companies have differentiated themselves, all with new ideas. Of course many of Trout's examples are limited to new ideas in advertising slogans or positioning statements, but many are based on real points of differentiation. This is a critical distinction.

If marketing is about anything it is about getting and keeping customers by differentiating what you offer from your competition. This has never been made clearer than in the title of Trout's book. If you do not distinguish your offering you will not survive. This cannot, however, be some arbitrary scheme dreamed up by advertising and marketing. The market—the public, the people, the Jonathan Lebeds, like Dorothy and the Tin Man—will see right through you.

Trout mentions several ideas or areas for differentiation: attribute ownership, leadership, heritage, market specialty, being the first, being the latest. This is essentially an update or variation on the checklist of *p*'s that marketers have used for years: product, process, pricing, positioning, packaging, and publicity. And the latest two *p*'s, which relate particularly to the Web, pass along value and permission. All of these areas require attention. They are worthy of critical review, but the single most important area is not on the list—the only *p* that really matters—is people. How is your offering going to help me? What does your heritage, or leadership, or attribute ownership do for me? How will your product or service save me time, make my life easier, richer, or more fun?

Ideas That Matter
Ideas that matter are ideas that contribute to the well-being of people. This is not some altruistic concept unconnected to doing business or to making money. Every business is entitled to make a profit and to do so they usually have to sell or market their products and services. There is abundant evidence that both of these can be done while focusing on ideas that benefit people.

A case in point from Trout is the Englewood Hospital and Medical Center located in Englewood, New Jersey. In an effort to serve the local Jehovah's Witness community that refused blood transfusions because of their beliefs, the Center developed techniques and procedures to provide "bloodless surgery." This became their point of differentiation and today they serve patients from around the world who prefer not to lose blood during operations.

Another example is Michael Dell's decision to bypass retailers and sell his computers direct to customers at a lower price than his competition. This stunned competitors such as IBM and Compaq when the company began in 1984, but today Dell is the world's leading producer of computer products and services. Using its direct business model, it designs and manufactures products and services to customer requirements, and had sales in the last four quarters of nearly $37 billion.

Lands' End, an early adopter of Web technology, has added one feature after another to its site to benefit its customers. For those who want their clothes to have a tailored fit, they simply answer a few questions about measurements and body type, and LandsEnd.com custom-crafts one-of-a-kind items to the customer's specifications. Today Lands' End has the largest business volume apparel Web site in the world.

One more example comes from Seth Godin. Dutch Boy paint made the process of painting easier and more fun by getting rid of the old paint can. Dutch Boy introduced a new twist and pour container that's easier for customers to carry, to open and close, and to pour. This simple packaging innovation increased sales and broadened distribution, all at a higher retail price.

"That is marketing done right," Godin says, "Marketing where the marketer changes the product not the ads."[2]

More Ideas That Matter

Godin's comment is perceptive beyond the Dutch Boy example. It reflects an uneasy shift occurring within the advertising, marketing communications, and graphic design industries, and among marketing departments within companies. They all seem to know change is afoot, but many are struggling with what it all means.

In the spring of 1999 *The Cluetrain Manifesto: The End of Business as Usual*, was launched on the Web with ninety-five theses, all basically saying that business doesn't have a clue about the Web, the changes occurring as a result of the Web, and people's real feelings toward management and big business. The book appeared around the end of 2000 with more of the same. The *Cluetrain* was a slap in the face, a wake-up call, a kick in the butt to anyone even remotely connected to marketing, advertising, and PR, which means about 90 percent of corporate America. It was the forerunner to FuckedCompany.com and it carried even more weight because the guys who put this together were not young, hip, dot.comers, but wizened old fixtures of the high-tech and marketing establishment. Rick Levine was a long-time engineer and Web architect for Sun Microsystems; Christopher Locke, a consultant, writer, and frequent speaker, worked with icons such as IBM, MCI, and Carnegie Mellon; the Silicon Valley marketing veteran Doc Searls is the senior editor of *Linux Journal*; and Boston based high-tech marketer David Weinberger has written for *Wired, Information Week* and the *New York Times*.

Here's Doc Searls on marketing: "Everyone of us knows that marketers are out to get us, and we all struggle to escape their snares. We channel-surf through commercials; we open our mail over the recycle bin, struggling to discern the junk mail without having to open the envelope; we resent the adhesion of commercial messages to everything from sports uniforms to escalator risers. We know that the real purpose of marketing is to insinuate the message into our consciousness, to put an axe in our heads without our noticing."[3]

And Chris Locke speaking of the Web, "Why is a medium that holds such promise—to connect, to inspire, to awaken, to enlist, to change—being used by companies as a conduit for the kind of tired lies that have characterized fifty years of television? Business has made a ventriloquist's trick of the humanity we take for granted. . . . The corporation pretends to speak, but its voice is that of a third-rate actor in a fourth-rate play, uttering lines no one believes in a manner no one respects."[4]

In the fall of 1999 another manifesto appeared; the *First Things First 2000* manifesto signed by thirty-three graphic design luminaries. The message was similar. It was a call for designers and art directors to protest the rampant consumerism of corporate America. "Designers who devote their efforts primarily to advertising, marketing, and brand development are supporting, and implicitly endorsing, a mental environment so saturated with commercial messages that it is changing the very way citizen-consumers speak, think, feel, respond, and interact."

"We propose a reversal of priorities in favor of more useful, lasting, and democratic forms of communication—a mind shift away from product marketing and toward the exploration and production of a new kind of meaning. The scope of debate is shrinking; it must expand."[5]

The distinction between the messages of these two manifestoes is insightful. Designers are calling for an expanded debate regarding rampant consumerism while *Cluetrain* (essentially the voice of Web users) is saying the debate has already begun, and people are winning:

- Thesis # 73—"You're invited, but it's our world. Take your shoes off at the door. If you want to barter with us, get down off your camel!"
- Thesis # 94—"To traditional corporations, networked conversations may appear confused, may sound confusing. But we are organizing faster than they are. We have better tools, more new ideas, no rules to slow us down."

But the common theme of both messages is even more important. Comments on the *Cluetrain* from Thomas Petzinger Jr. of the *Wall Street*

Journal nicely sum up the underlying premise. "The idea that business, at bottom, is fundamentally human. That engineering remains second-rate without aesthetics. That natural, human conversation is the true language of commerce. That corporations work best when the people on the inside have the fullest contact possible with the people on the outside."[6]

Then the market crashed. Through the end of 2000 and most of 2001 many people sighed with relief. The dot.com thing was a fluke, we have nothing to worry about, we can continue doing what we have always done. We do not have to think.

Nothing could be further from the truth. The economy is in the tank. Advertising agencies are struggling to stay alive. Publications that rely on advertising are wafer thin. Graphic designers are asking if they have a future at all. And unemployment lines are filled with software engineers, programmers, and corporate middle management. Yet, as we have already seen, the Web continues to grow, in breadth and depth, and in frequency, length, and consequence of use. And it has only just begun.

Ideas Change Industries—Sometimes

One of the difficulties with all of the recent focus on innovation, creativity, and new ideas is the lack of attention to old ideas. The things we do without thinking about them. This is what the two manifestoes are really about; the need to pay attention to the things we take for granted. The things that used to be important, but today linger on as primary activities only because no one has stopped to say, Why are we doing this?

Carly Fiorina, CEO of Hewlett-Packard, has a motto that drives decisions at HP: "Preserve the best, reinvent the rest." This requires looking at what exists and asking Why? This concept of business reinvention has been around for some time but it is worth reviewing. Theodore Levitt addressed the issue in 1964 with the following two examples:

"The railroads did not stop growing because the need for passenger and freight transportation declined. That grew. The railroads are in trouble today not because the need was filled by others (cars, trucks, airplanes, even telephones), but because it was not filled by the railroads themselves. They let others take customers away from them because they assumed themselves to be in the railroad business rather than in the transportation business. The reason they defined their industry wrong was because they were railroad-oriented instead of transportation-oriented; they were product-oriented instead of customer-oriented.

"Hollywood barely escaped being totally ravished by television. Actually, all the established film companies went through dramatic reorganizations. Some simply disappeared. All of them got into trouble not because of TV's inroads but because of their own myopia. As with the railroads, Hollywood defined its business incorrectly. It thought it was in the movie business when it was actually in the entertainment business."[7]

Over ensuing decades more businesses realized the old boundary rules of industries no longer applied and if they were to thrive or even survive they must redefine their business. What had been product businesses became service businesses. Newspapers were no longer in the newsprint business but rather in the "information communication" business. The *Wall Street Journal* used to be about the business of work. Now it's about "the Business of Life." Pharmaceutical companies, although they may still manufacture products, are now in the health, medicines, and lifestyle business. "Life Is Our Life's Work" at Pfizer. Some of the slogans you hear may not ring true, but as Charles Handy said, "When our language changes, behavior will not be far behind."

Businesses have also begun to cooperate with other businesses, forming new alliances. IBM, which was widely known for the "heavy iron" it delivered as mainframe computers throughout the seventies, eighties and well into the nineties, was late in coming to the desktop revolution, but is today in the business of providing information services. "The company no longer gives away its services to sell its goods. Indeed the deal is reversed: IBM will buy its clients' hardware if they'll contract with Global Services to manage its information systems."[8] In October 2002 IBM acquired the consulting business of PricewaterhouseCoopers, and in March of this year it took over the management of American Express' computer systems, from mainframes to desktops.

The changes in the world of business over the last decade have been so disruptive that entire industries are no longer the same. Yet advertising, marketing, and graphic design are doing more or less the same things they have done for the past forty years.

Advertising and Marketing

Advertising is still essentially in the business of buying and selling ad space on behalf of clients, ostensibly to help sell products, services, brands, companies, and even values. Yes, there have been changes in recent years. The old standard 17.65 percent markup has dwindled to 15 or even 11 percent, some client companies have tried to institute "performance-based payments," separate media companies do most of the buying now (though often owned by the same holding company), and agencies have been pushing hard for a convergence with Hollywood as entertainment has become a memorable component of commercials. Innovation in advertising in the past decade has consisted primarily of new ways to interrupt Web users' experiences with flashing banners, pop-ups, pop-unders, and page-filling ads. Marketing continues its direct barrage of "buy now" and "get one free" coupons, mailers, and tchotchkes through every possible channel. However, it has discovered the indirect channels of "buzz" and "viral" messages, which are at least less interruptive than pop-ups.

Even with these changes, the underlying premise of advertising and marketing remains the same: to continuously sell new customers on behalf of its clients, or sell more stuff to existing customers—ideally both.

Advertising related to the Web was a complete disaster throughout the nineties. Rance Crain, editor-in-chief of *Advertising Age*, noted that the "dot.com advertising outburst did colossal damage to advertising's reputation among the nation's CEOs . . . so pointless, so tasteless, so stupid that it shook the faith of corporate chieftains in the power of advertising."[9] What about the faith of the consumer? That was lost a long time ago. Advertising has not been believed for years. Nearly everyone—even within the industry—agrees that the 3,000 or more individual messages we are bombarded with each day has gotten way out of hand. Pop-up ads on the Web got so out of hand (according to Neilson/Netratings, they doubled in the last quarter of 2002) that America Online offers a pop-up ad blocker feature to its subscribers.

So, why do advertising agencies continue to do the same thing? For the very reason we all do; it is easier—always easier—to do what we have done before. Human habits do not change quickly, even in an industry that touts its own creativity. And particularly in a multi-billion dollar industry that supports millions of people; one that grew as industry grew, and is a large and integral part of the American and global economy.

But businesses changed, the economy changed, and there are tiny signs that advertising may finally be changing too. The example given earlier of Macromedia launching blogs with the introduction of new products is a truly innovative way to market. It makes use of the unique capability of the Web without being abrasive or offensive. It allows useful, valuable conversations to happen among the parties who are interested, without interrupting everyone else. Viral marketing on the Web is similar. It is based on people talking to people, not corporate pummeling. The recent introduction of AdWords by Google is another example. The small text-based ads that appear on the right-hand side of a results page are keyed to the words that are used for a search. It is clear that these are ads, but they are non-obtrusive and they are relevant to a searcher's request. They can also be purchased at a very reasonable rate because the cost of the ad is tied directly to the results, which are monitored in real time. Keep your fingers crossed; this just may be the beginning of advertising reinventing itself on the Web.

Graphic Design

Having begun as the stepchild of advertising—closely connected to producing the art required for ads—graphic designers grew up in the sixties and seventies as the handmaidens of industry; producing packaging, magazines, posters, identity programs, and annual reports. They have struggled for years to define the business they are in. Though it is primarily a professional-service business, some design companies clearly market from a product orientation—offering annual report, poster, branding, or CD package design. While others are more customer/service-oriented, offering "custom solutions" to business communications problems, or "integrated communications design" services.

During the eighties, graphic designers suffered a mild identity crisis and a financial blow as corporations adopted computers faster than designers, and desktop publishers mimicked the multiple graphic styles of the day. In the nineties, the graphic design industry was slow again and webmasters and software engineers took over the first decade of the Web.

Many webmasters were homegrown, having learned HTML and some basic software tools when in high school or college; they could easily sell their services to businesses—including graphic design businesses—that did not understand how the Web worked. As the Web became more sophisticated, engineers played a larger role, and in combination with marketers and venture capitalists, built the large Web consultancies during the dot.com explosion.

Today, Web designers are suffering from identity confusion. Experience designers, information architects, engineers, graphic designers, interface designers, and Web business strategists are struggling to define their individual roles and market their specific or collective services. Unfortunately, when you listen to the chatter on the Web, graphic designers are barely in the fray. And they should be. The Web desperately needs the intelligence, the aesthetics, the creativity, and wit that graphic design has brought to print communications for years. And it needs to be more than a surface—a skin laying on top of the complex structure beneath. It needs to be more than an animated flash intro to another boring site. It needs to be intelligent design, top to bottom.

Graphic designers experienced with magazine design, corporate literature systems, branding programs, and annual report design, have an opportunity to bring to the Web their expertise in establishing visual themes, structuring complex information, and balancing visual continuity with spontaneity. This is their opportunity to produce "more useful, lasting, and democratic forms of communication,"[10] to a make a difference in this new portion of our visual culture, and to make a difference in people's lives.

Designers who understand that ideas matter, that implementing valuable ideas matters even more—and that the Web is a great resource for doing both—discovering and implementing ideas which are beneficial to people, can use this knowledge to make a substantial difference for their clients and their own business success.

19

What Customers Want

As we know, the ultimate customer of any Web site is always the user—the visitor to the site. And there will be many visitors, each with their own goals, their own idiosyncrasies, and their own pressures, which the design of your site must take into consideration. The fictional character process outlined earlier is one good way to approach meeting their needs. As we have seen, this process also helps to minimize the ego friction among the various teams and team members, any one of whom may be the customer of the Web design consultant.

It is impossible to know with any degree of certainty the specific wants and needs of each of these people. But there are common wants and needs—common habits or practices—for almost all people, and these are critical to the marketing of a site, or marketing the consulting services required to design and build a site. In fact, they are critical to all marketing.

Trust and Credibility

We all know it is utter nonsense that you can't judge a book by its cover. We can judge books by their covers, and we do all the time. We also judge people on first impression. The way they look, their gait, their laughter, or tone of voice often contributes more to our impression than the specifics of what they say. We generally respond to people who make us feel good. People with whom we are comfortable, at ease. People we think we can trust. We respond the same way to Web sites.

Ones that give us a sense of comfort, ease of use, and trust are the ones we frequent. Whether our judgment about books, people, or Web sites is correct or valid is another question. That will be determined with each successive step we take in the relationship.

We all know intuitively that this is the way we make decisions. Yet we continually deny it, claiming to be rational, logical human beings. We turn to research reports, focus groups, and best practices to support our decisions. Fortunately, there is increasing evidence to support the fact that we make decisions based on our emotions and justify the decisions based on facts.

One such example comes from what is believed to be the largest Web credibility study to date, which was issued at the end of October 2002 by Consumer Web Watch. The consumer-driven study titled *How Do People Evaluate a Web Site's Credibility?* was prepared by Stanford University's Persuasive Technology Lab and invited more than two thousand people to rate the credibility of Web sites in ten content areas. The results surprised those involved in the study. They found that "when people assessed a real Web site's credibility they did not use rigorous criteria." This did not match what had been said in an earlier study from April of 2002. In this poll of 1,500 adult U.S. Internet users, people said that certain elements such as privacy policies were vital to the credibility of the site. But in the new study, based on real reviews of real sites, the statistics showed "that the average consumer paid far more attention to the superficial aspects of a site, such as visual cues, than to its content. For example, nearly half of all consumers (46.1 percent) in the study assessed credibility of sites based in part on the appeal of the overall visual design of a site, including layout, typography, font size, and color schemes."

"This reliance on a site's overall visual appeal to gauge its credibility occurred more often with some categories of sites than others. Consumer credibility-related comments about visual design issues occurred with more frequency with finance (54.6 percent), search engines (52.6 percent), travel (50.5 percent), and e-commerce sites (46.2 percent); and with less frequency when assessing health (41.8 percent), news (39.6 percent), and nonprofit (39.4 percent) sites."[1]

Consumer Web Watch concluded that they, "along with librarians, and information professionals, must increase efforts to educate online consumers so they evaluate the Web sites they visit more carefully and make better educated decisions, particularly when it could adversely affect their pocketbooks or health situations." This is undoubtedly worthwhile and would be beneficial to Web consumers, but it will not make a substantial difference in people's initial actions. We will continue—as we have since the beginning of humankind—to make our initial decisions on the basis of our perceptions, using logic to help verify our emotional choices. Even Aristotle said it is not enough to appeal to reason and logic, you must appeal to the emotions. What Consumer Web Watch referred to as "superficial aspects" are in fact very real and important components of our everyday process of thinking and decision-making.

Since the early seventies, cognitive neuroscientists have shown that the one rational human brain that is supposed to be in control of each of us does not really exist. "The brain does have supervisory systems in the prefrontal lobes and anterior cingulate cortex, which can push buttons of behavior and override habits and urges. But those systems are gadgets," Steven Pinker says, "with specific quirks and limitations; they are not implementations of the rational free agent traditionally identified with the soul or self."[2]

The most notable examples come from the "split-brain" test conducted by neuroscientists Roger Sperry and Michael Gazzaniga. They have shown that when the corpus callosum which joins the cerebral hemispheres is severed, each hemisphere can act on its own without the advice or consent of the other. "Even more disconcertingly," says Pinker, "the left hemisphere constantly weaves a coherent but false account of the behavior chosen without its knowledge by the right." For example, "if the patient's left hemisphere is shown a chicken and his right hemisphere is shown a snowfall, and both hemispheres have to select a picture that goes with what they see (each using a different hand), the left hemisphere picks a claw (correctly) and the right picks a shovel (also correctly). But when the left hemisphere is asked why the whole person made those choices, it blithely says, 'Oh, that's simple. The chicken claw goes with the chicken, and you need a shovel to clean out the chicken shed.'"

"The spooky part," Pinker continues, "is that we have no reason to think the baloney-generator in the patient's left hemisphere is behaving any differently from ours as we make sense of the inclinations emanating from the rest of our brains. The conscious mind—the self or soul—is a spin doctor, not the commander in chief." And the spin doctor is creating stories to help us justify the decisions we have made intuitively.

What do online customers want? The same thing offline customers want. They want respect. They don't want you to waste their time. They don't want to feel stupid. They want to be engaged emotionally and intellectually. But the emotions come first. Even when a Web visitor is under extreme time pressure to find a fact, get an answer to a question, or make a purchase, the ease and comfort she feels with a site—based on intuitive response to visual cues such as download speed, color and typefonts, balance of graphics and text, and clear navigation—will drive her decisions. This does not mean that visual cues—color, typefont, layout, and navigation—on a Web site are everything. It does mean that these elements play a much larger role and have much more influence in determining the visitor's reaction, in building trust, and establishing credibility, than has been credited to them in the past.

Confidence and Reliability

One of the biggest problems with the Web during the dot.com explosion was the extreme tendency to over-promise and under-deliver. Nearly every site stated, "We are here to help you, send us your questions, we want to hear from you." So people sent in their questions, and waited for a response. And they waited. And they waited. It is amazing to me that the great majority of Web sites continue to do this today. Even many transaction sites have outdated information, out-of-stock inventory, and do not respond effectively when asked why. To be told by a customer service rep, "Our Web site is two to three months behind on updating for discontinued items," is not a satisfactory answer. My confidence in your business has just been shattered.

If you expect to do business on the Web, any business—whether information-based, a service provider, a consultant, or selling products— you must be prepared to respond. Why is this so difficult for people to understand, even after ten years of the Web? It is no different from the business rules that exist offline. If you promise to deliver products between certain hours and you don't, you have lost a customer. Technology is not a magic bullet that relieves you of responsibility. In fact, the responsibility is even greater because the consumer's expectations are higher. Everyone is pressed for time. They want answers, accurate answers, and they want them now.

Web design consultants have an obligation to help their clients understand the ultimate customer's expectations, and the potential threats to their confidence in the company, caused by ill-conceived, poorly designed, malfunctioning, or unattended Web sites. Following are a few areas of special concern.

Corporate Strategy

I was recently handed a terrific business card from Terri Langhans of Maverick Marketing in California. Actually it was a stack of ten cards with a rivet through one corner holding them together so each card could be fanned out. The first card contained the following simple but powerful words: "No one cares about your boring business." When you turn the card over, the copy on the backside read: "They care about themselves. Yet most of your marketing is all about you. It boils down to a blatant sales pitch, punctuated by a boastful, long-winded description of the product or service. Blah, blah, blah."

Strategy may be important to your business, to your bankers and investors, to designing and building your Web site, but it is not important to 99 and 44/100ths of the visitors to your site. Langhans is dead-on; visitors don't care about your boring business—most will not read your strategy statements. They care about the influence your strategy has on them. The questions that must be asked are: What do you have to offer them? Can they easily find it? How quickly will you fulfill the promise when they take you up on the offer? And, are your people and your systems all integrated into one network ready to respond?

When a customer starts the purchase process of a ticket from Ticketron.com, she is notified that she has approximately two minutes to complete the transaction. Why? Because when she starts the process, the ticket is automatically taken out of inventory. If she does not complete the transaction in time, the system puts the ticket back for someone else to buy. That's integration strategy that works—for the customer and for the business.

Sales and Marketing

On another card from Langhans the front of the card reads: "There's a darned good reason Oprah never started a Brochure-of-the-Month club." On the back it says: "Who would join? No plot. No characters. Just lots of bullet points and the obligatory photo of the product, boss, and/or building. What a shame." Where is the personality? Where is the distinctive difference?

I can't tell you how many times I have received calls from marketing people saying they need a brochure and would like a proposal from me outlining our costs. My first question is always, "Why do you want a brochure?" Invariably there is a lull on the phone, and I feel like I have asked something that is not supposed to be discussed. The brochure is a given. It is standard procedure. It is a marketing cliché. Which is why so many Web sites are nothing more than brochures. If this is all that sales and marketing can do with their Web presence, they should not waste the company's money. The standard brochure on the Web does nothing to improve customer confidence or company reliability. The same brochure off the Web often does damage to a company's credibility because it is seen as nothing more than another contribution to the environmental waste stream. At minimum, offer your brochure as a PDF file that visitors can print out for themselves if needed. Or think of your brochure as an interactive possibility on the Web. Think of it as a blog.

Information Technology

An IT department that has been given responsibility for the corporate Web site or sites frequently calls us in. Surprisingly, the technology people often realize that the site is not a technology issue. It has just been dumped in their lap. They know it is a core strategy issue and they need help with the internal communications strategy to get everyone on board. It is senior management who does not realize the full impact that design of information technology—information access, storage, integration, and untethered flow, both internal and external—has on the confidence consumers have in their business.

•

Consumers now have several years of online experience with companies like Ticketron, Amazon, FedEx, eBay, Expedia, and PayPal. They expect more than brochures. They expect quick, accurate response from systems that work and from people online ready to help them. This increased expectation demands greater reliability, not just of systems, but also more importantly of management.

The difficulty is getting management to understand that although the well-designed Internet strategy may reduce cost, improve efficiency, strengthen relationships, even provide new revenue streams, it will not happen overnight and there will be disruption in different departments along the way. It is like trying to explain to future parents that their lives—the joys of children not withstanding—will never be the same.

We may not know what each Web customer wants or needs, but we do know that they are now in the drivers seat. And that they share some common habits and desires: most of their decisions will be intuitively made, and they are looking for companies they can trust, that are credible, responsive, and that they can rely on. These principles should support design decisions as marketing and Web strategy are developed.

20

A Value Proposition for the Web

The foundation of business building and marketing on the Web is the ability to create a *mutually beneficial relationship* between an organization and its various audiences at a single point of contact. No other communications channel affords the *opportunity to create an interactive experience* that can convey brand attributes; tell the business story; begin a conversation with customers, suppliers, employees, and community members; *provide multiple action points* through a single interaction; and track and *compile data* on all of the activity in real time. This is the fundamental value proposition of the Web. It contains several key phrases that are easy to overlook or misinterpret and are therefore called out below for additional comment.

A Mutually Beneficial Relationship
This is the single most important aspect of the Web, yet companies continue to misinterpret its meaning. If your Web site is a one-way street you have missed the point. Information must flow both ways, and must be beneficial to both parties. If you are showing off your products or services but not allowing visitors to act on what they see—request more information, fill out an application, make a reservation, request a proposal, make a purchase, make a suggestion, all online—you are not only wasting their time, you are wasting your time. When a visitor is engaged with your site and is ready to make a purchase, but must print out an order form and fax it to the company, you have interrupted the natural flow of information, delayed the process by using two different

systems, and involved more people in the process than are required if the transaction happens online.

This is about building a relationship between the organization and its audiences. It is not about Customer Relationship Management. Almost all CRM or ECRM (Electronic Customer Relationship Management) programs are written from the business point of view. They are focused on selling—up-selling, cross-selling, "would you like fries with that?" Customers will tolerate some of this, and it may be appropriate under the right conditions, but as John Hunter, senior vice president of Customer Service at QVC reported, ". . . we've found that maximizing the sale generally doesn't help to achieve customer loyalty and repeat purchases. Building trust and consistency in consumer relationships is the key to success in the retail business."[1]

Hunter avoided the CRM vendors who pushed cross-selling technologies and developed his own browser-based customer-service system, based on how QVC representatives interact with their customers. "CRM is not just about slick technology and seeing how much you can sell to your customers today," Hunter says, "it's about building relationships so that you can sell to them tomorrow." Over three-quarters of the customers of QVC rate the company seven out of seven for trustworthiness. And those customers repurchase at a rate 80 percent higher than ones who rate the company a six. They are also the ones willing to recommend QVC to a friend.

To be mutually beneficial a site cannot be all about selling, it must let the visitor's voice be heard. Building a relationship with customers, suppliers, and employees requires mutual participation, respect, and trust. That is the key to success in any business.

Opportunity to Create an Interactive Experience

It seems that many companies have mistaken activity for interactivity. Adding Flash presentations that function like television commercials is not providing an interactive experience. Interactivity means reciprocal action. The visitors to your site must be able to take action. At the very least they should be able to click on items shown and get more information. And the information should be right there, not at the end of a phone call. They should be able to do something with the information—respond to it, add to it, save it, pass it on.

In October of 2002 the designers from 37 Signals, LLC posted a surprising research brief on their site titled, "Sites That Don't Click." It reported, "37 Signals reviewed the homepages of ten prominent retailers and found that they all displayed product images that were either 1) non-clickable; or 2) clickable, but did not lead to a page where the featured product could be purchased. Even worse, several high-profile retailers featured products on their homepages that were nowhere to be found within their sites."[2]

Several of the companies included in the survey such as Abercrombie.com, BananaRepublic.com, ExpressFashion.com, Gap.com, have since corrected the problem. Others (at this writing) have not. By comparison, LandsEnd.com always has a clickable image on the homepage and on the front page of each section such as Women, Men, Kids, For the Home, and Luggage. But that is only the beginning. Following are some of the other interactive experience features of LandsEnd.com:

- *Lands' End Live.* This appears throughout the site and allows customers to talk directly by phone or "chat" online with a customer service representative at any time.
- *My Virtual Model.* Visitors provide body measurements, hair and skin color, and body and face shape, and a 3D personal model is rendered. The visitor may then "try on" clothing items. This may be saved on the site, sent to friends, or used on other Web sites who participate in the My Virtual Model network.
- *Shop with a Friend.* This unique service allows two shoppers to browse through items on the site together, communicate with each other in the process, and add items to a single shopping cart.
- *My Personal Shopper.* This is a "personal wardrobe consultant" who will suggest outfits or items that best suit the shopper's taste, based on clothing preferences provided earlier.
- *The Alumni Collection.* This service allows shoppers to select their favorite college team logo and have it added to the garment of their choice.
- *Lands' End Custom.* Customers answer a few simple questions about body type and measurements and Lands' End custom tailors clothing to fit.

There are "seasonal" experiences as well, such as the Swim Finder for appropriate swimwear in the summer and Outerwear Finder to help customers in the fall. The latter includes a tutorial on outerwear layering techniques.

The opportunities to create these types of interactive experiences abound. And they are not the exclusive domains of retail- or product-based sites. With a little thought they may be designed into any site in any industry. Look for what irritates your existing customers, suppliers, and employees. Can you save them time? Reduce their stress? Improve their personal satisfaction? Add some fun? Provide them with simple tools to do things for themselves?

Provide Multiple Action Points

This does not mean putting a pull-down menu of many departmental e-addresses on a general purpose "contact us" form. A contact us page is a requirement and should be available throughout the site, but it should be structured from a potential visitor's point of view, not from the company point of view. It should also be more than just an e-mail form. Postal addresses and at least primary phone numbers are essential. And while we're talking about contacts, how about some people? I am constantly amazed at the number of sites that do not have these two basic things. When people cannot find an address or a phone number on your site they have good reason to suspect that you are not a real company. When they can't find people they usually get frustrated and leave. Most people do not want to do business with sales@, market-ing@, or corpcom@. People want to work with Alice, or Tom, or Shareen—not Mr. Anonymous.

Of course, "contact us" is only one action point. One of the essential values of the Web is that you can—and should—have multiple action points. All of the interactive experiences suggested above are action points. And they are more important than the "buy now" button that many companies overemphasize. Most visitors want to review, compare, discuss, and even haggle over price or features before they buy. Provide them with calculators, comparison charts, industry studies, estimate forms, feedback from other customers, discussion channels with employees, a ranking mechanism to record their likes and dislikes. The list can go on and on, and it will be different for each department within a company. Will all of these tools be used? Certainly not by everyone. The point is, when clearly organized multiple possibilities for action are offered, more and different kinds of visitors will respond.

Several years ago, the vice president of marketing for an East Coast printer told me he had placed a "request-a-quote" form on the home page of the company Web site. He was not a fan of the Web and did not expect any results. So he was very excited the following month when he received, via the Web form, a request from a designer in Chicago to bid on printing a major corporate annual report. The VP immediately called the designer to thank him for the opportunity to bid and said he had already assigned a Chicago sales rep to his account. The designer's response was, "I don't want a sales rep calling me. I don't have time to schmooze with a salesman. That's why I used your online form. Just get me the numbers and then we'll talk."

Some people want to talk, others want to shop, and others just want to get on with things. Multiple action points allow you the opportunity to appeal to each.

Track and Compile Data

There's no question that the Web is a measurable medium. It may be the most measurable medium we have ever had. There are numerous off-the-shelf tools that can be used to track every conceivable activity on your site; where visitors are coming from, where they are going, what they are doing, and how much time they spend doing it. For any marketer this is important information, but it is only important if you can make sense out of all of the available data. It is easy to talk about capturing "eyeballs" or hits or unique sessions, but it doesn't mean anything unless you have an objective. Tracking and analyzing Web data must begin with the question; What do you want to know? The second question is Why?

The NetIQ Corporation, publishers of WebTrends, a leading analytics software, breaks down Web analysis into three levels:

- *Traffic Reporting* provides basic site activity information, such as number of visitors, sessions, page views, and time spent, viewed by day, week, month or year.
- *Visitor Behavior* offers insight into the dimensions of visitor activity and behavior on the site. Where are visitors coming from, and leaving from, and how are they responding to certain portions or elements of the site.

- *Customer Behavior* gives you individual visitor activity merged with general site activity to provide an in-depth view of specific customers' interactions with your organization.

Looking at the data in these types of reports, you can see trends, benchmark key numbers such as number of visitor sessions, or time spent in particular areas of your site, or areas where people seem to leave. You can then make changes in your site and, tracking the data, see if the changes are getting more reaction or less. When a new marketing campaign is launched, offline or on, you can immediately see the results, where visitors are coming from, if they are clicking through the area you want them to, if they are making the purchase, etc. Again, based on the statistics, changes can be made to the campaign or to the site and the trends tracked once more. The idea is to use the data to continuously improve the value of your site. This means improving the relationship with your visitors. Offering them a better, more useful, experience.

One of the things LandsEnd.com did a couple of years ago after realizing that too many shopping carts were being abandoned, was to install an inventory alert function that tells shoppers when a requested item that is out of stock will be available; offers to send an e-mail notice when the item is in stock; and provides alternative items that are available immediately. This kind of dedication to continuously improving the value for the customer has helped make LandsEnd.com the largest volume apparel Web site in the world.

The Fundamentals

There you have it. The four critical advantages of the Web that must be used effectively for marketing and business success on the Web: Building a mutually beneficial relationship, creating an interactive experience, providing multiple action points, and tracking and compiling data on all of the activity in real time. Each advantage reinforces the others to provide a rich, valuable experience for your visitors. And this, along with a little common sense and courtesy, can lead to long-term, valuable business relationships.

21

Building One-to-One Relationships

The concept of one-to-one marketing has been promoted in the context of valuable business relationships for at least ten years now. The idea is to provide products and services to one customer at a time by identifying and meeting his or her individual needs. Then repeat this process with each customer many times to build long-term relationships. Rather than concentrating on selling one product to many customers, the one-to-one strategy is to concentrate on one customer and sell that customer as many products as possible. Amazon began by selling books. Now it offers you games and toys, clothing, electronic products, and tools and hardware. The whole concept of one-to-one rests on information technology being able to personalize and customize products and services.

Finally, the personalization technology required to accomplish this is here. Although it is still difficult and expensive in relation to its returns, many of the things it is supposed to do are now possible. The problem is not the technology; it is the focus of many marketers trying to adopt the one-to-one strategy. In and of itself, the idea of mass customization is appealing, but to be effective, the focus must be primarily on pleasing the customer, not satisfying the demands of the technology or the demands of the marketer. Ideally, the desires of the customer and the marketer can be met but only if the focus is correct.

The Tickler File

Tickle: 1 a: to excite or stir up agreeably; PLEASE; b: to provoke to laughter or merriment; AMUSE.

Years ago I read an article somewhere that I now wish I could find. It was about a car salesman who was considered the best car salesman in the country. He had hundreds of customers and they all seemed to love him. They relied on him for all kinds of advice having to do with cars, but also for advice having nothing to do with cars. As I recall, several of his customers were quoted in this article and talked of this man as if he were a member of their immediate family. He was invited to family affairs including weddings and graduation ceremonies. He also seemed to love his customers. He went to their affairs. He visited them in their homes. And he sent lots of cards and notes: birthday cards, anniversary cards, congratulations cards on a new baby or new job, and get-well cards after a sickness.

In the article the salesman explained how he managed to keep up with all of his customers. He kept a "tickler file," a catalog of cards on which he made brief notes each time he spoke to a customer. Something to "tickle" his memory about items of specific interest or dates or life events that the person had mentioned. He organized the cards by date into monthly and then weekly groups. Each morning—maybe it was each weekend, or maybe both—he would review his stack of cards for the upcoming week or day. He explained that this was about business, but more importantly it was about people. He liked people. He loved people, and this method assured him that he would not forget the things in their lives that were important. It allowed him to stay in close touch with many, many people.

Today, what this salesman called a tickler file has been transformed to CRM, or ECRM. It just doesn't have the same ring, does it?

Pleasing People

The underlying principle of CRM is more or less the same as the tickler file. That is, the idea is the same; organizing personal data—interests, statistics, preferences—in relation to a calendar and to an inventory of products and services, for easy recall. Whether the users of these programs care about people is another question.

I am actually a fan of personalization technology. This is the under-pinning of CRM. I like it when 1to1.com (the Peppers and Rogers Group site, the people who are most responsible for promoting all of this) addresses me by name. I'm sure Don Peppers doesn't know me from Adam. Neither does Jeff Bezos at Amazon. Although I frequently use Amazon.com, I am not interested in a long-term relationship with the company. Neither of these companies is my "friend." I am aware that this is only a software program calling up my name from a data-base. But I also know, with reasonable certainty, that when this is done correctly and the software program addresses me by name, it will do "friend-like" things. It will provide me with what I am interested in based on the profile or preferences I have provided. Like Lands' End, it will try to accommodate my wishes on my terms—anywhere, anytime. It will give me what I have requested, or notify me when it will be available. It may make a few alternate suggestions, but it will not insult me with a barrage of things I don't care about. If it does, I'm gone.

Pleasing people is what personalization software is all about. At least that's what it is supposed to be about. The whole idea of using software to help people and businesses deal with the increasing complexities of life is great. This is what it should do. The way businesses, consultants, and tech-nologist talk about it, however, is horrible. The language used is downright scary. And even worse, the users of this language don't realize how fright-ening they sound. They don't realize what damage they are doing to peo-ple's perception and adoption of the very technologies they are promoting.

To begin with, the question of who owns the customer should never come up. Businesses do not own customers. Period. Businesses serve peo-ple. When someone talks about owning customers they reveal their per-spective as inside-out—business first, people second. Today, the perspective that works is just the opposite; outside-in—people first, business second.

Don Peppers and Martha Rogers, the highly acclaimed one-to-one marketing consultants and best-selling business authors, have a book out called *REAL IMPACT: Increasing Your Return on Customer*. They contend that focusing on share-of-customer by using today's technology is what will drive future business growth, and businesses should re-think their success metrics based on this premise. These are very smart people, but their language is awful. *Return on Customer*? Please, this sounds like a bad movie. Virtually all the life and personality have been squeezed from this expression. Even the acronym ROC is hard and less fluid than ROI (Return On Investment).

Much of what Peppers and Rogers have suggested in the past has been great. The idea of demographic market segmentation giving way to one-to-one marketing is terrific. No one ever liked being lumped into a generic market segment anyway. But when phrases like share-of-market are replaced by share-of-customer, I get nervous. Who is going to get what part? I guess Nike, Reebok, and Bass will fight over my feet, Levis, and Geoffrey Beene will claim my legs, Van Heusen and the Gap get my chest and arms, and all of them, plus the *Wall Street Journal*, *Harvard Business Review*, CNN, NPR, and Gumpta, will squabble over my brain. Yikes!

Forget terms like CRM, ROC, and SOC (share-of-customer). Pleasing people is what Web designers need to focus on. It is also what business leaders should focus on. If you please people first you might actually sell them more. Think about the language you are using from the customer's perspective not the business perspective. Think about your customer database as a larger and easier-to-use version of the salesman's tickler file. It should tickle your memory and your customers fancy.

Convenience, Choice, and Value

When Sam Walton started Wal-Mart he said, "I'm going to go twenty miles outside of town and build a store. And I'll offer value merchandise and people will come."[1] Everyone thought he was nuts. But people came. Even though it may have been inconvenient, customers were pleased because they were presented a wide choice of great products at great value. In 2002, Wal-Mart earned $244 billion.

In July 2002, Joe Fedele, a grocer in New York, launched FreshDirect.com, an online grocery service catering to demanding New Yorkers. Many people think he is nuts. Webvan, the spectacular dot.com grocery store that burned through over $1 billion dollars, had just closed shop in July 2001.

"[Webvan] tried to change behavioral pattern with convenience," Fedele says. "And convenience doesn't change behavioral pattern—especially with food. You go to the butcher with the best meat. You go to the best bagel shop for the crustiest bagels. You go to one deli for smoked salmon and another for fresh mozzarella. Choice and value change patterns of behavior."[2]

With over 15,000 products, including thirty different cuts of steak, parbaked bread, Braeburn apples from New Zealand, and the best Bucheron cheese I've ever tasted—all at 10 to 35 percent less than the supermarket—FreshDirect certainly has choice and value.

Like Wal-Mart, technology controls much of Joe Fedele's operation. But technology is not what it's about. FreshDirect's slogan: "It's all about the food." It buys direct from farms, dairies, and fisheries, so the food is much fresher and less expensive. It has a state-of-the-art food-processing facility in Queens where it butchers the meat, cuts up the fish, roasts coffee, bakes its own bread and pastries, and ripens fruit and vegetables in nine separate, temperature-controlled environments. Software monitors just about everything, including food deliveries, which are tracked and managed much like FedEx. Fedele says he can locate any order at any time, within twenty feet.

This is all about laying the groundwork for a relationship with customers before they even get to the Web site, because it is about providing the best possible quality, a broad choice, and lower prices. When personalization is added through the Web site, it takes the experience and the value to a whole new level. FreshDirect.com is very nicely designed. The color palette is soft and refreshing with a minimum of supermarket banners. Organization of products and information is clear and clean in appearance, even with fifteen major categories of food and ten to twenty-five sub-categories in each. The navigation is very intuitive. The copy is minimal but sufficient, and crisply written.

Each major section of the site such as Deli, Meat, or Seafood introduces the visitor to one of FreshDirect's food handlers like Katie Mitchell, a.k.a. Katie Lady from the Deli and Cheese department. She has eight years of experience bringing cheeses and deli foods to people in such places as Artisanal, Balducci's, Zabar's, and Fairway Markets. The vignettes are brief but informative. They are very personable and the people seem knowledgeable and likable.

Each individual food item such as white cauliflower florets, found under Broccoli and Cauliflower in the Vegetable department, has a photo, a short descriptive block of text and a link to detailed nutritional facts. There is much more: a photo tour of the facility; seasonal recommendations by department managers; your own account that stores order status and purchasing history; a help desk with phone numbers and e-mail; and of course all of the company and policy information. This is a very rich and enjoyable site, and I am not a shopper.

The order status is particularly nice because you can add items to your shopping list over time until you are ready to place the order. But you can also do a quick order using your last list, which contains all of the details—quantity, size, cost—and can be modified as you like and placed again. This site is all about building one-to-one relationships because it is focused on pleasing the people who visit and buy.

The final touch is personalization; specialty items such as the Bucheron cheese carry the preparation date and the name of the customer it was prepared for in discreet type on the label next to the "best to use before" date. This does make it seem like it was prepared just for you. I'm hooked.

New Media Strategies

All of the attention given to personalization technologies over the last few years has forced advertising and marketing people to rethink their media strategies. In October 2002, Opt-in News reported, "Seventy-three percent of media buyers that currently use opt-in e-mail marketing feel it is the most responsive form of marketing available producing better results than television, radio, print, and direct mail."

It is unquestionable that opt-in e-mail works. It's easy, personal, inexpensive, interactive, and direct. People can and do skim and respond immediately. Even with this it should be used with extreme caution. People are exhausted from spam. And they are mad. With the new laws being passed, which were mentioned earlier, you could easily find that the response you get is a charge, or worse, a lawsuit for spam.

The best way to avoid this is to use only your own opt-in list, never one you get from someone else. In requesting permission to e-mail from your site, show respect for the privacy of your visitors and give them more than a yes or no choice. Let them decide the frequency and relevancy of subject matter they want. This type of permission-based, opt-in e-mail, offering respect and relevance to potential customers is one of the most effective electronic marketing tools available today.

•

With all of the attention given to electronic tools, to personalization and customization technologies, the most important thing to remember is that one-to-one relationships in business are not new. They have existed since the beginning of time. The best relationships in my life have nothing to do with technology. This is probably true for most people, and is an important perspective to keep in the front of your mind, in both sides of your brain, while developing marketing plans on the Web or off.

22

Integrated Marketing Communications

Integrated marketing is one of those terms that in the past got brought up and bandied about by marketers every five years or so and then slipped into the background again. I think this was because different media—radio, television, print, outdoors, etc.—were, well, so different. Each had different presentation characteristics, production methods and standards, appealed to different people in different environments, and was controlled by different advertising or marketing people. In the past, integrating campaigns cross-media was difficult to accomplish.

This has all changed. The same group of people who are producing print ads, e-mail newsletters, and outdoor posters can, on the same desktop computers, design broadcast-quality television commercials. The music, voice, and sound effects used for radio commercials may be mixed on the same desktop computers, by the same group of people who are producing the CD-ROM or online interactive presentations. As important as all of these changes are, they are not the biggest change.

Integrated marketing is no longer only about consistent messaging in appropriate media. Today it is about integrating appropriate messages with communications systems that provide real-time feedback and opportunities for action.

Traditional Integrated Campaigns
It should go without saying that any traditional marketing campaign that does not integrate across media will be less effective than campaigns

that do integrate media. This does not mean that many traditional channels—television, radio, print, outdoor, online, environmental, viral—must be used. It simply means that when multiple channels are used they should be coordinated to support one another. The whole—when it is planned as a whole—is nearly always greater than the sum of its parts. In marketing it can be substantially greater.

The reason for integration is simple. Most people ignore most marketing messages. Numerous reports have shown that of the approximately three thousand advertising messages an American individual is exposed to on a daily basis, they notice about eighty and react to only ten. Most researchers agree that no more than a dozen or so messages will be remembered. The more frequently a consumer sees the same message the more likely it will be recalled. Unfortunately many marketers respond to this by delivering more messages. And people respond to this by working harder to ignore them. This has been a continuously escalating, outrageously expensive, self-defeating spiral for years.

Fortunately, permission-based marketing has begun to catch on, more businesses are realizing that constant selling does more harm than good, and more consumers using the Web realize their voices can be heard. A prime example is the fifty million people who signed in the first three months of the national "Do Not Call Registry," launched by the Federal Trade Commission on June 27, 2003, to block telemarketing calls. For marketers this means much more careful selection and integration of messages and media than ever before.

Rather than sending more messages in the same media or even different media, integrated campaigns use multiple media by playing to the strengths of each medium while keeping the critical elements of the campaign the same. Reviewing the strengths of separate media only highlights the value of new media. Television is primarily image-based mass distribution with little immediate response unless the audience makes a phone call or visits a Web site. Radio and magazine ads on the other hand can be more in-depth and more targeted to a niche but also do not allow for action other than a phone call, snail mail coupon, or an e-mail address. The same is true of traditional direct mail.

Meanwhile, e-mail can be targeted to specific individuals, prompt immediate action, and offer immediate connection to the action point, which of course is a Web site. It can also be easily passed on to others.

Remember that your Web site is now the nerve center of all business communications. This is particularly important for marketing.

Although integrated messaging and an integrated look and feel have been the mainstay of some marketers in the past, and integrated "traditional" media campaigns will continue, effective campaigns today require more attention to the integration and efficient use of new information "sharing" systems rather than old broadcast media.

A Smart Integrated Approach

My wife, Cheryl, first heard of FreshDirect.com a year ago when she was given a small flyer as she came out of our local supermarket. The flyer introduced the concept of FreshDirect and highlighted the essential benefits: higher quality, lower prices, better selection, and expert food knowledge. It also stated that delivery was not yet available in our neighborhood, but when it was, she would be entitled to a $50 discount on her first order. It encouraged her to visit the site and register to be notified when delivery would be available—which she did. Apparently many other people in the neighborhood did also. FreshDirect has used this method of building desire until they have enough response to justify the expense of establishing delivery to a particular community.

Sure enough about three months later, Cheryl received an e-mail from FreshDirect saying delivery would be available in our neighborhood on a certain date, and confirming the $50 discount offer on her first order. How could we pass this up? Cheryl placed her first order before going away for the weekend and asked for delivery Sunday evening between 7:00 and 9:00. Shortly after returning home, we received a phone call, half-an-hour before delivery to confirm that someone was home. When the delivery was made, the delivery guys would not accept a tip. This is a FreshDirect policy (and unheard of in New York City). The next day Cheryl received an e-mail from FreshDirect inquiring about her satisfaction with the service. It included a brief, nine-question survey and a $10 discount on her next order if she responded to the survey.

When I asked Cheryl recently about other messages she may have received, she responded, "They told me what I wanted to know, when I needed to know it and that was it." There must be more than that,

I thought, so I asked again. And she replied, "They deliver great food at a great price, it's very convenient, and there's no other nonsense."

In recent weeks we have noticed more FreshDirect trucks in the neighborhood making deliveries and I have seen other FreshDirect people passing out their flyer on the street. But neither of us has seen any advertising other than the original flyer. (There may be advertising that we just have not seen.)

Marketing integration is occurring in two places here. One apparent, that is, the colors, brand identification, and key benefits seen on the flyer; the Web site, the trucks, and clothing worn by the people on the street and making the deliveries. This is extended by the buzz of people talking about FreshDirect in the neighborhood parks and at school. The other is less apparent, but in many ways more important. It is all of the information systems integration, internal to FreshDirect.com, that allows them to collect and track the neighborhood data from their site; purchase, prepare, pack, and deliver the food, and use the purchase and delivery data to meet, and yes exceed, their customers' expectations.

Case Study: Eye-One Color

GretagMacbeth, a worldwide leader in color management and measurement solutions, came to Waters International in the beginning of 2001 with a great challenge. They had been working for a couple of years on shifting their company from being a hardware manufacturing company to a software and solutions company, and had developed a new digital product or digital system of products, which they wanted us to help them launch globally, with an introduction in April at the Seybold conference, the leading graphic arts conference in the United States.

GretagMacbeth has had a superior reputation in color measurement tools for the graphic arts industry for years. Their color instrumentation and color viewing booths are standard fare in printing plants around the world. But this new system of products was different. Not only was it digitally based for measuring, managing, and communicating color information from computer screens to color printers, it was designed for the creative community: art directors, designers, illustrators, and photographers. The launch of this product system was also to be the first public notice of the shift in corporate orientation from manufacturing to software, from the old world to the new "cool color company." What a great assignment. And what a tight deadline. We had three months to the conference.

After a quick but extensive review of internal marketing plans, new product documents (the product was still in development), discussions with management, and a trip to Regensdorf to meet with developers and managers involved, we developed an integrated launch campaign that centered around the Web. The idea was to create a new Web site based on the name of the product, Eye-One. The new site would be substantially different in look and feel, and content and tools, than the existing corporate site, which had been in existence for a few years. EyeOneColor.com would be the hub for all other collateral and advertising that would be designed to drive traffic to the site.

After development of a mood board to establish the look and feel, an initial set of three print ads were developed for placement in multiple publications around the world targeted to photographers, designers, and art directors. Each ad contained very colorful items each showing a face with only one eye. The first was a doll, custom-designed by doll designer Peggy Flynn from California. She produced fifty, one-of-a-kind dolls as giveaways to the first people to register on the site. We also commissioned limited-edition posters created by internationally known graphic artists, namely Jose Ortega, Grant Richards, Michael Mabry, Jennifer Sterling, and Francois Robert. These were raffled off at the conference and offered while they lasted to people who registered at the site. Other media included small banner ads developed for online place-ment with the conference and other related sites, and an interactive CD-ROM presentation that was used at the conference and also raffled off to the audience. The CD contained multiple points that link to the Web site. The site of course includes much information about the new products but it is also rich with information about color.

As soon as the products were available, just shortly after the confer-ence, which was hugely successful, we added a freeware section to the site where visitors could download the first level of software at no charge. And a support section was added where people who had the product could register its serial number and have direct access to technical support. GretagMacbeth also made available one complete product system to be given away each month to a randomly selected registered visitor on the site (this is continuing at this writing).

Even with the events of 9/11 occurring just five months after the conference and the subsequent downturn in the economy, the campaign was very successful. And it continues today with e-mail iSpots, fifteen-second commercials sent to opt-in lists that allow immediate action and have pass-along value; placement of small space ads on industry e-mail newsletters all of which link to the site; and new print ads that lead interested people to specific "landing pages" on the site where they can interact directly with the company.

Although this story is about marketing products, and an integrated use of traditional and new media, you can see that the emphasis was and is on using the Web to provide a location where people can easily get what they want—the full range of products, service, support, and knowledge—and they can get it without a lot of hassle. This is what GretagMacbeth has done with the development of their products. The Web site and the marketing program are simply extensions of this thinking.

As Thomas Vacchiano, CEO of Amazys Holding AG, parent company of GretagMacbeth, said in January 2003, "Color management, once the exclusive realm of graphic arts experts, is no longer a niche application. The success of our latest generation of color management solutions is a testimonial to this trend. In taking ease-of-use to a new level, these solutions fit into real-world workflows and make consistent color reproduction accessible for a wider range of markets . . . ."

Ease-of-use, integrated information systems, real-time feed back, and opportunities for immediate action are now critical ingredients for effective integrated marketing communications.

Removing the Axe

Marketing is no longer about putting an axe in people's heads. It is about carefully taking it out. It is about reuniting our left brain with our right, letting emotions mingle with reason, rejoining our personal lives with our business lives, and working together as consumers and producers to improve the condition of all our lives. The man behind the curtain has been exposed. He knows it and we know it. So now we can all get over it and move on.

Perception is everything. And the Web is where perceptions are now traded. Companies like GretagMacbeth, FreshDirect, Lands' End, QVC, and many others are using the Web to market without offense by developing new ideas, asking permission, sharing information, and making access and action easy. They are providing mutually beneficial locations with multiple points for activity and continuous conversation. They are integrating systems with people for the benefit of people. And in the process they are also making money.

Increasing Returns

During the nineties it seemed that everyone learned the language of finance. As the stock market soared, American cab drivers barely able to speak English were heard on their cell phones discussing investments. Bartenders talked with their beer-drinking patrons about spectacular market returns. The acronym ROI moved out of the boardrooms and executive offices of corporate headquarters into the living rooms, dens, and street corners of the country.

Now three years after the market crash many are still waiting for the next big thing; the "killer app" in technology, biochemistry, telecommunications, and energy—there must be something. Meanwhile the very concept of return on investment has shifted. It is no longer strictly about financial gain, and has not been for some time. As we shall see, there are other ways to measure returns, to create increasing returns, and to realize more valuable returns. There are now multiple "economic" viewpoints. This does not mean that money is no longer important. Designers, like everyone else, still need to get paid.

And they will. The discussion that follows touches on machines getting smarter, the world getting smaller, processing power continuing to increase, *communications moving even faster, and the role of design growing exponentially. There are also some general guidelines for current Web site costs, the language of proposal requests, and ways to look at possible returns for business. Designers who keep up with these continuing changes in technology, business, language, personal creativity, and global interaction become more important and more valuable to their clients.*

We will discover that the role of our business language is beginning—ever so slightly—to change. Avoiding the traps of design-speak, biz-speak, and tech-talk adds to our credibility and broadens our perspective. To help align our communications with humanity's conscience, we must acknowledge both the importance of globalization and the risk of a singular American point of view. And adopting some basic technology parameters while following universal, human principles, just may lead us to a new, golden era of design.

23

Faster, Better, Cheaper

Every time I hear "faster, better, cheaper," it gives me the willies. I actually feel my heart pumping, my blood running faster. I get jumpy and nervous and irritable. The difficulty I experience is because this phrase is so often interpreted to mean; "fast and cheap, and that's better." There is a huge difference. Without quality, fast and cheap is mere clutter.

Too many Web sites still look and work as if the companies they represent believe that fast and cheap is best. Most successful Web sites, like successful companies, reflect the knowledge that reducing cost and time are critical, but not at the sacrifice of quality—quality of products, service, and purpose. Speaking to this issue in relationship to his suppliers, Lands' End president Richard Anderson says, "We customarily say to them, 'What can we add to this product to make it better?' This is a far more welcome question to good suppliers than the one they more frequently hear: 'What can we eliminate from this product to make it cheaper?' It invites them to do their best and they appreciate the chance to do so."[1] This is true of most people; they want to do their best. They want to make a contribution, and to be proud of their work.

But they also want things fast. And companies want, and need, to reduce their costs. Everyone today is in the business of managing speed, quality, and price. All three are closely connected to our economic, social, and psychological well-being. As we shall see in the following sections, achieving high marks in all three is not only increasingly important, it is increasingly possible.

The Need for Speed

"No matter how fast a movie goes these days—or a situation comedy, a newscast, a music video, or a television commercial—it is not fast enough," James Gleick says in his book *Faster*. ". . . the viewer at every instant is in a hurry. That's *you* pressing the gas pedal. Give you a full second of blank screen, and your thumb starts to squeeze the change-channel button . . . ."[2]

It is amazing how much our minds can absorb in a split second. How hungry we seem to be for speed, for motion, for entertainment. We have a nearly unquenchable thirst for sensual stimulation. "Speed is the form of ecstasy the technical revolution has bestowed on man," says novelist Milam Kundera. Yet the Web, by comparison to movies and television, seems slow and clunky. The five to ten seconds we wait for a download is unbearable. As a result, businesses and computer users at home are opting for faster connection speeds.

In January, Nielson/Netratings released a report that Internet users accessing the Web via a broadband connection in December 2002 increased by nearly 60 percent from a year earlier; meanwhile, people logging on through a slower dial-up connection declined by 10 percent. It is not surprising that the increased importance of connection speed is attributed to the shift in content from predominantly text and static graphics to streaming video and other motion graphics. After all, this has become our popular language. We have been building and sharing it now for over fifty years, and we are finally growing accustomed to its influence.

"We have learned a visual language made up of images and movements instead of words and syllables," Gleick says. "It has its own grammar, abbreviations, clichés, lies, puns, and famous quotations. Masters of this language are the artist and technicians, Muybridge descendants, who create trailers for movies and thirty-second commercials and promotional montages of film clippings. And we in their audiences are masters, too, understanding the most convoluted syntax at a speed that would formerly have been blinding . . . . We absorb information in volume, with true virtuosity."

And it's a good thing, because the increase in information we have seen so far is nothing compared to what's coming. Industry estimates are that the total amount of information in the world will double every two to three years. Fortunately our technological processing power has been doubling at a slightly faster rate. Moore's Law (every eighteen months, processing power doubles while cost holds constant) has held remarkably constant for over thirty years. And new developments in chip technology, computing architecture, and software and system design indicate it will hold for at least another fifteen years. Recent developments in molecular electronics are leading some forecasters to suggest that it may continue for another fifty years. Biological computing is becoming a reality. DNA chips have been available in labs since 1996, and a DNA computer for commercial lease was not far behind.

IBM and other leading computing companies have introduced the concepts of self-configuration, self-protection, self-healing, and self-optimizing to computers. These systems have millions of lines of code built in to provide a certain level of intelligence. The vision shared by many in the industry, "is that currently disconnected applications and Web sites will automatically share information and transactions without human intervention. For individual consumers, a typical scenario might be a hotel rental or car reservation being automatically modified according to an airline itinerary."[3]

The Net Effect

The idea of currently disconnected applications and Web sites automatically sharing information has terrific potential for increasing speed or saving time, and for reducing costs, but it requires vigilant attention by designers. Transactions without human intervention will be terrific only if they meet the human need. While recently planning a trip to the Thousand Islands area on the St. Lawrence River, I went to Expedia.com to book a flight into Syracuse, New York, and rent a car to drive north. Booking the flight was no problem but reserving a car could only be done in combination with reserving a hotel room in Syracuse. This is dumb. I did not plan to stay in Syracuse. This has nothing to do with technology. The technology required for my requested transaction is available, but in this case, it is being used for the wrong purpose. It is being driven by a business decision that does not correspond to my need.

All Web designers should understand the premise of Web services, the unfortunately confusing name that has been given to the new but rapidly growing application-to-application communication technology. It is essentially a metalanguage: an XML envelope that wraps around HTML to become a self-describing component that can locate and engage other self-describing components (other Web Services) to carryout complex transactions. Application-to-application communication has been technically feasible for some time but has been limited by the proprietary languages of individual applications. Web services change this. They are not services so much as they are standards, offering a common language to describe how data is structured, and providing protocols defining how applications can make and respond to requests from other applications.

Web services will grow rapidly over the next few years as more and more devices connected to the Web become available. Transactions between a service company and the user of that service will be transformed as applications find, connect, and communicate with one another, on their own. If designed to meet not only the application need, but also the human need, this advancing technology is what will allow us to thrive in the expanding sea of information.

Another technology that may be a big help is holographic data storage. This is a theory that has been around for almost forty years and is now becoming reality. The idea is that storing data in three dimensions rather than in two, which is the way data is currently stored, will make storage devices far more efficient. "Theoretical calculations suggest that it will be possible to use holographic techniques to store a terabyte (1,000 gigabytes) of data on a CD-sized disk. Today's DVDs, by comparison, have a storage capacity of less than twenty gigabytes."[4] Data retrieval speeds will also be much faster (approximately sixty times faster than current DVDs) allowing for quicker sifting through huge amounts of information to find useful relationships.

The difficulty with holographic memory has been finding the right photosensitive substance for recording the data. Many companies have been addressing this problem including IBM, which has a number of promising "test platforms" in research; Aprilis, a company in Maynard, Massachusetts, that expects to have a two hundred gigabyte product available in 2005; and Prolight Technologies, a company in Cambridge, England, which plans to launch the first product to use holographic technology—a disk of five hundred gigabyte capacity—in 2004.

Another tool in the works that will bear on our speed and survival is the Electronic Product Code (EPC). The Auto-ID Center, a nonprofit global research organization headquartered at MIT, has estimated EPC technology could be commercially applied by 2005, at least in niche applications. The EPC is similar to (but will probably not replace for several years) the Universal Product Code (UPC), the bar code seen on nearly all products. The idea behind EPC is to allow computers, using a Radio Frequency ID system (RFID), to identify any object, anywhere, instantly without human intervention. For example, any shelf or container could also be an EPC reader, and automatically know what it contains. The checkout clerk at a store will no longer have to hand-scan individual items.

Tiny tracking devices using RFID tags will soon be powerful and cheap enough to be used nearly everywhere. In 2001, John Patrick, former vice president of Internet technology at IBM, said in the next five to ten years we will likely see one hundred times more speed and one thousand times more connected devices when we use the Internet. Meanwhile, Forrester Research has predicted 14 billion devices will be connected to the Internet by 2010. This is an incredibly expanding opportunity for designers—all designers. And if we design our objectives, our connections, our interfaces, and our presentations well, the speed of the systems just might allow us to slow down and smell the flowers.

Competing on Quality

Just a few years before Arthur Andersen imploded in 2002, two harried executives from Andersen's Business Consulting group in Amsterdam decided they had had enough of the relentless pressure of corporate life. Pim Bouwman, in charge of change management with the firm, and Olivier Meltzer who headed a strategy group, were vacationing together in Tuscany, watching the old men of the village gathering for coffee and talk, when they decided to quit Andersen and build better lives for themselves and their families.

In 1999, after teaming up with Paul Duurland and gardening designer Jacqueline van der Kloet, one of the premier tulip experts in the Netherlands, they created TulipWorld.com, now the fastest-growing online shop for Dutch flower bulbs.

The Dutch flower bulb is the quintessential product of the Netherlands. Approximately seven million of them are exported each year and nearly half go to American gardeners. But the bulbs most gardeners get from American retailers, such as Home Depot and Wal-Mart or through mail-order bulb companies, are often small and poor quality. This is the opportunity the founders of TulipWorld discovered and exploited. "Unlike giant retailers, we know that bulbs aren't a commodity," Meltzer explained. "They are a product of nature, and there's an enormous difference in quality and size. In a typical U.S. warehouse, sellers just don't care. So suppliers deliver smaller bulbs at lower quality because retailers want the cheapest of the cheap."[5]

From the beginning, the focus of TulipWorld has been on quality. Its bulbs are grown by small, specialized growers offering unique species found only in Holland. They offer great prices because they don't spend money printing and mailing catalogs. And they focus on the gardener. The Web site reflects this focus on quality. It is so rich in easily accessible information it is like having your own personal gardener to advise you. And so colorful it almost feels like a garden itself. It is filled with high quality photographs, extensive information on planting, storing and caring for bulbs, and a garden-style advisor wizard that helps visitors select flower colors or play with harmonies and contrast around primary garden colors when designing a garden.

TulipWorld's approach to marketing is similar to its take on business; it's all about partnering to improve the quality of life. The company joined forces with the National Family Partnership, an American nonprofit organization, to provide red tulip bulbs for schoolchildren to plant during Red Ribbon Week. TulipWorld provided 500,000 bulbs in 2002 and in return gained access to 70,000 email addresses. It then donated a portion of the proceeds to NFP's drug-education programs.

Focusing on quality—of product, knowledge, Web site experience, and people's lives—has helped grow TulipWorld's business and its reputation. "TulipWorld is not just another pretty online catalog," the reviewer from *Plant & Garden* cheered, "This is online merchandising at its very best."[6]

Expanding with Quality

Italy has long been known as a center of design excellence, from fashion and art to furniture and architecture. It is also a country where family tradition is important—and the Pianezza family is one of its textile design dynasties. Located in the Lake Como area, they have been passionate about quality for years, as they supplied fabrics and textile design for such well-known and demanding labels as Versace, Armani, and Gucci.

In 1999, Paolo Pianezza saw an opportunity to extend his business by using the personalization technologies of the Web to custom-design products for individuals. He owned thousands of magnificent textile patterns, collected over the years, some passed down from his grand-father who started the business in the late 1800s. And he had developed an innovative method of inscribing messages onto the silk, discreetly along the hem of a scarf or the back of a tie. All that was required was a database of patterns and a method by which customers could select or specify what they wanted. ". . . but it needs to be well designed," Paolo exclaimed in the planning stages of his concept. "People need to see what they are buying, they need to be able to find and feel the quality of our work."

This was the birth of Baldoria.com, an Internet store that provides luxury accessories—scarves, ties, and foulards—hand-sewn from the finest Italian silk. The site is a visually rich environment of color, texture, pattern, and personal assistance. As Christina Stubbs reported in *Red Herring*, "The Baldoria Web site is a beautifully designed electronic version of a salon, complete with a virtual assistant named Andrea. Customers can select swatches and have products monogrammed; Andrea will suggest matching shirts and make gift recommendations."[7]

The Andrea wizard also tracks the visitor's pattern browsing history, placing selected patterns on the side, much like an in-store assistant at a fashion salon might place selected items on a table for final review before purchase. Andrea will also assist the store visitor with the language to be inscribed as a personal message. Each item is then handmade by the designers in Como. As the Web site says, "In Baldoria, the item you choose does not exist until you create it." And when it is delivered direct from Como two weeks later (free of all delivery charges), the packaging is as special as the product. Each item is hand-wrapped onto wooden spindles and inserted into silver metal canisters, which are then encased in cardboard tubes to insure that the fabric is as fresh when received as when it leaves the factory.

Similar to TulipWorld, Pianezza launched its online business just as the dot.com world imploded, but they survived, even thrived, because of their focus on quality, selling online products primarily to American and Japanese markets. In early 2001, Baldoria added a limited-edition collection to its site including cashmere scarves for men, and skirts and tops for women. And the following year the Pianezza family exhibited their first line of women's clothing, offline, under their own label in the fashionable showrooms of Milan.

Quality of Life

"I've always been the type of person who holds onto things . . . "[8] artist John Freyer begins his book *All My Life for Sale*. The book, published in late 2002, is just one result of a project Freyer started two years earlier in an attempt to simplify his life by getting rid of things.

Returning to the University of Iowa where he was a graduate student in August 2000, Freyer found his house overflowing with stuff; miscellaneous stuff he had accumulated in the previous year on the streets and in the flea markets of Iowa City. He felt trapped by the things he owned and determined to sell what he didn't need, pack the remaining things that would fit into the trunk of his car and move back to New York.

After selling a few items on the Internet auction eBay, he decided it would be interesting if he had his own dot.com where he could design an online catalog. A search for available domain names having to do with sales ultimately resulted in the name: allmylifeforsale.com. Freyer invited friends to a party at his house to help him label and price all of his possessions, then he began the process of writing descriptive text, photographing, and posting six hundred items to his Web site which linked to eBay for bidding. And people bid, and bought: his toothbrush, half-a-bottle of mouthwash, a plastic toy Cadillac, a box of taco shells, old comic books, nearly all of his clothes, un-opened Christmas presents for his parents, even his shaved sideburns in a plastic bag. Simon Garfield, a reviewer for the *Sunday London Observer*, said ". . . it soon became clear to those reading his sales-pitches that he was selling something other than just his belongings: himself. Freyer was cleansing his soul as well as his apartment, the ultimate consumer's detox.

His pure project had several messages: everything in life is for sale; every object is useful to someone; spent objects can be reborn; the Internet is the best shop in the world."[9]

But it was even more than that. People not only bought, they began to send notes and John Freyer responded. By late August 2001, he had sold nearly everything he had and decided that it would be nice to meet some of the people with whom he was corresponding and revisit some of his things in their new homes. He set off for Portland, Maine, to visit his saltshaker, and spent the next three months traveling across the country meeting and staying with the purchasers of his stuff, posting photographs and commentary to the Web as he traveled. This soon became the book, which Winda Benedetti, a reporter for the *Seattle Post-Intelligencer*, captured well in the following comment: "In a culture that encourages—no, celebrates—consumption on a massive scale, *All My Life for Sale* is a refreshing look not so much at the things we own but at the stories that attach themselves to those things . . . and the new stories that develop when you let them go."[10]

Freyer realized that the sale of his things on the Internet did more than give him the freedom he originally sought. "In fact," he says, "I no longer wanted to escape . . . I no longer wanted to move to New York. I now know that it is possible to engage the broader culture from somewhere besides the big city." He had designed and sold his book, sold the movie rights in late 2002, his Website is now owned by the University of Iowa Museum of Art, one of his chairs is in the Museum of Modern Art, his bag of Porky's BBQ Pork Skins is in Japan, and he has an enormous community of networked people who share his sense of a quality life.

The Bargain

The increasing connections and communication speed brought about by technology, and the ability to improve the quality of products, services and the excitement of life, all offer possibilities to interaction designers. They also go hand-in-hand with reducing business costs, which designers need to understand. Seeing how reduced costs fits with increasing speed and quality—grasping the real implications of faster, better, cheaper—or increasing returns, requires an understanding of exponential growth, which is what Moore's law is all about.

There is an old fable about a king, a peasant, and a chessboard, which may be used to explain the concept. In this story, the king is indebted to the peasant for saving his life and asked the peasant what he would like for a reward. The peasant responds that he would simply like one grain of rice on the first square of his chessboard and then twice as many grains on each succeeding square. The king is so struck by the apparent simplicity of the request that he immediately agrees.

Only after the kings' assistants had filled the twentieth square with rice did the king realize his mistake. The first fifteen squares were relatively easy to fill, requiring only a few bags of rice. The next five squares required multiple bags, and by the time the twenty-eighth square was reached, it required an entire room filled with rice. (This is approximately how many times computer processing power has doubled since Moore introduced his law in 1965.) To fill the last square, the sixty-fourth, would require rice grains represented by a two followed by nineteen zeros. This has been estimated to require the entire surface of the earth to produce and would weigh approximately 100 billion tons. This is the way exponential growth works. It is nearly beyond comprehension. Which is why Economist Paul Romer says, "We consistently fail to grasp how many ideas remain to be discovered. . . . Possibilities do not add up. They multiply."

In eighteenth-century America, at the height of the agrarian economy, more than 80 percent of the workforce was involved in farm labor. "Today, less than 3 percent of the population work on farms."[11] Yet we produce more food for more people at less cost than ever before. This is an example of increasing returns. We are producing more and distributing more with less effort because of the multiplying technological possibilities.

We haven't gotten it all right yet. The quality of some of the food is still suspect. There is huge waste, and there are far too many people on this earth who are starving, or living in abysmal conditions without the basic requirements to sustain life. This, however, is not a technology problem. It is not even a problem of priorities. Virtually everyone who thinks agrees that these problems urgently need to be solved, and that we have the technological and economic knowledge, capacity, and resources to do so. The problem is communications. It is systemic to businesses, social organizations, and political institutions that are still mired in the mud—the protective, unconnected, corrupt communication models of our past.

The possibilities of improved speed, enhanced quality and reduced costs brought about by network technology are clear. They have been repeatedly demonstrated. The goal now is to bring social, political, and business systems up to speed, to assure that faster and cheaper is actually better, to put the emphasis on quality—on real benefits for people. And this is a design problem. It is a problem of intent. This is where designers who are familiar with the Web, who understand its potential, and who know how to develop for its best use, can make their contribution count. They can help their clients—businesses, nonprofit organizations, financial institutions, government entities—realize how increased speed, reduced costs, and improved quality fit together. All three are now possible and essential, but the real benefits accrue, the returns increase, the possibilities multiply, for those that focus on quality—of communication, of products and services, and of life. This is the "faster, better, cheaper" that can lead to a sustainable future for all people.

24

Economic Possibilities

Just before the beginning of the last century, America took over England as the world's leading manufacturer and shortly afterward the mass production economy began. It took about fifty years for this to shift to the consumer economy, and another twenty before we realized it was really a service economy, and we could no longer add and subtract the cost of widgets to determine our profitability.

Fifteen years later we became an information economy and spread our new currency to many other countries. It took only ten years after that for the network economy—where connections are more important than information—to explode around the world. And, in the last five years we have created at least five additional views of the economy:

1. *The Experience Economy.* Goods, services, information, even connections become commodities, and value is determined by experience.
2. *The Entertainment Economy.* All commodities gain value relative to their entertainment quotient.
3. *The Creative Economy.* New ideas from creative people in creative communities equal increased value.
4. *The Hydrogen Economy.* Hydrogen will replace fossil fuel to create the first global democratic energy regime.
5. *The Support Economy.* We move from transaction to relationship economics, from "managerial capitalism" to "distributed capitalism."

The growing rate of new economic possibilities is mind-boggling. I'm sure there are many more than what I have listed and others with which I am not familiar. My landlord is not familiar with them either.

He still expects money for the rent. And my bank expects money for the mortgage. All of the designers I know want money for their services, and our clients expect to make money from their businesses. Although there are many new ways to look at value, particularly as it relates to our expanding knowledge brought about by the Web, most companies are still dealing in dollars.

At least that is where they begin.

What Will It Cost?

What will it cost? is always one of the early questions asked of a Web designer. It can only be answered by the designer asking a number of other questions. The simplest of these questions is: What are you willing to spend? This is rarely known. Even when there is a budget number allocated it is often incorrect because the people who established the budget frequently do not really know what they want to accomplish. As mentioned earlier, this is the single most important question: What are you trying to accomplish? And it is not easy to answer.

Many companies begin by outlining a Request for Proposal (RFP). This is an important step, but it should not come first. When writing an RFP people often let the "proposal" aspect—the legal, financial, and responsibility issues—cloud their thinking. These are important issues, but only after the company has the overall and detailed business objectives of the initiative clear. Web design consultants can often help companies through this process.

In a recent RFP that I received, the most prominent statement under Web design was: "The Web design should follow current best practices and be open architecture for future expansion and integration." This is really nothing more than a hedge clause, and not a very good one since "best practices" is open to broad interpretation. It would be OK, except that they did not bother to tell me what they wanted to accomplish other than to "redesign" the site. Design is about intent. What's the intent? "To give it a new look and feel" or "incorporate our new identity" are not sound objectives unless your site is already working at 500 percent. Specific, measurable goals for a site redesign should be something like: increase our membership by

30 percent over the next twelve months, deliver 20 percent more leads to our sales team, improve our conversion rate by 5 percent, reduce our administrative costs by 12 percent, etc.

In the same RFP the company made another frequent mistake: using acronyms, "popular language" or software names that are more confusing than clarifying. Under the subtitle "additional responsibilities of supplier" was the statement: "Evaluate and suggest appropriate content management processes and tools for use by our employees after initial set-up." This is not an unreasonable request, but the RFP did not provide any sense of the size of the company, the number of employees who may be involved, or even the departments who would change or provide content. Certainly the details of this are part of the evaluation process, but the basic information is relative to the objectives, and without it a proposed cost is nothing more than a guess.

Today, third-party content management systems (CMS) range in price from $99 for a basic Web site administration tool for a small site to $100,000 and more for managing database content in multiple areas such as product list and prices, press releases, HR benefits, etc. And there are literally hundreds of packages in between.

Besides that, the quality of a number of off-the-shelf CMS tools is highly questionable. In response to the popularity of content management tools, Forrester Research did a "tech ranking" comparison in 2002 of nine products from content management suppliers. The results showed that most could handle Web site administration, but some exhibited "catastrophic deficiencies" when accessing databases, workflow systems, e-mail systems, and ERP applications.

A content system, which provides page templates, is essential for most business sites. To change a navigation label or piece of repeating type that visitors find confusing, is a simple matter with templates. It may take days, even weeks without templates, as each page must be changed by hand. This has tremendous bearing on the cost of original design and development, and maintenance once the site is launched. All the same, companies should not talk about content management systems unless they are very clear about what they want the system to do.

It is preferable for them to talk in terms of specifics: "We want to be able to change the text and images in this area (or these areas) of the site on our own without having to write code." It is also helpful to know the frequency and amount of information that may be changed. If there are hundreds of items, whether images, text blocks, news stories, prices, etc., it is best to handle them in a database. Are they in a database now, or will this need to be created? If the database exists, what's the platform?

Another thing that is helpful to know is the process for specific content development. For example, press releases; do one or two people write and post releases a couple of times a month, or do multiple people pass drafts back and forth with an outside PR firm and then through an internal approval process on a daily basis? If it is the latter, how much of this process do you want online? (The answer to this question should be all.) Administrative tools can be quite simple—cut and paste text into a window and hit a button to make it live—or more complex with various permission levels and approval methodologies built in. And of course, the price will vary accordingly.

The cost of Web site design and development is still truly all over the lot, particularly in a tight economy. As recently as a year ago we bid on a Web redesign project on which four other firms—all from the East Coast—also bid. The RFP was reasonably clear and well written and each of the bidding firms had at least one face-to-face meeting with the prospect, a small public company. The five fixed-fee proposals ranged from $35,000 to $750,000. Something is dreadfully wrong. Clearly, the deliverables here were substantially different, or somebody—either client or design firm—was going to take a bath.

Although clarifying the specifics in RFPs is important, it is even more important in the design firm's proposal. The overall objectives for the design or redesign of the site must be clearly stated up front, with specific business objectives detailed, and clearly stated criteria for success. The methodology of development should be outlined with specific tasks detailed in each phase, and a clear list of deliverables at the conclusion of each phase. There should be a general schedule tied to each phase with greater detail to be added later, and there should be a change-of-scope process outlined. Most companies today request fixed-price proposals. All the more reason why the deliverables need to be detailed.

All of the comments on writing RFPs are the same for designers writing proposals. They should avoid acronyms, and not use popular language or broad terms. For example, the following statement was seen in a recent proposal: "We will add an e-commerce component for the store and include testing it for usability." What does this mean? Would this be a PayPal account which cost nothing to set-up and only takes about five minutes to do, or will this firm work with the prospect company to establish a merchant bank account, which costs more, requires more time and more credit worthiness, but is much more secure? Each of these has their place on the Web, but the statement does not indicate which approach will be provided.

Testing for usability—this is a whole world in itself. There are usability-testing firms that charge from $10,000 to $25,000 for a single session with ten to twelve testers. There are expert site evaluators who charge from $7,500 to $25,000 for their reports. And there are some testing software packages that range from $5,000 to $50,000 a month. And of course there are many testing arrangements shared by the developers, the client, and their friends. (Read Steve Krug's *Don't Make Me Think* to find out more about this.) If the designer is thinking about the last choice but the prospect thinks she is talking about the first choice, someone is going to get hurt.

The most important thing to remember about a proposal is that it's not about "the number." It is about the specific details of the what, how, and when, that the number represents.

What's the Return?

Five years ago everyone was trying to find a way to make money on the Web. Many companies are still trying to figure this out, while many others are making a bundle. The difference in most cases is that the successful ones do not focus on making money. They focus on improving business. This also means improving life. They look for ways in which they can provide their products and services differently—higher quality, less cost, more convenience, and broader choice. They seek new ways to strengthen relationships, extend their reach, customize their offer, and find new opportunities through improved functionality and usability of their Web sites. FreshDirect, EyeOne, LandsEnd.com, TulipWorld, and NMWA are all good examples.

Calculating the return on your Web investment with a traditional ROI formula—increased revenue or decreased cost divided by the cost of the investment—can be done, and it should be calculated in each department within your company. Risks should be analyzed in each area as well. Both ROI and risk should be looked at from an external as well as internal perspective.

This gets difficult because some areas, such as "improved customer relationships," seem hard to quantify. Keep in mind that "return" does not just mean increased sales by customer, and "risk" is not only financial loss from customers. Areas that may be affected by integrating more customer transactions through the Web include: reduced transaction time, reduced need for support, or increased cost of support, reduced training costs, fewer returns, fewer errors on your site, increased delivery costs, reduced call center costs, or increased participation in other areas of the organization. The entire process from solicitation of customers to follow-through after an initial transaction should be reviewed.

The outcome of this will be substantially different from industry to industry and from large operations to small. One advantage smaller businesses have over large ones is they do not have huge antiquated information systems in place. For billion-dollar corporations the integration cost for customer relationship programs and supply chain management systems frequently take three to four years to complete and costs run into the tens of millions of dollars. Smaller organizations can integrate many of their communications operations for under one million dollars, and "Mom and Pop" businesses for a fraction of that.

Keep in mind that this is not about systems. It is about information—how to make information useful and usable by the visitors to your site. A Forrester Research report in June 2001 titled "Get ROI from Design" had the following to say regarding Web usability:

Although companies don't typically measure return on user experience, there is strong connection between design success and business success. When redesigns focus on solving specific business problems, they can:

Boost revenue. By moving its product selection closer to the homepage, Skechers made it easier for customers to begin their top task—shopping for shoes. The changes helped increase holiday sales by more than 400 percent.

Lower support costs. Lucy.com found that improving descriptions and images on product pages meant that users did not have to call or e-mail customer support with simple questions like "What does a shirt look like from the back?" The changes paid off when product-related inquiries dropped by more than 20 percent.

Reduce development waste. Optavia, a usability consulting firm, advised one client to drop an expensive personalization project when early user testing showed that visitors had no interest in customized content.

Affect customer satisfaction. The experience that users have with a site ties directly to customer satisfaction. For example, Amazon let customer service slip in mid-2000. When this happened, Amazon fell behind its competitors in three categories—for the first time.

The return on your investment will ultimately be determined by the way you treat your customers, partners, and employees. Show them respect—provide them what they need, when they need it, in a manner they really like—and the possibilities for continuing returns will be high.

The critical thing for consultant designers to keep in mind when determining cost or figuring out financial returns is that their job is to help their client understand the real values. For example, purchasing an appropriate content management system may cost $25,000. But integrating the system, training to use the system, and the effectiveness of the system itself may cost that much again. Designers need to spend time talking through this with their clients. If there are items or processes that the client thinks are too expensive, detail the benefits in terms of time saved and returns, and provide options that are less expensive, but explain the reasons why. The more knowledge you provide your client, the more valuable you become.

25

The Circle of Language

Have you noticed how everyone is talking faster these days? It's like there is just not enough time to get all the words out, so we speed up our tongues, abbreviate words, and use acronyms for nearly everything in our talk and even more so in our e-mails. As we do so, our language becomes proprietary. Is there really so much to say and so little time that we should risk understanding?

Herbert Simon, economist and behavioral scientist from Carnegie Mellon, says, "A wealth of information creates a poverty of attention." The more data available, the more difficult the focus. This is a central problem of communications design, distilling information to its essence and shaping that to a purpose. In this process, the exclusivity of the language we use and the speed with which we use it is one of the most difficult barriers to overcome. But there are signs that suggest our words are beginning to change and, as we have already seen, visual communication has become far more important. It just may be that design is the metalanguage we need to clarify what is going on, and to lead us to a brighter future.

Just Before Dawn

Tim Sanders, a senior executive at Yahoo! had the nerve to write an article, published in *Fast Company* in February 2002 titled, "Love is the Killer App," in which he says, "The most powerful force in business isn't greed, fear, or even the unbridled force of competition. The most powerful force in business is love." I say he had the nerve to write this because it takes nerve—assurance, strength, fortitude—to use a word like love in the context of business. He goes on to say, "The most profound transformation in business . . . is the downfall of barracudas, sharks, and piranhas and the ascendancy of nice smart people with a passion for what they do." Is this naïve idealism, youthful exuberance? Or is there some underlying truth that Sanders has touched on? The possibility of a change—a major change—in the way business perceives itself?

Granted, this was published just five months after the horror of 9/11, and America was still in a state of extreme emotional shock. All the same, it is a far cry from typical business talk. Where is the macho, the bravado, the steely determinism that has been the voice of business for so long? What happened to *The Art of War*, the bible of many business strategists?

Sanders did not use the acceptable language of business. What he did is like using the language of ballet to talk about football; describing a quarterback *stiff-arming* the opposing tackler as *port de bras*. Or saying a *grande jeté* instead of a *hell-of-a-jump*. The language of football is short, quick, and brusque. The language of ballet, of course, is French, but it is fluid and harmonious. Interestingly, the visual activity of football and ballet is often very similar. Watch a game on television (without the sound) while listening to Chopin and you will notice amazing moments of synchronization.

But the similarities go beyond the visual. Each is an organized team of people, collaborating to carry out specific objectives. They work from detailed plans and the precision and timing of individual movements are critical to the group's success. Yet the labels we use for the activities of each are substantially different. This variance is more important than the differences in the languages of French and English, it has to do with a fundamental difference in the purpose of the activities. Football is competitive. Ballet is cooperative.

The thrust of Sanders' article is about the shift occurring in our understanding of the fundamental purpose of business. The old concepts of crush the competition, screw the supplier, bigger is better, and faster is best no longer hold up. Business has always emphasized competition; today it must focus on cooperation. This does not mean that competition is wrong, over, dead. Competition is a fundamental survival skill; without it we would never have made it back to the cave after our first emergence. But in our increasingly interdependent, networked world the values of cooperation, of partnership, of sharing in business, cannot be denied. To fully embrace this value, requires a change in language.

Aside from the gang of deplorable acronyms used in technology talk, one of the most overused words in business language today is "customer." We are implored to listen to the customer, respond to the customer, embrace the customer, and indeed, there are times we should. But excessive focus on the customer blinds us to new possibilities. Design is not only about listening to the customer. It is about knowing when to listen and when to act—when to make subjective decisions and when to make decisions based on sustaining visual, technical, economic, or ethical integrity. To preserve the integrity of strategic business initiatives, management must sometimes do unmanagement-like things.

"Good management was the most powerful reason [leading firms] failed to stay atop their industries," Clayton Christensen says in *The Innovator's Dilemma.* "Precisely because these firms listened to their customers, invested aggressively in technologies that would provide customers more and better products of the sort they wanted, and because they carefully studied market trends and systematically allocated investment capital to innovations that promised the best returns, they lost their positions of leadership."[1] For consultant designers this is particularly important. Customers often do not know what they want, much less what they need. Because of the pressure for speed we are all inclined to make quick decisions and settle for "good enough." But designers have an obligation to themselves and their clients to speak up when good enough is just not good enough.

"I don't know" is another piece of language that needs to change. It needs to be used more frequently. In the past, this phrase was unacceptable in business. You were supposed to know, to have done the research, to have the facts. The work must still be done, but even when you have all the facts, you often don't know. The good news is, that's OK. Not knowing opens up a world of new possibilities.

Many business people do not know what design is. They do not really understand what they are requesting from a design firm. Steve Jobs says, "We don't have a good language to talk about this kind of thing. In most people's vocabularies, design means veneer . . . . But to me, nothing could be further from the meaning of design. Design is the fundamental soul of a man-made creation."[2] In design for business, the languages of line, form, color, typography, and texture are like the language of love. They often shatter the bounds of business reason, but they can make the human spirit soar.

Designers have an obligation to help their customers understand the meaning and value of design and in order to do so, they must stop themselves from using popular biz-talk when it makes no sense. Phrases like "owning the customer," "customer centricity," and "using best practices," should be deleted from the business language database. They are vague, sweeping generalizations that contribute nothing to people's understanding.

In connection with the problem of language, philologist Wilhelm von Humboldt has stated, "Man lives with his objects chiefly—in fact, since his feeling and acting depends on his perceptions, one may say exclusively—as language presents them to him. By the same process whereby he spins language out of his own being, he ensnares himself in it; and each language draws a magic circle round the people to which it belongs, a circle from which there is no escape save by stepping out of it into another."[3]

The language in a room full of doctors is different from the language in a room full of lawyers, or a room full of anthropologists, or car salesmen, young mothers, marketing managers, designers, programmers, impoverished children, or wealthy executives. Each is caught up in the language of its own world. Like the light from campfires scattered along the beach on a cool night, each group huddles close to the warmth of familiarity. Each reinforces its own condition, its optimism, its language by telling its own stories. Each group is nearly oblivious, only slightly concerned with the distant glow of neighboring fires. At dawn we will see the similarities, the universal traits of the human condition.

"We are in the twilight of a society based on data," Rolf Jensen says. "As information and intelligence become the domain of computers, society will place more value on the one human ability that cannot be automated: emotion. Imagination, myth, ritual—the language of emotion—will affect everything from our purchasing decisions to how we work with others."[4] More importantly it will affect how successful we all are with our lives.

Tim Sanders, like the authors of *The Cluetrain Manifesto*, and the signers of *First Things First* 2000, has stepped out of his circle. He escaped the snare of business language, tech-talk, and design-speak and stepped into the larger circle of human concerns. By daring to call the word "love" a killer app and emphasizing "nice people" in business, he has signaled a shift toward the inclusion of emotional concerns in business decisions. This does not mean that we all need to start getting sappy, teary-eyed, or overly sentimental, but with some effort we may finally achieve an appropriate balance, and thereby expand our circle to include many more.

Design as a Metalanguage

Looking at almost any Apple product we begin to understand Steve Jobs' comment, "Design is the fundamental soul of a man-made creation." What is that gut feeling we have when we look at the new Power Mac or the iMac or iPod that makes us want to touch it, to pick it up, to own it, or to just continue looking at it? It sounds almost too simple, but it is design. Then how do we explain the difference between the design of the Apple products and the design of intricate sixteenth-century Turkish tiles from the Ottoman empire; or the design of brilliantly patterned wooden animals from Oaxaca, Mexico; or the colorful beaded dolls from the coast of New Guinea; or the design of the Opera House in Sydney, Australia; each of which can produce similar gut reactions, yet each is substantially different in line, form, color, and materials?

It is not the singular quality of line, or form, or color in the Apple products or the Turkish tiles, or in any product or message for that matter, which we respond to. It is the totality of these elements—the way line, form, color, texture, pattern, purpose and meaning all fit together—that creates a whole far superior to the sum of its parts. Design is a holistic language that speaks not just to emotion or just to reason, but to both sides of the human brain.

Like Web services, the new metalanguage—a transformative language about language—which allows computers to speak to one another, design may be thought of as the metalanguage for humans, one which speaks more clearly, more universally, more comprehensively than any other language we have. A language that may be used effectively on the Web to help us cross borders, not create them. A language that may help us preserve cultural characteristics while sharing universal concerns. By thinking of design as the metalanguage of humans, the circle of language on the Web can be expanded to include everyone.

26

Golden Music

Shortly after 9/11, the Poynter Institute, a school in St. Petersburg, Florida that teaches skills and ethics to professional journalists, posted a notice on its Web site inviting news editors who design front pages to send an electronic copy of how they told the 9/11 story. In one day, hundreds of front pages from all around the world were recorded on the Poynter site. From Appleton, Wisconsin, to Göteborg, Sweden, from Madrid to Lisbon to Sydney, Australia, to Chennai, India, and Cebu City, Philippines, the images and the words are very similar and all are dated 9/11 or 9/12. An event that happened here was reported visually and verbally in print around the world in less than twenty-four hours.

Since then our world has gotten even smaller and faster. It is unquestionable that we are now living in the global village. For the first time, we are beginning to *see* the global society. This represents enormous opportunity and responsibility for designers. As we shall see, both begin by understanding and abiding by the rules of global citizenship. This requires cautious use of the increasingly popular word globalization, which is already tainted with an unmistakable American ring. It is perceived by many as the Americanization of the world, and many countries and people are not interested.

Communication between people is the essence of human society. It is the lifeblood of all business, institutions, social organizations, and local and global governments. But when the communication needs of individual organizations or businesses or governments take precedence over the human need—when they are out of sync with humanity's conscience—they eventually disappear. Darwinian principles prevail. Life clings to what works.

Removing the Straitjacket

In Thomas Friedman's bestselling treatise on globalization, *The Lexus and the Olive Tree*, he proposed names for three major forces that have been shaping our world for the past thirty years and have become critically important to the survival and future prosperity of countries, companies, and individuals. The three names are the "Golden Straitjacket," the "Electronic Herd," and the "Microchip Immune Deficiency Syndrome or MIDS." Although the names he created and the thesis that supports them are fascinating, he exhibits a frightening bias toward the Americanization of the world and the importance of mega-corporations and institutions.

Two of the three premises Friedman proposes deserve expansion and at least one of those requires a better name. The third—Microchip Immune Deficiency Syndrome—is the most on-target. This is the name for a disease which he suggests was responsible for the collapse, or the radical restructuring, of a number of countries as well as companies, all at approximately the same time, including IBM, General Motors, East Germany, the Soviet Union, Asian capitalism, Chinese communism, and Brazilian state-owned industries.

Friedman says that MIDS is the "defining political disease of the globalization era." The name itself is less important than the appropriateness of a biological metaphor to discuss what we generally think of as independent economic, technological, political, or managerial problems. These are no longer stand-alone or even stand-apart issues. They have not been for years. They are intimately connected, and that is exactly his point. They are part of the complex network of information-porting veins that feed and monitor and adjust a growing global organism. Friedman mistakenly suggests that companies and countries must "inoculate themselves against changes brought about by the microchip, and the democratizations of technology, finance and information."

Following are Friedman's indications of MIDS to be on the lookout for: The symptoms of Microchip Immune Deficiency appear when your country or company exhibits a consistent inability to increase productivity, wages, living standards, knowledge use, and competitiveness, and becomes too slow to respond to the challenges of the Fast World. Countries and companies with MIDS tend to be those run on Cold War corporate models—where one or a few people at the top hold all the information and make all the decisions, and all the people in the middle and the bottom simply carry out those decisions, using only the information they need to know to do their jobs.[1]

The *Boston Globe* on September 30, 2001, reported the following, "In an era when terrorists use satellite phones and encrypted e-mail, U.S. gatekeepers stand armed against them with pencils and paperwork, and archaic computer systems that don't talk to each other." This sounds like a serious example of MIDS in America. This disease is apparently just as real as SARS (Severe Acute Respiratory Syndrome). America needed to go back for additional shots.

Since 9/11 we made extensive upgrades and changes to at least some American systems and policies as evidenced by the televised "shock and awe" presentation of the war on Iraq, but we have barely begun to understand the breadth and depth of changes that still need to occur. Friedman places little emphasis on the "fourth democratization," which is the cure for MIDS. This is the redistribution of power, the decentralization of information control, and the sharing of information and systems with all people. This may be best explained by looking at Friedman's limited view of the Electronic Herd. He defines the herd as "all the faceless stock, bond and currency traders sitting behind computer screens, moving money around with the click of a mouse from mutual funds to pension funds to emerging market funds, or trading from their basements on the Internet."

In actuality, the herd is much larger today, is moving much more than money, and it is not just the currency and pension fund traders (which Friedman calls shorthorn cattle) or the multinationals involved in direct foreign trade, (longhorn cattle) or the entrenched leaders of government. Yes, these exist and they are major forces, but what the fourth democratization is about is giving the power of information to ordinary people. People like Jonathan Lebed and Marcus Arnold, and Rey Ramsey, David Prendergast, and Rajeswari Pingali. The herd is comprised of all the Lands' Ends, Kimcos, NMWAs, GretagMacbeths, FreshDirects as well as the Joe Fedeles, Pim Bouwmans, Olivier Meltzers, Paul Duurlands, Jacqueline van der Kloets, the Pianezza families, John Freyers, and literally millions more. It is you, the Web designer.

It is not longhorn or shorthorn cattle. It is people. People moving alone or in small groups but swelling to an occasion that demands a response. People who want a good life, and want others to have one, too. An example of the power of the network, or the herd, is the $10 million that was raised in two weeks of 2003 for Presidential candidate, Howard Dean. This was accomplished through Meetup.com; a relatively new site that takes an interesting twist on the approach to community building. It does not have a community as such on the Web; rather it is a service that helps people get together off the Web.

Using an advanced technology platform and a global network of local venues, Meetup helps people self-organize local group gatherings on the same day in multiple locations. From politicians to soccer moms, poker players to beagle lovers, Meetups can happen in up to 580 cities in forty-two countries (at this writing) in local cafés, restaurants, bookstores, and other local establishments. This is a free online service and they have nearly 500,000 people signed up for over 1,300 topics. This is the fourth democratization in practice.

The last Friedman name is his worst. "The Golden Straitjacket is the defining political-economic garment of this globalization era," Friedman says. To wear this jacket, a country or company must adopt or show solid evidence that it is moving toward adoption, of a number of free-market rules, most of which seem fine—shrinking bureaucracies, balanced budgets, privatizing state-owned industries, opening banking and telecommunications systems to private ownership—although Friedman does not define how all of this may be evaluated.

The concept is the tighter you wear the jacket—meaning the better you adhere to the rules—the more gold you produce. There are two things wrong here. First, no one—*no one*—wants to wear a straitjacket. Any group of people trying to accomplish something certainly need a common goal, general guidelines, and some underlying principles about how to achieve the goal. As groups get larger the guidelines become rules and the rules in governed societies become laws. But putting on a straitjacket, even if it is pure gold, suggests you are going to prison or an asylum. No one wants to do either.

The second problem is worse. "Once your country puts on the Golden Straitjacket," Friedman says, "its political choices get reduced to Pepsi or Coke—to slight nuances of taste, slight nuances of policy, slight alterations in design to account for local traditions, some loosening here or there, but never any major deviation from core golden rules." My god, this is a prison. We will all be wearing the same gold striped straitjackets. No, it's worse than prison. This is putting on a burial robe. There is no creative spirit left, no room for initiative, no space for dreams, all human desire has been extracted. Certainly, there are alternatives.

Jamming

Watching a small group of musicians at a jam session or improv performance is always amazing to me. The way they communicate with one another while playing—with a nod, a tipping of their instrument, or just a glance. They pass the lead from one performer to another and another, and then soften the tempo of one group while another takes off with a long riff. Another musician may arrive, make a few instrument adjustments and fit right into the flow. They move the rhythms and harmonies and melodies along, around, and back and forth, building to a final crescendo or breaking into separate paths, seemingly without effort.

Of course, there is effort. There is musical knowledge and experience, or a musical sense within each of the performers. Though many great musicians don't read musical notation, each performer can feel the vibes of the others and of the group, and tune his performance as he plays. What makes a good jam session great is the love the players have for what they are doing. Sure it's work, but you can tell when they are really having fun.

Walter Thompson, a musician, composer, and conductor, leads improv performances with large groups of musicians, as well as dancers, actors, poets, and visual artists all working in what Thompson calls structured improvisations or, sound paintings. This started about twenty years ago when he began developing specific communication gestures for various musical activities. His sound painting has evolved into a system of over 700 gestures with which music, theatre, dance, and film scores can be realized spontaneously. When all of the performers are on, a Thompson jamming performance can be stunning.

The language of music—of jamming—is like the language of design; it goes where words cannot reach. Jamming is the way the electronic herd really works on the Internet. It is individual players "feeling" one another out. Sure, there are business players, and there are huge institutional and government players too, and there are increasing numbers of automated systems which are sensing other systems and responding to the system and to peoples' needs. But jamming is what we are all doing. It is still pretty crude, often downright ugly, but we are learning. Some may yearn for a Walter Thompson-type conductor, but this is one point on which Friedman is correct, there is no conductor for the network. There is no leader. No one is in charge. It is up to each of us—as individuals, small groups, businesses, and large institutions. We get into the swing, follow the lead, take the lead and pass the lead along.

We do not have to put on a straitjacket, adorn a prescribed uniform, or move in unison. Yes, we need to understand some basics, and then we just have to jam with our ideas, voices, images, numbers, music, and motion. Some of this will be about understanding markets, or selling products, services, or ideas. Other parts will be about solving communications problems, business problems, institutional problems, government problems, and people's problems. All of it is about solving design problems, about agreeing on intent and moving in unison toward it.

Many designers love to refer to themselves as problem solvers, and often they are. But so is everyone else. My building superintendent is the best problem solver I know, I call him in the morning when my faucet has dripped through the night. When I return in the evening the problem is solved. Rarely do I dwell on which magical tool, what method, whose process or which best practice he may have used. My dentist, lawyer, accountant, wife, and my children are problem solvers too. They are also problem creators, but that's another story.

Designers—all of us—do more than solve problems. We are dreamers, tinkerers, fiddlers, dabblers, putterers, inventors, explorers, myth-breakers, and language-makers. Likewise, the Web is more than a problem solution. It is more than a store to sell products, a medium in which we communicate, a system for collecting and storing data, more than a repository of all the facts and figures that comprise our history, and more than the tsunami of additional data we will soon face. It is all of these things and still more. It is a jamming arena.

A marketplace of perceptions. The central nervous system of a global organism. A space in which we increase our capacity to dream, explore, tinker, fiddle, dabble, putter, create, and destroy.

If we adhere to a few functional rules, cooperative development of open tools, and interoperability standards, and we uphold the global human right to equality, honesty, courtesy, respect, and responsibility, then we get to participate in the creation of golden music which just may allow us—all of us—to reach unimaginable levels of creative, economic, and human prosperity.

The global opportunities for Web designers are abundant and the responsibilities are clear. Participation in forming and following the rules of global citizenship is up to each of us. Ultimately, the Web we design will reflect the balance we achieve between freedom and authority; private ownership and public good; local and global control; institutional and individual need; technical and human growth. It will transport the lifeblood of human society. The problems may yet be substantial, but the prizes may well be invaluable.

In the *Power of Myth*, Joseph Campbell tells a wonderful story of the time he was in Japan for an international conference on religion. He overheard another American delegate, a social philosopher from New York, say to a Shinto priest "We've been now to a good many ceremonies and have seen quite a few of your shrines. But I don't get your ideology. I don't get your theology." The Japanese priest paused as though in deep thought and then slowly shook his head. "I think we don't have ideology," he said. "We don't have theology. We dance."[2]

And so it is with Web designers, all of us—interface or interaction designers, experience or functional designers, business and government designers. Before the fiddlers flee, while there's still time for romance, we must crank up the music and dance.

Resources

The real business of Web design can best be learned by using the Web. It is rich with practical, educational, and inspirational resources. Following is a short list of starting points for information on Web standards, interaction design, functional development, usability, and business use.

Web Standards
World Wide Web Consortium
www.w3.org

Created in 1994 to promote interoperability and an open forum for discussion about the future of the Web, this is the primary membership organization establishing the standards and guiding the design and development of the Web.

Web Standards
www.webstandards.org

The Web Standards Project (WaSP) is a grassroots organization founded in 1998 to promote core Web standards and encourage browser makers to do the same. The goal is to ensure simple, affordable access for all people.

Web Services Interoperability
www.ws-i.org

An open industry organization chartered to promote Web Services interoperability, the WS-I site provides white papers on interoperability standards, the latest news on Web Services, and provides guidance and resources for developing interoperable Web Services.

Interaction Design
Web Page Design for Designers
www.wpdfd.com

Articles, news, product reviews, and editorials covering the world of Web design. This site includes sections on typography, graphics and color, tricks and tips, navigation, and links to many other web design resources.

Webmonkey
http://hotwired.lycos.com/webmonkey

Billed as the *web developer's resource*, this site is filled with design knowledge, information, and resources for the front end and back end of sites. It has easy to read sections divided into categories for beginners, builders, and masters.

Boxes and Arrows
www.boxesandarrows.com

This site has a growing collection of articles and reviews on information architecture and design written by practicing designers and architects. It is simple and clean, and the content provides a rich overview of current thinking on "experience design."

A List Apart
www.alistapart.com

Each week the group at A List Apart adds another feature on the art of webmaking. From layouts to programming, using Flash, CSS, or XML, this site is rich with shortcuts, tricks and advice on how to make the most of your web design efforts.

Babble
www.babblelist.com

This is a mailing list site for advanced Web design issues. There is a steady exchange of questions and responses, information and practices from designers and developers who are currently creating Web sites.

Blogroots
www.blogroots.com

This site is all about blogs, blogging, and blog rolls. It provides news and reviews of blogging tools and services and the lastest happenings in the world of Weblogging.

Metafilter
www.metafilter.com

Metafilter is billed as a community blog. It also happens that a number of the participants seem to be Web designers and programmers. The posts range widely from politics to art to religion and everything in between.

Functional Development
Builder
www.builder.com

As the name suggests, this site is targeted to the web developer. A wealth of information and resources for the functional designer includes product reviews, books, online courses, white papers, and discussions on a number of programming issues.

Web Review
www.webreview.com

A publishing venture of CMP Media, LLC, this site is geared to the professional software developer. It covers the languages, platforms, tools, new technologies, and tricks of the trade used by software developers.

Web Dev IQ
www.webdeviq.com

This site has a broad collection of articles, tips, product reviews, and press releases covering such topics as best practices, Web standards, design and graphics, programming and scripting, Web tools, and more. Multiple newsletters are available.

•

Usability
Interaction Architecture
www.asktog.com

Bruce "Tog" Tognazzini is a principle in the Nielson Norman Group, a company focused on human-computer interaction. He is the author of *Tog on Interface* and *Tog on Software Design* and a highly regarded consultant on interaction design and architecture.

Good Experience
www.goodexperience.com

This is the newsletter site for Creative Good, the world's first user experience consulting firm, founded by Mark Hurst in 1997. In 2003, Mark also launched thisisbroken.com a collection point for bad user experiences which highlights the need for better customer experience.

Asilimar Institute for Information Architecture
http://aifia.org

Founded in late 2002, the AIFIA looks like it could become "the" representative organization for information architects. Critical professionals in the field have dedicated their efforts to advancing the design of shared information environments.

Advanced Common Sense
www.sensible.com

This is the home of Steve Krug, the best usability expert around and the author of *Don't Make Me Think*. The site is not deep, but provides his workshop schedule and basic information.

Louis Rosenfeld
http://louisrosenfeld.com

Lou Rosenfeld is an information architect and coauthor of Information Architecture for the World Wide Web, regarded as the bible of information architecture. This is his blog site with workshop and speaking schedule, but also contains useful information and some tools.

Business Use
Webopedia
www.webopedia.com

This site is an online dictionary and search engine for computer and technology terms. It contains brief explanations of such things as object oriented programming, document object model, or the difference between Java and Javascript.

Gartner, Inc.
www3.gartner.com

This is the site of a leading research and advisory firm with over a thousand analysts and consultants that provide information and advice relative to business and technology. Many reports are available online, most require payment.

Forrester Research, Inc.
www.forrester.com

Forrester focuses on the business implications of new technology. The site is filled with research reports covering business, marketing, and technology strategy. There is a fee for most, but some commentaries on trends and new product releases are free.

JupiterResearch
www.jupiterresearch.com

A division of Jupitermedia Corporation, this site provides a spectrum of news, information, media resources, and research related to the Internet industry and graphics professionals. Jupiter Research is focused on emerging technologies and provides industry specific analysis for a price. Information may be gleaned for free from attached analysts' Weblogs.

Notes

THE PROMISE

Alvin Toffler, *Future Shock* (New York: Bantam Books, 1971)
Alvin Toffler, *The Third Wave* (New York: William Morrow, 1980)
Alvin Toffler, *PowerShift* (New York: Bantam Books, 1990)

Chapter 1

1. CERN—Conseil Europeen pour la Recherche Nucleaire
2. Tim Berners-Lee, *Weaving the Web* (New York: Harper Business, 2000)
3. Evan L. Schwartz, *Webonomics* (New York: Broadway Books, 1997)
4. Berners-Lee, *Weaving the Web*
5. The idea of tell, sell, link, and think as the four steps required to acquire a customer, comes from Rich Everett, manager of interactive communications for Chrysler Corporation. Evan L. Schwartz, *Webonomics* (New York: Broadway Books, 1997)
6. Berners-Lee *Weaving the Web*

Chapter 2

1. "About Fast Company," fastcompany.com, downloaded December 2002
2. Tom Steinert-Threlkeld, "Can You Work in Netscape Time?" *Fast Company*, November 1995
3. Schwartz, *Webonomics*

4. John Hagel III, Arthur G. Armstrong, *Net.Gain* (Boston, MA: HBS Press, 1997)

5. Patricia B. Seybold, *Customers.com* (New York: Times Books, 1998)

6. Kevin Kelly, *New Rules for the New Economy* (New York: Penguin Books, 1998)

7. Ibid.

Chapter 3

1. Michael Pollan, *The Botany of Desire* (New York: Random House 2001)

2. Melanie Austria Farmer, "Net Consulting Firms Fight Growing Competition," CNET News.com, September 27, 2000

3. "About Fast Company," fastcompany.com, downloaded December 2002

4. Christopher Locke, foreword to *The dot.bomb Survival Guide* (New York: McGraw-Hill, 2002)

5. David S. Greene, inkwell.vue 158: digitalmass.boston.com

Chapter 4

1. James Surowiecki, "The New Economy Was a Myth, Right?" *Wired*, July 2002

2. Ibid.

3. Noel M. Tichy and Stratford Sherman, *Control Your Destiny or Someone Else Will* (New York: Doubleday, 1993)

4. Arrow Electronics, Inc., Annual Report 2002

5. Paul Romer, "Ideas and Things," *The Economist*, September 11, 1993

6. Kelly, *New Rules for the New Economy*

7. Ibid.

8. Hagel, Armstrong, *Net.Gain*

9. Ronald Bailey, Cato Institute, "The Law of Increasing Returns," *The National Interest*, March 18, 2000

10. W. Brian Arthur, "Increasing Returns and the New World of Business," *Harvard Business Review*, July–August 1996

11. Beth Cox, "Value Pricing Key to Boosting Profits," *Jupiterresearch*, February 26, 2003

12. Press Release, "Today's *Wall Street Journal*," Dow Jones, April 9, 2002

Chapter 5

1. Berners-Lee, *Weaving the Web*

2. "Impact: Initiatives & Products," About CAST, CAST.org, downloaded March 15, 2003

3. "Watchfire Acquires CAST's Website Accessibility Technology," watchfire.com/news, *Press Release*, August 6, 2002

4. "February, 2003 Meeting Overview," Accessibilityforum.org, downloaded March 16, 2003

5. "World Wide Web Consortium Issues User Agent Accessibility Guidelines 1.0 as a W3C Recommendation," *W3C Press Release*, December 17, 2002

6. "Counting on the Internet," pewinternet.org/reports, December 29, 2002

7. "Antonia 'Toni' Stone," ctcnet.org, *Biography*, December 2002

8. Curtis Sittenfeld, "From the Digital Divide to One Economy," *Fast Company*, December 2002

9. Ralph King, "Crossing the Great Divide," *Business2.0*, January 2002

10. "GRHF on the Road," hsph.harvard.edu, *Global Reproductive Health Forum Newsletter 1.1*, downloaded March 17, 2003

11. Dan Lee, "Philanthropy Meets Technology," *Mercury News*, December 17, 2002

Chapter 6

1. Direct Marketing Association, *Direct Marketing News*, October 4, 2002

2. Ben Worthen, "Easy as A, B, C, D, E, F, G, H, and I," *CIO*, January 1, 2003

3. Susannah Patton, "IM Goes Corporate," *CIO*, January 1, 2003

4. Geoffrey A. Fowler, ". . . Find a Blog," *Wall Street Journal Online*, November 18, 2002

5. Daintry Duffy, "Blogging for Bucks," *CIO*, January 1, 2003

6. Bob Tedeschi, "For the Web Generation Travel is Self Service," *New York Times*, October 20, 2002

7. Robyn Greenspan, "E-Banking Blooming, But Needs New Apps, Best Practices," *CyberAtlas*, February 20, 2003

8. George Packer, "Smart-Mobbing the War," *The New York Times Magazine*, March 9, 2003

Chapter 7

1. Kelly, *New Rules for the New Economy*

2. Steven Pinker, *The Language Instinct* (New York: HarperCollins Books, 1994)

3. Kmnetwork.com, this web site is touted as the World's most reputed Knowledge Management resource. It is also one of the ugliest.

4. Richard Lederer, *The Miracle of Language* (New York: Pocket Books, 1991)

Chapter 10

1. Ellen Lupton and J. Abbott Miller, *Design Writing Research: Writing on Graphic Design* (New York: Kiosk, 1996)

2. Naomi Klein, *No Logo* (New York: Picador USA, 2001)

Chapter 12

1. This conceptual model of the three primary qualities of technology-based products—desirability, capability, viability—comes from Larry Keely, president of Doblin, a leading innovation strategy company.

2. Charles F. Wilkinson, *The Eagle Bird* (Boulder, CO: Johnson Books, 1999)

Chapter 13

1. The original title for Temple Grandin's book was *A Cow's Eye View*.

2. Temple Grandin, *Thinking in Pictures* (New York: Vintage Books, 1996)

3. Oliver Sacks, *An Anthropoligist on Mars* (New York: Knopf, 1995)

4. Pinker, *The Language Instinct*

Chapter 15

1. Charles Handy, *The Age of Unreason* (Boston, MA: HBS Press, 1990)

Chapter 16

1. Michael Lewis, *Next* (New York: W. W. Norton, 2001)
2. Ibid.
3. James Gleick, "Tangled Up in Spam," *New York Times Magazine*, February 9, 2003
4. Ann Mack, *IQ News Daily Briefing*, April 9, 2003
5. James Gleick, "Tangled Up in Spam"
6. Alorie Gilbert, "Jury: eBay Guilty of Patent Infringement," *CNET News.com*, May 27, 2003
7. Harlan Cleveland, "How can intellectual Property Be Protected?" *Change*, May 1989
8. Tim Berners-Lee, "World Wide Web Consortium Approves Patent Policy," *W3C Press Release*, May 21, 2003

Chapter 17

1. Doc Searls, *The Cluetrain Manifesto: The End of Business as Usual* (Cambridge, MA: Perseus Publishing, 2000)
2. Lewis, *Next*
3. Theodore Levitt, *The Marketing Imagination* (New York: The Free Press, 1986)
4. Ibid.
5. Ibid.
6. Kelly, *New Rules for the New Economy*
7. Richard Florida, *The Rise of the Creative Class* (New York: Basic Books, 2002)
8. Keith H. Hammonds, "No Risk, No Reward," *Fast Company*, April 2002
9. Personal conversation with Judith Jedlicka
10. Seth Godin, "In Praise of Purple Cows," *Fast Company*, February 2003

Chapter 18

1. Jack Trout, *Differentiate or Die* (New York: Wiley, 2000)
2. Seth Godin, "In Praise of Purple Cows"

3. Searls, *The Cluetrain Manifesto*

4. Ibid.

5. Carolyn McCarron, "First Things First: A Second Look," *Communication Arts*, May/June 2000

6. *The Cluetrain Manifesto: The End of Business as Usual*, downloaded from cluetrain.com, March 24, 1999

7. Theodore Levitt, *The Marketing Imagination* (New York: The Free Press, 1986)

8. B. Joseph Pine II, James H. Gilmore *The Experience Economy* (Boston, MA: HBS Press, 1999

9. Kirk Carr, "The Advertising Standards We Honor," *AdAge.com*, August 27, 2002

10. Carolyn McCarron, "First Things First: A Second Look," *Communication Arts*, May/June 2000

Chapter 19

1. "How Do People Evaluate a Web Site's Credibility? Results from a Large Study," *Consumerwebwatch.org*, October 29, 2002

2. Steven Pinker, *The Blank Slate* (New York: Viking, 2002)

Chapter 20

1. John Hunter, "I Want My QVC," CIO, June 1, 2003

2. "Sites That Don't Click," 37 Signals Research Brief, October 2002

Chapter 21

1. Patricia O'Connell, "Can FreshDirect Bring Home the Bacon?" *BusinessWeek Online*, September 25, 2002

2. Ibid.

Chapter 23

1. Richard Anderson, "The Land's End/Supplier Connection: A Series of Valuable Partnerships," Our Company, LandsEnd.com, downloaded March 2003

2. James Gleick, *Faster* (New York: Pantheon, 1999)

3. Lisa DiCarlo, "IBM Leaves Dinosaurs Behind," *Forbes.com*, September 29, 2002

4. "Light on the Horizon," *The Economist*, July 31, 2003

5. Colin Bell, "Stop . . . And Sell the Flowers," *Fast Company*, May 2003

6. From PressQuotes at Tulipworld.com

7. Christina Stubbs, "The Ties That Bind," *Red Herring*, November 1999

8. John Freyer, *All My Life for Sale* (New York: Bloomsbury, 2002)

9. Simon Garfield, "The Man Who Sold His Life for $6,000," *Sunday London Observer*, December 8, 2002

10. Winda Benedetti, "In 'All My Life' a man learns it's not the stuff, it's the stories," *Seattle Post-Intelligencer*, November 19, 2002

11. Julian L. Simon, *The Ultimate Resource 2* (Princeton, NJ: Princeton University Press, 1996)

Chapter 25

1. Clayton M. Christensen, *The Innovator's Dilemma* (Boston, MA: HBS Press, 1997)

2. Steve Jobs, Interview, *Fortune*, January 24, 2000

3. Ernst Cassirer, *Language and Myth* (New York: Dover, 1946)

4. Rolf Jensen, *The Dream Society* (New York: McGraw-Hill, 2001)

Chapter 26

1. Thomas L. Friedman, *The Lexus and the Olive Tree* (New York: Farrar, Straus and Giroux, 1999)

2. Joseph Campbell, Bill Moyers, and Betty Sue Flowers, *The Power of Myth* (New York: Doubleday, 1988)

Index

Abercrombie.com, 179
abundance, 31
  vs. scarcity, 34–36
access
  for disabled, 40–42
  for disadvantaged, 42–47
The *Accessibility Forum*, 42
accountability, 38
accounting, 37
  history of, 132
  as software, 130
ACLU. *See* American Civil
  Liberties Union
acronyms, 213
  overused, 220
action, ideas and, 68
action points, multiple, 180–181
Active Server Pages (ASP), 103
  functional designers and, 129
administrative tools, 107
Adobe Systems
  The *Accessibility Forum* and, 42
  Web Accessibility and, 42
advertising
  direct, 94
  site map and, 83
  space allotments, 88
  success drivers and, 66
  Web, 167–168
Advertising Age, 167
AdWords, 168
aesthetics, 113
The Age of Unreason (Handy), 138
AIGA. *See* American Institute of
  Graphic Arts
airlines, 52
ALA. *See* American Library
  Association
All My Life for Sale (Freyer), 207
Amazon
  Bezos, Jeff and, 185
  confidence in, 176
  Miller-Williams and, 38–39
  one-to-one marketing and,
    183
  patent infringement and,
    147–148
  personalization and, 53,
    96–97
Amazys Holding AG, 195
ambiguity, in language, 61
America Online, 144
  IM of, 50
  pop-up ads and, 167
American Association of Public
  Accountants, 132
American Civil Liberties Union
  (ACLU), 147
American Express, 166
American Institute of Graphic
  Arts (AIGA), 18–19
American Library Association
  (ALA), 147
America's Second Harvest, 45
analogies, 137
analysis, 67
Anderson, Richard, 200
Andreessen, Marc, 15

Netscape and, 16
animal management, 120
annual reports, 140
Apple Computers, Inc.
  The *Accessibility Forum* and, 42
  contributions of, 43
  design and, 222
  Miller-Williams and, 38–39
application-to-application
  communication, 203
Aprilis, 203
Aristotle, 172
Armstrong, Arthur, 19
Arnold, Marcus, 145
  Electronic Herd and, 225
Arrow Electronics, Inc., 33–34
The Art of War, 219
Arthur Anderson, 204
Art@Work, 159
AskMe.com, 145
ASP. *See* Active Server Pages
assets, 31–32
Association for Computer
  Machinery, 9
Atlantic Monthly, 9
Automated Distribution
  Center, 33

Baldoria.com, 206–207
Banana Republic, 179
  personalization and, 96–97
banking, 53
Barlow, John Perry, 147
Barnes&Noble.com, 147–148
B2B sites, 24
B2C sites, 24
BCA. *See* Business Committee for
  the Arts
Beamer, Norm, 148
beauty, 113
Beehive, 45
Bell, Alexander, 12, 59
Benedetti, Winda, 208
Berlin Wall, 37
Berners-Lee, Tim, 6
  CERN and, 15
  Internet and, 36
  Internet tools of, 11
  interoperability and, 133
  on policy, 148
  W3C and, 11
  on Web Accessibility
    Initiative, 42
  Web and, 8–9
  on Web goals, 40
best practices, 62–64
beta versions, 17
Bezos, Jeff, 185
Bias for Action, 68
bill payment, online, 53
Bina, Eric, 15
biological computing, 202
Blogger.com, 50
Blogroots, 50
blogs, 50–51
  Macromedia and, 168
  motivation of, 64
blood transfusions, 162

bloodless surgery, 162
blueprints, 85
Bobby, 41
Body Shop, 94
Boo.com, 25
boom economy, 22
Boston Globe, 225
boundaryless organization, 82
Bouwman, Pim, 204–205
  Electronic Herd and, 226
Brand Standards, 99–100
brand(s), 22, 31, 92
  cohesion, 99
  confirmation, 94
  extensions, 94
  function of, 92–93
  impressions, 94
  loyalty, 94
  message, 94
  visualization, 97–99
  vs. logos, 92
broadband connectivity, 201
brochures, 175
brochureware, 19, 28
  advantage of, 36
  cost of, 49
Brown-Forman, 159
browsers, 133
buckets, 85
budgets, 66
Burger, Warren, 146
Burns, Kathy, 80, 80
Burson-Martella, 141
Bush, George W., 55
Bush, Vannevar, 9
business, 1, 115
  basics, 22
  communications papers, 22
  creativity in, 159–160
  foundation of, 177
  management, 62–64
  metaphors, 137–138
  models, 22
  objectives, 68
  people, 116
  product *vs.* service, 166
  purpose of, 156
  reinvention, 165–167
  site map and, 83
  success drivers and, 66
Business 2.0, 18
Business Committee for the Arts
  (BCA), 159
business design
  team, 141–142
  viability and, 142
Business Week, 18
buttons
  dimensionalized, 90
  style guide and, 99
buzz messages, 167

C coding, 129
call-outs, 99
camelephant, 139
Campbell, Joseph, 229
CAN-SPAM Act, 145
capability, 117

·